THE
J. I. PACKER
COLLECTION

SELECTED AND INTRODUCED BY

ALISTER E.
MCGRATH

THE

J. I. PACKER

COLLECTION

REGENT COLLEGE PUBLISHING
VANCOUVER, BRITISH COLUMBIA

This edition published 2009 by special arrangement with
Inter-Varsity Press, 38 De Monfort Street, Leicester LE1 7GP

REGENT COLLEGE PUBLISHING
5800 University Boulevard
Vancouver, British Columbia
V6T 2E4 Canada
www.regentpublishing.com

Typeset in Great Britain
Set in Minion Condensed

Library and Archives Canada Cataloguing in Publication Data

Packer, J. I. (James Innell)
[Selections]
        The J.I. Packer collection / selected & introduced by Alister McGrath.

Includes bibliographical references.
ISBN 978-1-57383-414-8 (pbk.)

        1. Theology, Doctrinal. I. McGrath, Alister E., 1953- II. Title.
III. Title: James Innell Packer collection.

BX5199.P22A25 2009   230'.3   C2007-903268-0

Contents

Preface

On a cold and misty February morning in 1991, I travelled from Oxford to Cambridge to give a lecture. To my delight, I found that I had an unexpected travelling companion on this journey between England's two leading universities. James Innell Packer had just visited a colleague in Oxford, and was also on his way to Cambridge. We spent the three-hour journey talking about his life and times. As we parted at Cambridge coach station to go our separate ways, I knew that J. I. Packer's biography had to be written. It was a task that took me five years to research, and I count it time extremely well spent.[1]

Packer is a man of ideas – a theologian with that rare gift of being able to communicate his ideas to a variety of audiences. I personally have found those ideas encouraging and challenging, and have found that interacting with Packer is an immensely rewarding experience. We all need to deepen our grasp of our faith; engaging with an articulate and intelligent writer such as Packer is an ideal way of stimulating that process of development and enrichment. Packer, the son of a railway clerk, rose from his humble beginnings to become one of the most influential theological and spiritual writers of the twentieth century. The readers of *Christianity Today* named him as one of the greatest influences on their lives, placing him second only to C. S. Lewis. There is no doubt that Packer's substantial body of writings makes him one of the most attractive and rewarding of modern evangelical authors. Many have found interacting with Packer's works a deeply rewarding experience, leading to a deepened understanding of their faith and a longing to go further and deeper into its intellectual and spiritual richness.

Yet Packer is more than just a first-rate writer; he has been deeply involved in the shaping of British and North American evangelicalism in the second half of the twentieth century. His personal vision for the development of the evangelical movement may be seen as having proved to be of decisive importance in defining evangelical attitudes in a number of areas, and stimulating debate in others. Packer represents that rare species – a major theologian with an awareness of the importance of institutions and individuals for the shaping of the Christian life. Packer is, of course, an immensely prolific writer, who has authored some 300 works throughout his long career. While coming to terms with such a substantial literary output may well be rewarding, it is also immensely time-consuming. It is this consideration which gave rise to the present book, which aims to present some core theological writings from Packer's massive oeuvre, along with introductory and explanatory material to enable readers to gain the most from engaging with them.

Whether his readers agree with Packer or not, he is a writer who stimulates reflection on their part. Many of those who diverge from his viewpoint nevertheless find that his writings represent classic statements of the questions under consideration, which must be taken seriously in modern evangelical theological debate. To engage with Packer is to wrestle with much of the theological heritage of the Christian tradition, particularly the Reformed and Puritan school, as applied to the modern situation. As Packer put it: 'I theologize out of what I see as the authentic biblical and credal mainstream of Christian identity, the confessional and liturgical "great tradition" that the church on earth has characteristically maintained from the start.'[2]

Packer's is a highly significant achievement, which demands careful study. The best place from which to start this process of engagement is a brief overview of Packer's career, to which we now turn.

Notes

1. Alister E. McGrath, *J. I. Packer: A Biography*, Grand Rapids, MI: Baker Book House, 1997; United Kingdom edition published as *To Know and Serve God: A Biography of James I. Packer*, London: Hodder and Stoughton, 1997.
2. J. I. Packer, 'On from Orr: The Cultural Crisis, Rational Realism, and Incarnational Ontology', *Crux* 32/3 (September 1996), pp. 12–26; quotation at p. 12. (See essay 15 in this collection.)

Acknowledgments

I gladly acknowledge the assistance of many who helped bring this volume into being. In particular, I would like to thank Sandra Goundrey-Smith, who provided invaluable assistance with the transcription and editing of texts. Inter-Varsity Press were everything that a publisher should be, and it is a particular pleasure to thank Colin Duriez for his advice and encouragement as this work was put together. Many thanks are also due to Dr J. I. Packer for his gracious collaboration with this project, without which it could never have taken place.

J. I. Packer:
an introduction

James Innell Packer was born in the English cathedral city of Gloucester on 22 July 1926.[1] His father was a clerk who worked for the Great Western Railway; his mother had trained as a teacher in Bristol, prior to marrying Packer's father. In September 1933, at the age of seven, Packer began to attend the National School in Gloucester. It was at this time that an incident took place which had a major impact upon his development. He was chased out of the schoolyard into the main road outside the school, straight into the path of an oncoming bread van. He was seriously injured, and was obliged to remain away from school for some time. He suffered a head injury, still visible to this day, which necessitated his wearing a metal plate over the damaged area of his forehead until he left school. As a result, Packer found himself reading books when other boys of his age played sports. At the age of eleven – when all his friends at school were being given bicycles as presents – Packer found himself the initially puzzled, but ultimately gratified, recipient of the gift of a second-hand typewriter. Anyone seeking an explanation of Packer's love of reading or facility in writing need look no further than here for a partial explanation.

In September 1937, Packer changed schools, and became a student at the Crypt School, Gloucester, where he would remain until he went up to Oxford in 1944. It is fair to say that Packer had little interest in religion at this stage. His interest in Christianity would be quickened through reading some of the core writings of C. S. Lewis to be published around this time, including the talks which Lewis gave for the British Broadcasting Corporation in 1942. Packer began to find himself persuaded of the truth of Christianity, but nothing more. At this stage, his concerns were perhaps more tightly focused on the study of classics, and the possibility of going up to Oxford University to study this subject in greater detail. In late 1943, Packer learned that he had been awarded the Hugh Oldham scholarship, which would allow him to study classics at Corpus Christi College, Oxford.

So Packer began to study Literae Humaniores (as Oxford likes to refer to classics) in October 1944. The Second World War was still in progress, and Oxford was suffering economic and social deprivation, along with the rest of the country. It was not an easy time to be a student. Yet Packer's memories of wartime discomforts must be set against an experience which would change the remainder of his life. On 22 October 1944, Packer was converted. As he later explained matters, he heard an evangelistic sermon which made him realize that he was not a Christian, despite his belief in the truth of the Christian creeds. He lacked personal commitment. He made the decision to commit himself to Christ.

This decision caused him to reconsider his plans for the remainder of his life. Instead of becoming a classics scholar, or perhaps a classics teacher at an English school, he turned his thoughts to ministering to the people of God. He was accepted as an ordinand (that is, as a trainee clergyman) by the Church of England, and was initially minded to begin his preparation for ministry at Wycliffe Hall, Oxford, immediately after completing his classics studies. In the event, another possibility presented itself – that of taking the academic year 1948–9 out, and doing some teaching at Oak Hill College, London. Oak Hill was one of a number of colleges, along with Wycliffe Hall, which the Church of England recognized as offering accredited training for its ministry. At that stage, the college needed someone who could teach Latin and Greek for a year. Packer took the position, and found it to be a landmark in his personal development. In the first place, he found that he seemed to have an innate ability to teach. This suggested to him that his future might lie in some form of theological education. Second, he realized the importance of gaining a research qualification in theology.

Both these thoughts remained with him as he began his preparation for ministry at Wycliffe Hall in 1949. After gaining First Class Honours in theology at Oxford, Packer applied to undertake research at Oxford on the theology of one of the leading Puritan writers – Richard Baxter. Packer had grown to respect the Puritans during his days as an undergraduate, and had been one of the founders of what came to be known as the 'Puritan Studies Conferences' in 1950. It seemed to him that an obvious way of gaining academic respectability and deepening his knowledge of the rich Puritan heritage was to study Baxter in greater detail. Although the resulting DPhil thesis (Oxford does not use the abbreviation 'PhD') has never been published, it remains a landmark in Puritan studies, and is widely referred to in the academic literature of the subject.

Packer left Wycliffe Hall in December 1952, and took up his first – and only – parish appointment as curate of St John's Church, in the Birmingham suburb of Harborne, close to Birmingham University. During this time, he married Kit Mullett. However, Packer's conviction that his future lay in theological education suggested that he ought to be seeking a position in a theological college (as English seminaries are known). In January 1955, Packer moved to Bristol. He had been appointed as a residentiary tutor at Tyndale Hall, another of the Church of England's theological colleges. Here he would develop his reputation as a Christian speaker and teacher. He would also gain a reputation as a writer. It was during his time as tutor at Tyndale Hall that he wrote two of his most important early books, *'Fundamentalism' and the Word of God* (1958) and *Evangelism and the Sovereignty of God* (1961). These works revealed Packer as a theologian of Reformed convictions with that rarest of abilities – communication skills.

Yet Packer could not remain in this relatively junior position permanently. He moved to Oxford, to take up the position initially of Librarian (1961), and then Warden (1962) of Latimer House, a newly established evangelical research centre designed to provide theological encouragement and support for the growing evangelical presence within the Church of England. During this time, Packer began to emerge as a statesman within the evangelical constituency of the Church of England. He mounted what is generally accepted to be the most effective evangelical response to John Robinson's *Honest to God*. More importantly, Packer was one of the strategists who plotted the trajectory by which evangelicalism could regain a significant presence within the English national church. A disastrous public argument broke out between John R. W. Stott and Martyn Lloyd-Jones at an Evangelical Alliance meeting in October 1966 over whether evangelicals should stay within their denominations and reform them from within (the position of Packer and Stott), or leave them to form a separate evangelical congregation (the position of Lloyd-Jones). The National Evangelical Anglican Congress, held at Keele in 1967, is widely regarded as one of the most important events in the history of English Christianity during the twentieth century; Packer may be regarded as its theological architect, and Stott as its statesman.

Packer's major achievements during his time at Latimer House may have suggested to some that he remain there, and continue its mission indefinitely. Yet Packer sensed the need to move on, preferably returning to theological education. His growing first-hand experience of North American models of theological education suggested to him that there was a need for the widespread adoption of American models, particularly the idea of parity within theological faculties. To be able to ensure that such insights were adopted, Packer would need to have a senior position within such a college – such as that of Principal.

After much heart-searching, and not without considerable personal anguish, in 1970 Packer decided to accept the principalship of the college which he had earlier served as tutor – Tyndale Hall, Bristol. He knew that he was entering into a difficult situation. There was considerable tension within both the student and staff bodies over a failed merger proposal with a neighbouring theological college. Within a year, tension flared again, when it became clear that the future of Tyndale was under threat. The college could be saved only if a merger could be negotiated with two other Bristol colleges. The negotiations were tortuous and exhausting. They ended successfully with the creation of Trinity College, Bristol, which incorporated Tyndale Hall. Packer would serve as Associate Principal of the new institution. The period from 1970 to 1972 was probably one of the most stressful in Packer's life. Yet it was during this period that he authored what is widely regarded as his greatest work – *Knowing God*, which was completed in August 1971, and published in 1973.

In many ways, Packer's years as Associate Principal of Trinity College were happy, allowing him time to read and write, and particularly to visit North America, and establish his reputation as a speaker and writer in that region. Nevertheless, he was not entirely at ease with his position. He felt that the situation in the Church of England was increasingly such that he had little contribution to make to that church. He was also aware that his close personal relationship with the Principal of Trinity, Alec Motyer, which went back over many years, meant that it would not be easy to remain at Trinity once Motyer left. Motyer, a gifted pastor as well as teacher, had made it clear that he would not remain at Trinity for ever, leaving Packer with the impression that it might be wise to prepare for the future.

He found himself being increasingly drawn to North America, where he was a known presence. Packer had a high regard for the faculty structure of North American seminaries, which he regarded as superior to their British equivalents. Eventually, Packer accepted an offer to join the faculty of Regent College, Vancouver, from 1979. Regent College was then a fledgling institution, which had yet to attain its present size and international reputation. Packer would serve under its then Principal, James M. Houston, whom he had known from his days in Oxford in the late 1940s. Packer's time at Regent was not without its controversies. Perhaps the most significant of these was the debate which broke out over the extent to which evangelicals should collaborate with Roman Catholics over shared theological and moral concerns. This debate concerned the document *Evangelicals and Catholics Together*, which was published in May 1994, with Packer as one of its signatories. Despite major changes in Regent's faculty, size and administration over the years, Packer remained its most widely known and admired faculty member until his semi-retirement in 1996, at the age of 70.

The purpose of this book may be stated simply as follows. It aims to facilitate the process of engagement with Packer's ideas, by offering its readers sixteen of Packer's finest shorter writings. The work can thus be thought of as a 'sampler', or a 'reader', which brings together certain core writings for detailed study. These have been chosen on the basis of three criteria. First, the works should reflect Packer's personal interests. Throughout his long career, Packer has shown that there are a number of major theological issues which he regards as being of special importance – such as the authority of Scripture, the relation of theology and spirituality, and the importance of 'great tradition' Christianity. This collection of essays reflects those concerns. Readers can thus be assured that they will have gained an understanding of both Packer's approach and his emphases through using this book.

Secondly, the works should represent every phase of Packer's career. It is important that readers of this work should have access to works drawn from throughout Packer's long career. Packer became involved in very specific discussions and controversies at various stages in his career, and it is important to allow readers to study those views against the original context. It is also interesting to observe developments in Packer's writing style over the period of nearly half a century covered in this work.

Thirdly, the works must be complete in their own right. Extracts from longer books by Packer have been avoided, in that it is often necessary to read the entire work to appreciate the significance of the section being abstracted. Each of the works printed here is self-contained, and has not been abbreviated or truncated.

Yet it is not enough simply to reprint Packer's ideas. They need to be introduced and explained. This is why I opened with a biographical essay, setting Packer against the backdrop of the development of evangelicalism in England and North America during the critically important fifty-year period 1945–95. In addition to exploring Packer's intellectual development over this period, I note major phases in his career as a scholar and writer.

The sixteen essays now follow. Each is framed by an introduction and a concluding set of study questions. The introduction sets the background to the essay, allowing readers to understand the background against which it was written, and alerting them to points of particular interest or importance in advance. It also identifies other writings by Packer which are of revelance to this theme. The text is then reproduced, with certain minor editorial alterations designed to be helpful to readers – for example, Hebrew and Greek works are transliterated, and bibliographical details of cited works slightly fuller than those originally provided are offered to enable readers to trace them more readily than might otherwise be possible. The concluding study questions are designed to assist engagement with the text, both by inviting readers to ensure that they have understood what is being said, and by encouraging them to interact further with Packer's ideas.

Notes

1. For full details of Packer's life, see Alister E. McGrath, *J. I. Packer: A Biography*, Grand Rapids, MI: Baker Book House, 1997; United Kingdom edition published as *To Know and Serve God: A Biography of James I. Packer*, London: Hodder and Stoughton, 1997.

1. 'Revelation and inspiration' (1954)

J. I. Packer has always been aware of the importance of affirming and defending the authority of Scripture. This became of particular importance within British Christianity as a result of the 'Fundamentalism Controversy' of 1955-7. By the early 1950s, the word 'fundamentalism' had come to mean something like 'unthinking, dogmatic, narrow-minded, and unscholarly'. Liberal writers, particularly within the Church of England, encouraged the direct identification of 'fundamentalism' with 'evangelicalism'. Thus Billy Graham, who became well known in England during the early 1950s on account of his evangelistic crusades, was widely ridiculed by the intellectual élite of the Church of England at this time as a 'fundamentalist'. This attitude was reinforced by Michael Ramsey, then Bishop of Durham, who published an article entitled 'The Menace of Fundamentalism' in 1956, which accused Billy Graham of being heretical and sectarian. Ramsey – who later became Archbishop of Canterbury – clearly had his sights set on John R. W. Stott, who was then emerging as a significant spokesman for the growing evangelical constituency. It was clear that a response was needed to these critiques of biblical authority. In 1956 Stott himself fired off a broadside in an important pamphlet, entitled *Fundamentalism and Evangelicalism*, which sought to place clear blue water between the two movements.[1] Yet it was clear that something more substantial was needed. As events proved, the definitive evangelical response came from Packer, in the form of his first book, eventually entitled *'Fundamentalism' and the Word of God*, which was published in 1958.

17

It is often suggested that Packer's first book was written in direct response to A. G. Hebert's book *Fundamentalism and the Church of God* (1957), which was severely critical of what Hebert termed 'fundamentalism'. The truth is slightly more complex than this. Packer had written on the general theme of the inspiration and authority of Scripture earlier in his career. In 1954, Packer contributed a major article on 'Revelation and Inspiration' to the second edition of a one-volume Bible commentary co-edited by his friend Alan Stibbs. This important article was constructive in its approach, and did not engage in argument with critics of the evangelical position. Yet it was clear that there was a need for Packer to expand this work to deal with the new 'fundamentalism' debate. This he did in the form of a lecture given to the Graduates' Fellowship meeting at London in 1957, with the title 'Narrow Mind – or Narrow Way?' The text of this lecture was a mere 7,000 words in length; Packer wrote this up, in the light of his conviction that it was necessary to engage with the issues – and especially the critics of evangelicalism – in greater depth. In particular, he felt the need to engage directly with Hebert's depiction and criticisms of evangelicalism. An article on 'The Fundamentalism Controversy', which he published in the spring of 1958, provided him with the opportunity to gather his thoughts on Hebert's work, and begin to assemble the elements of an informed and articulate evangelical response. One of Packer's goals was to show the critics that their criticisms fell wide of their intended targets. The book virtually wrote itself, and ended up as 55,000 words in length. As Packer himself recalls, it seemed 'to spring full-grown from the womb'. Ronald Inchley, Publications Secretary of the Inter-Varsity Fellowship, was expecting a 6,000-word pamphlet; after eighteen months, a typescript nearly ten times that length landed on his desk.

'*Fundamentalism*' *and the Word of God* established Packer as a major figure in relation to the evangelical defence of the authority of Scripture, and laid the foundations for his involvement in the 'Battle for the Bible', which broke out within North American evangelicalism in the late 1970s and early 1980s. Important though Packer's polemical writings on this issue may be, many argue that his finest discussion of this theme is to be found in the 1954 article 'Revelation and Inspiration', in which he sets out the basic components of a responsible evangelical attitude to Scripture. To this article we now turn.

Related works by Packer

'*Fundamentalism*' *and the Word of God*, London: Inter-Varsity Fellowship; Grand Rapids, MI: Eerdmans, 1958.
'The Origin and History of Fundamentalism', in T. Hewitt (ed.), *The Word*

of God and Fundamentalism. London: Church Book Room Press, 1960, pp. 100–127.

'Encountering Present-Day Views of Scripture', in J. M. Boice (ed.), *Foundation of Biblical Authority.* Grand Rapids, MI: Zondervan, 1978, pp. 61–84.

'Upholding the Unity of Scripture Today', *Journal of the Evangelical Theological Society* 25 (1982), pp. 409–414.

'In Quest of Canonical Interpretation', in R. K. Johnston (ed.), *The Use of the Bible in Theology: Evangelical Options.* Atlanta, GA: John Knox Press, 1985, pp. 33–55.

'Thirty Years' War: The Doctrine of Holy Scripture', in H. Conn (ed.), *Practical Theology and the Ministry of the Church.* Phillipsburg, NJ: Presbyterian and Reformed, 1990, pp. 25–44.

Revelation and inspiration

Christian theology as taught in the Bible is an organic unit, and should be studied as such. No part of it is properly understood except in relation to the whole. No single doctrine is mastered till one knows its place in the system. Our aim in this article is to formulate the view of revelation and inspiration which the Bible teaches and which underlies this Commentary [the *New Bible Commentary*]. Accordingly, our first task must be to indicate the relation in which these topics stand to the rest of Christian truth. The doctrine of biblical inspiration, as we shall see, is a part of the general doctrine of revelation, which in its turn derives from, and must be constructed in terms of, the fundamental doctrines of creation and redemption. In the following exposition we shall try to exhibit these connections, and so to gain a fully biblical understanding of the subjects in question.

Revelation

The English word 'revelation' may be taken either actively or passively. In the former sense it means that activity of God whereby he makes himself known to men; in the latter, the knowledge thus imparted. The biblical idea of revelation must be elicited by means of a broad induction of evidence, of which the briefest outline must here suffice.

The Old Testament

The Old Testament constantly affirms that Israel's existence and history as a nation, and her religion as a church, were wholly the result of divine revelation. God had revealed himself in covenant to Abraham, as his God, and had pledged himself to continue in covenant with Abraham's seed (Gen. 17). Accordingly, he had brought them out of captivity into the promised land, and made them a nation to serve him (Exod. 6:2–8; 19:3–6; Ps. 105:43–45). He had given them his 'law' (*tôrāh*; lit. 'instruction'), and taught them how to worship him. Throughout their history he raised up a succession of spokesmen to declare to them 'the word of the Lord'. Again and again at decisive moments he demonstrated his own complete control of circumstances by foretelling what he would do for them before the event (cf. Is. 48:3–7).

Israel was very conscious of the uniqueness of her relationship to God (Ps. 147:19–20). True religion was, to her, precisely the knowledge of Yahweh, and presupposed Yahweh's self-disclosure in covenant. Lacking this, the Gentile world had fallen into idolatry. The revealed religion of Israel threw into relief the essential blasphemy of all other religion whatsoever. Hence, when God revealed himself to other nations, with whom he had not entered into covenant, it was exclusively in judgment upon them for their sins (Exod. 7:5; Ezek. 25:11, 17; 28:22–24).

The Old Testament verdict upon Old Testament revelation was that it was not a complete whole, but preparatory for something greater. The prophets looked forward to a day when God would reveal himself by mightier works than ever yet: he would raise up the Messiah, gather his scattered people and establish his kingdom among them. Heaven and earth would be *made* new (Is. 65:17–25); Israelite religion would be transformed (Jer. 31:31–34); and all nations would see and acknowledge the glory of God in Israel as never before (Is. 60:1–14; Ezek. 36:23). On this forward-looking note the Old Testament closes (Mal. 4).

The New Testament

The New Testament writers were convinced that the meaning of Jewish history and of the Old Testament was to be found in Christ: that, in other words, the course of events in Israel from the very beginning and the composition of the Old Testament over the centuries had been completely controlled by God with the incarnation in view. The implications of this claim led naturally to the fundamental theological idea in terms of which they expounded the subject of revelation. The idea is this: God, the sovereign Creator, who within his world 'worketh all things after the counsel of his own will' (Eph. 1:11), foresaw the ruin of the race through sin, determined to glorify himself by saving a church, and appointed his Son to effect its salvation by his mediatorial ministry. World history has been to date, and will be to the end, nothing more nor less than God's execution of the plan which he then formed in order to compass his goal. After the Son had been raised, exalted and enthroned in his messianic kingdom, he sent the Holy Spirit into the world in order both to complete the disclosure, which he had himself commenced while on earth, of his Father's purposes for the church, and also to bring his people, through faith in himself, into the possession and enjoyment of the salvation he won for them. The revelation of God's plan was duly completed by the Spirit, who made it known in full to the apostles; its performance will be completed by Christ at his 'appearing' (*parousia*), when the church will be made perfect.

This, in barest outline, is the dogmatic framework which underlies the New Testament teaching about revelation. It is most fully stated in Paul's Epistles (cf. Rom. 8:28–39; Eph. 1:3–14, etc.) and John's Gospel (cf. 6:37–45; 10:14–18, 27–29; 16:7–15; 17), but is more or less explicit everywhere. The main passages relating to revelation fall into three classes:

Passages concerning Christ's disclosure of God. The Son is the perfect image of the Father (2 Cor. 4:4; Col. 1:15; Heb. 1:3) and so is in himself a perfect revelation of the Father to those who have eyes to see (John 1:18; 14:7–11). All God's 'fullness' dwelt in the incarnate Son (Col. 1:19; 2:9). Those who understand the full significance of his life and death thereby understand the whole eternal purpose ('wisdom') of God for the church's salvation (Col. 2:2–3; 1 Cor. 1:24 and 2:7–10; see also next section). None can apprehend any part of Christ's revelation of his Father without supernatural spiritual enlightenment (John 3:3–12; 6:44–45; Matt. 16:17; Gal. 1:16).

Passages concerning God's disclosure of his plan. God's comprehensive scheme for the salvation of his elect out of every nation, Jew and Gentile alike, was the 'mystery', the divine 'wisdom', which God conceived before creation but concealed until the apostolic age. Now it was revealed, and the full meaning of Israel's election and history and of the Old Testament revelation for the first time became clear. All the time God's goal had been, not the salvation of one of the world's many nations, but the creation of a new nation, the members of which were to be drawn from every nation and to receive their spiritual nationality, not by natural, but by spiritual birth (cf. 1 Pet. 2:9, 10). The destiny of the regenerate was to be glorified, as their Head ('the first fruits' of the new race, 1 Cor. 15: 20, 23) had been already; and his very presence in heaven, 'the man in the glory', was a pledge to them that they would some day share that glory with him. Paul deals with the revelation of this mystery in several important passages which should be carefully studied (Eph. 1:8–12; 3:3–11; 1 Cor. 2:7–10; Rom. 16:25–26; cf. 11:25–36; 2 Tim. 1:9–11). The source of this revelation is God; the mediator of it is Christ (Gal. 1:12; cf. Rev. 1:1); the agent in its communication is the Spirit (1 Cor. 2:10–12; 2 Cor. 3:15–18; cf. 4:6; Eph. 3:5). In order that it might be conveyed to the church intact, the Spirit inspired the words of apostolic testimony (1 Cor. 2:13), as he had inspired the words of Christ (John 3:34; cf. 12:48–50). He caused the apostles to embody the revelation given to them in a 'standard of teaching', the 'pattern of the sound words' (Gk. *typos*, a 'pattern', 'standard'; see Rom. 6:17; cf. 2 Tim. 1:13). This is 'the sound doctrine' (1 Tim. 1:10; cf. 6:3; 2 Tim. 4:3; Titus 1:9; 2:1), the apostolic 'tradition' (2 Thess. 2:15; 3:6), the test and norm for the faith and life of the churches.

Passages concerning God's performance of his plan. As was said, God discloses his purposes by what he does as well as in what he says; and any action which marks a further stage in his plan of redemptive history may be called 'revelation'. The New Testament knows two such acts of revelation yet to come: the appearing of antichrist (2 Thess. 2:3, 6, 8) and the parousia of Jesus (1 Cor. 1:7; 2 Thess. 1: 7–10; 1 Pet. 1:7, 13). The latter concludes history and ushers in the day of judgment. Christ will then reveal by executive action God's eternal intentions with respect to the impenitent and the saints, wrath for the one and glory for the other (Rom. 2:5–10; 8:18; cf. 1 Pet. 1:5).

Such, in brief, is the biblical material from which the theological doctrine of revelation must be constructed. To this task we now turn.

The original revelation

The doctrine of revelation is grounded upon the fact that God made man in his own image, to know, love, worship, serve and so glorify him. We saw that man's religion, if it is to be true, must be grounded on God's revelation; and God accordingly revealed himself to Adam as fully as was necessary for Adam to live in fellowship with him. Adam knew God, then, first through his works of creation. The world on which he looked out bore eloquent testimony to the power and wisdom of its Maker. The created order, though since involved in Adam's ruin (Gen. 3:18; Rom. 8:19–22), still proclaims God's glory (Ps. 19:1f.; Rom. 1:19–20); much more must it have done so before. Adam knew God, too, by his knowledge of himself; as God's noblest creature, he was a part of God's revelation of his glory, as well as being its recipient. Again, God's works of providence brought him knowledge of his Maker's goodness. If, despite the chaos that has entered the world through sin, the course of events still bears this testimony (Acts 14:17), doubtless it did so far more clearly to Adam when he knew only the garden, the animals God had brought him to rule, and the wife he had made for him (Gen. 2:18–24). Finally, the testimony of God's works was supplemented by verbal revelation (how conveyed we do not know) as and when necessary (Gen. 2:16–17).

Much of this is necessarily obscure to us. The knowledge of God that Adam enjoyed in Eden before the fall is as far beyond our comprehension as is the knowledge of God which the church will enjoy in heaven after the resurrection. But the permanent characteristics of God's self-revealing activity are already here made plain, and it is worth our while to pause and note them.

The purpose of revelation. God makes himself known to man so that man may attain the end of his creation, which is to know, love and worship him. The transcendent Creator is inaccessible to his creatures until he discloses himself, and man's knowledge of God, where it exists, is correlative to and consequent on God's prior self-revelation. Adam in Eden needed revelation if he was to live in fellowship with God.

The means of revelation. Revelation is God's personal self-disclosure to his rational creatures. The relationship which it initiates is compared in Scripture to that of husband and wife, father and son, friend and friend (cf. Jer. 3; Hos. 11:1; Is. 41:8; Matt. 7:11; John 15:15; Eph. 5:25–27). Such a relationship could not be created apart from personal address by God to man. God must open his mind; he must speak. Action out of the context of conversation, movement divorced from explanation, is a very limited medium for making oneself known to another. It was not enough for Adam to see God in his works; he needed to hear his word, to receive verbal or propositional revelation.

Of course, there is more to self-revelation that merely communicating information about oneself, just as there is more to faith than a mere 'notional' acquaintance with truths. In human relationships, personal attitudes, by their very nature, cannot be expressed in propositional form. Their existence can be indicated, and their nature to some extent suggested, by speech, but they can be expressed, and so fully manifested, only by action. So, when God reveals his love to men, the depths of meaning contained in the words in which he avows it to them become clear only in the light of their experience of what he does for them. God's personal attitudes towards men, therefore, require works as well as words for their revelation. But this does not affect our present contention, which is, simply, that without words such revelation could scarcely take place at all.

The effectiveness of revelation. An unfathomable mystery underlies the claim that the transcendent, infinite Creator makes his thoughts known to finite man. But we may not imagine that God is somehow hampered or thwarted in his self-revealing action by the limitations of man's mind. That man's knowledge of God on earth is now, and was before the fall, imperfect, dim and inadequate to its object in very many ways, is not to be denied. But God made man's mind; and he made it as he did in order that man might be able to apprehend him in a manner perfectly adequate for the ends of his self-disclosure – i.e. for the development of the religious relationship which was man's destiny. He made Adam's mind such that Adam could not but apprehend as much of God as was disclosed to him. And when God reveals himself to sinful man, he restores to him his lost ability to recognize God's Word for what it is and receive it as such. The activity of trust which results from the exercise of this faculty is in Scripture termed faith; and in Hebrews 11:3 the faculty itself is so denoted. It appears correct to say that, in this sense, Adam in Eden had faith, and that it is no more than a restoration to man of what he lost at the fall when the Spirit implants the faculty of faith in those to whom God intends to make himself known.

When man fell, he jeopardized his status and corrupted his nature. God therefore adapted his self-disclosing activity to the new situation, integrating it into the redemptive process which he had at once initiated in order to remedy sin's effects. But the three features of revelation noted above remained, and remain, constant.

God revealed as Redeemer

Through sin, man lost his ability to apprehend creation's witness to its God. The meaning and message of the book remained the same, but he could no longer read it; the heavens proclaimed God's glory into deaf ears. 'They did not like ("did not see fit", RSV; "disdained", Moffatt) to retain God in their knowledge' (Rom. 1:28). Man had lost his natural inclination to love and serve his Creator; the idea of a life so spent was profoundly distasteful to him (Rom. 8:7). There remained in his heart an indelible sense of God, i.e. an awareness that there was something or someone greater than himself whom he should worship and serve, but he refused to let it lead him back to his Maker; for he was now under the sway of unbelief, which the Bible depicts as a positive, devilish thing, a passionate energy of blind denial, a resolute repudiation of the true God (cf. Rom. 1:21–32; Eph. 2:2–3; 4:17–19).

In this situation, the insufficiency of God's self-revelation in creation and providence is manifest. God still shows himself in his works (Rom. 1:19–20); but men shut their eyes, and 'hold down the truth in unrighteousness' (Rom. 1:18). Thus, the continuance of the original revelation leads none to the knowledge of God and serves only to leave the world without excuse for its ignorance of him. And, even supposing that fallen man succeeded in reading 'the book of the creatures' aright, what he read could only drive him to despair. For this general revelation (as it is best called) brings knowledge of a God who hates and punishes man's disobedience and ingratitude (Rom. 1:18), and says not a word about redeeming love. The good news that the God who is merciless to sin is at the same time merciful to sinners is made known only by special revelation, which centres upon Jesus Christ; and to this we now turn.

Since the fall, the Creator has been making himself known as Redeemer upon the stage of human history, working out the eternal purpose which, as we saw, constitutes the 'mystery' which the apostles declared. The whole plan hinged upon the earthly ministry of the incarnate Son. In the fact of Christ all the types, shadows and prophecies of the Old Testament found their meaning, so that by it Israel's Scriptures were fulfilled (cf. Matt. 5:17; Luke 24:27; John 5:39; Acts 13:26–33; Heb. 7 – 10). Again, upon this ministry all subsequent redemptive activity is grounded. When he ascended, Christ entered upon the exercise of his heavenly ministry, whereby he conveys to his people by his Spirit the benefits which he secured for them while on earth, and this ministry will not be completed until he perfects his church at his return. And only when the whole church is made perfect, possessing and exhibiting in all its fullness the glory of God (Rev. 21:11), and appearing with its glorified Saviour in a new-created universe (Rev. 21:1 – 22:5), will God's resources and intentions in redemption be fully manifested, and his purpose of perfect self-display be finally accomplished. Meanwhile, every act of grace brings it one stage nearer completion. The new creation, therefore, no less than the old, God's works of special grace as well as those of common providence, are works of revelation, every one of which declares the glory of God.

Verbal revelation

In the redemptive process by which the church is saved, verbal revelation has an indispensable place. First of all, it was an integral element in the series of acts by which redemption was wrought out. Without verbal revelation, Abraham would never have entered Canaan, nor Moses led Israel from Egypt, nor Jesus' life been preserved in infancy (cf. Gen. 12:1–5; Exod. 3:1–6:13; Matt. 2:13–15). Secondly, verbal revelation has always been necessary as a ground for faith. Its importance from this point of view is seen when we consider the soteriological significance of faith. Not merely is faith, as an activity, the instrument whereby a sinner lays hold of Christ and so obtains all the promised benefits, but also, as a faculty, faith is, as we saw, the organ of that knowledge of and fellowship with God from which man fell and to which redemption restores him.

Now, the object which brings this faculty into exercise is God's Word, as such (cf. 1 Thess. 2:13). Faith 'hears his voice' and responds to his Word of promise in trust and obedience. Without a word from God, faith cannot be (Rom. 10:17). The reason for this is clear. Without an explanatory word, God's redemptive action could not even be recognized for what it was. The creature, as we saw, cannot know the Creator's mind till he speaks. The case of the incarnation shows that the clearest revelation of God is nevertheless the most opaque to man. Christ, the personal Word of God, expressed and effected his Father's redemptive purpose completely. In him, God fully manifested himself in redemptive action; and, for that very reason, the fact of Christ utterly transcended man's powers of interpretation. 'It may be doubted', wrote B. B. Warfield, 'whether even the supreme revelation of God in Jesus Christ could have been known as such in the absence of preparatory, accompanying and succeeding explanatory revelation in words.' Even that is an understatement. How could man ever have learned the utterly paradoxical and eternally mysterious truth, that Jesus was God incarnate and put away the world's sins by dying on a cross, without being told? Accordingly, in order to make possible faith in Christ, God gave the world a verbal explanation of the fact of Christ. This was the gospel, the apostolic kerygma, which announces God's gift of the living Word and promises eternal life to those who receive him. It thus appears that the giving of propositional revelations concerning God's redemptive action in history is no mere adjunct or appendage to that action, but is itself part of it, as essential a link in the chain as the events with which those revelations are concerned. For God's redemptive programme includes the conveyance as well as the procuring of salvation, and is not complete until sinners have been restored to faith and knowledge of God through the gospel.

In form and substance, the gospel promise has been one and the same throughout redemptive history, from the time of Adam and Abraham to the present day, namely, a covenant on God's part to be the God of the one to whom he speaks and to safeguard and reward him, both in this life and the next, if he will trust and obey. Saving faith, therefore, has been the same thing from Abel's time onwards (Heb. 11:4). In content, however, the promise grew richer as time went on; for, within the framework of his covenant pledge, God gradually disclosed both the particular blessings which it included and also the objective ground – his own redemptive action – upon which it was based. This revelatory process continued intermittently for centuries. It was thus progressive: not in the sense that each new revelation antiquated the last, but rather in the sense that from time to time God underlined and amplified what he had taught already and added to it further intimations of what he intended to do until he had completed the pattern of truth which was to be fulfilled in

Christ. Then, at the appointed time, he sent his Son to achieve redemption and crowned the revelatory process with the unveiling of the gospel and the 'mystery'. From first to last, the progress of revelation had been closely interlocked with the unfolding of God's plan of redemptive history; and the interpretation of the fact of Christ, itself the complete disclosure in action of the Creator as Redeemer, completed it.

The means by which verbal revelation was given were many and varied. Sometimes an abnormal quality of experience was the vehicle of its reception. This was the case with visions, dreams, and prophetic inspiration, which seems to have ranged on occasion from the slow crystallizing of prolonged meditations at one extreme to the hurricane rapture of complete ecstasy at the other. Sometimes, again, God conveyed truth through his chosen organs of revelation merely by his divine concursus – by operating, that is, in and with them in the exercise of their own natural powers and so leading them to his truth through the normal processes of their own thought – historical research, exegesis of canonical Scripture, meditation and prayer, logical and theological reasoning. Much of the Wisdom literature, the Old Testament historical books and all the New Testament writings save the Apocalypse appear to have resulted from revelation of this sort. Limitations of space preclude any discussion of these modes of revelation. But it is important to notice before we pass on that there is in Scripture no indication of any difference in the purity and reliability of revelations mediated through these various kinds of experience. All organs of revelation, however limited they may appear in themselves, become in the hands of the sovereign God completely effective to the end for which he employs them.

Biblical revelation

In order to ensure the safe preservation of what he had revealed, God 'inscripturated' it. The book which he thereby produced contains, not all the verbal revelations ever given (cf., e.g., the reference in 2 Chr. 9:29 to prophetic books which have not survived), but those which were relevant for the book's designed purpose; which was, not merely to provide a ground for personal faith and guidance for individual Christian living, but also to enable the world-wide church in every age to understand itself, to interpret its history, to reform and purify its life continually, and to rebuff all assaults made upon it, whether from within, by sin and heresy, or from without, by persecution and rival ideologies. All the problems that ever faced or will face the church are in principle covered and solved in this book. For the Christian Bible, though a very human book, recording much sin and error, reflecting in many places the weaknesses and limitations of its authors, is yet – and this is the fundamental truth about it – a divine product, whose *auctor primarius* is God.

The proof of this divine authorship of the Bible (i.e. the proper ground of faith in it) may here be indicated. It is twofold:

The testimony of Christ (the external proof). This proof comprises two propositions. First, Christ's authority demands the acceptance of the Old Testament as divinely inspired. His witness concerning its character is unambiguous and emphatic. To him, it was not a miscellany but a unity, 'scripture' (singular: John 10:35), whose authority was permanent and absolute because of its divine origin (cf. Matt. 5:17–20; Luke 16:17; Matt. 19:4–6). Arguments from Scripture, therefore, possessed for him clinching force (Matt. 22:32, 41ff.; John 10:34–35, etc.). The emphatic 'it is written' was final, and settled matters. His whole ministry was one great testimony to his acceptance of the divine authority of the Old Testament; for he preached and healed and died in obedience to what he found written (cf. Matt. 8:16–17; 26:24, 54; Luke 4:18–21; 18:31–33; 22:37). He, the teacher to whom the Christian church professes subjection, was himself in everything subject to his Father's word in the Old Testament Scriptures. The apostolic writers everywhere echo this witness (cf. 2 Tim. 3:16; 2 Pet. 1:20–21, the phrase 'oracles of God' in Romans 3:2, and the quotation of Old Testament passages, spoken in their context by men, as words of God, or of the Holy Ghost, e.g. Matt. 19:4–5; Acts 4:25–26; 13:34–35; Heb. 1:6ff.; 3:7).

Second, Christ's authority demands the acceptance of the New Testament as possessing the same character as the Old Testament. Jesus taught his disciples to read the Old Testament Christologically, as a prophetic revelation of the things concerning himself (Luke 24:24–25, 44–45; John 5:39, 46). The apostles did so (cf. Acts 3:18, 24; 1 Pet. 1:10–12), claiming that it was written primarily for the guidance and benefit of Christian believers (cf. Rom. 4:23–24; 15:4; 1 Cor. 9:10; 10:11; 2 Tim. 3:16), and that it could not be understood at all by those who would read it in the light of Christ (2 Cor. 3:14–16).

Now, seeing that God had inscripturated his earlier, prophetic revelations so that they might be permanently accessible in an uncorrupted form for the benefit, not merely of old Israel, but of the church universal, it would have been an unaccountable departure from a way of working so well established, and so patently wise and desirable, had he done nothing similar when his crowning revelation was given to the world. The New Testament, therefore, was only to be expected. Against the background of this presumption, certain facts acquire unmistakable significance. (1) Christ promised the Spirit to the apostles so that they might remember and understand what he had taught them already (John 14:25–26) and receive the further revelations concerning himself which they could not as yet 'bear' (John 16:12-14). So equipped, they were to be his authoritative witnesses and interpreters to the whole church, in all ages and all parts of the world (John 17:20; cf. Matt. 28:19). How, we may ask, could Christ have envisaged this, unless he intended them to write their testimony? (2) The apostles claim that, in virtue of their possession of the Spirit, they teach and write the pure truth of God. They are verbally inspired (1 Cor. 2:13); and a genuinely 'spiritual' man recognizes this fact (1 Cor. 14:37; cf. Gal. 1:8; 2 Thess. 3:6, 14). These are unqualified affirmations; and there is no question but that by making them the apostles claimed, and intended to claim, an authority for their own sermons and letters no less absolute than that which they attributed to the Old Testament. (3) Paul quotes Deuteronomy and Luke together, and Peter refers to Paul's Epistles as part of the Canon of Scripture (1 Tim. 5:18; 2 Pet. 3:16). (4) Centuries of Christian exegesis have demonstrated that, theologically, the two Testaments together form an organic unit, each complementing the other in a harmonious testimony to Christ, each bringing to light more and more of the contents and meaning of the other in an endlessly fruitful dialectic of foreshadowing and fulfilment.

We conclude, that, in the light of Christ's evident intention that his apostles should write their testimony and his promise to equip them for the task, the claims they made for themselves and each other, and the quality of what they produced, lead us irresistibly to acknowledge the New Testament as the expected and needed completion of the Old Testament.

The testimony of the Spirit (the internal proof). We saw that it is by the use of the faculty of faith that we discern God's Word for what it is. Faith sees the real nature of that at which it looks. This has been the church's experience down the ages. Since it is the Spirit who implants faith and works in believers their acts of faith, the presence of this conviction is termed the Spirit's witness.

The Bible, then, is the revealed Word of God, in the sense that in its pages God speaks his mind – all his mind – concerning his purpose for his people. To call the Bible a record of, or a witness to, a revelation made in history is insufficient. The Bible is all this, and more. It is not merely a report of what God said: it is what he says, here and now. It is itself a link in the chain of God's redemptive action. Its contents, heard or read, are the means whereby, on the grounds of the historical ministry of Christ which it records and explains, and through the regenerating action of the Spirit who works in and with the Word, sinners come to know the Father and the Son. It is not the Word of God in the sense that every separate sentence, including the words of evil men, expresses his mind or reflects his will. 'God's Word written' is the Bible as a whole, or, more accurately, the theology of the Bible, that organic unity which our fathers so happily and suggestively termed 'the body of the divinity'. Here is the image of God's mind, the transcript of his thoughts, the declaration of his grace, the verbal embodiment of all the treasures of wisdom and knowledge that are hid in his Son. And here faith rests.

Inspiration

The meaning of inspiration

Inspiration is not itself a biblical word. It is usually, and most conveniently, defined as a supernatural influence of God's Spirit upon the biblical authors which ensured that what they wrote was precisely what God intended them to write for the communication of his truth, and hence could be truly termed 'inspired', Gk. *theopneustos*, lit. 'breathed out by God' (2 Tim. 3:16). We have already dealt with this subject in constructive statement, and confine ourselves here to the correction of some misconceptions.

The 'inspiration' which secured the infallible communication of revealed truth is something distinct from the 'inspiration' of the creative artist, which does not. The two things should not therefore be confused. Nor does inspiration always imply an abnormal state of mind in the writer, e.g. a trance-state, a vision, or the hearing of a voice; nor does it imply the obliteration of his personality. God in his providence prepared the human vehicles of inspiration for their task, and caused them in many, perhaps most, cases to perform it through the normal exercise of the powers he had given them. Many states of mind, as we saw, were compatible with inspiration. There is no reason to think that the authors were always aware that they were being inspired in the sense defined, i.e. that they were writing canonical Scripture. Nor is there any ground for asserting that an inspired document could not in God's providence have been compiled from sources by an ordinary process of historical composition, or passed through various editions and recensions before reaching its final form. All that is claimed is that the finished product is *theopneustos*, precisely what God intended for the communication of saving truth.

Since truth is communicated through words, and verbal inaccuracy misrepresents meaning, inspiration must be verbal in the nature of the case. And if the words of Scripture are 'God-breathed', it is almost blasphemy to deny that is free from error in that which it is intended to teach and infallible in the guidance it gives. Inerrancy and infallibility cannot be proved (nor, let us note, disproved) by argument. Both are articles of faith; corollaries of the confession, which Christ's teaching demands and the Spirit's testimony evokes, that canonical Scripture was breathed out by God who cannot lie. He who denies them thereby shows that he rejects the witness of Christ, the apostles and the historic Christian church concerning the nature of 'God's

Word written', and either does not possess or has not understood the
testimonium Spiritus Sancti internum.

The problems of inspiration

No Christian doctrine is free from problems; and that for a very good reason.
God has put forward his truth as an object for faith, and the proper ground of
faith is God's own authoritative testimony. Now, acceptance on grounds of
another's authority and acceptance on grounds of rational demonstration are
two distinct things. Man's original sin was a lust after self-sufficient knowledge, a craving to shake off all external authority and work things out for
himself (cf. Gen. 3:5–6); and God deliberately presents saving truth to sinners
in such a way that their acceptance of it involves an act of intellectual repentance, whereby they humble themselves and submit once more to be taught by
him. Thus they renounce their calamitous search after a self-made wisdom (cf.
Rom. 1:22; 1 Cor. 1:19–25) in order to regain the kind of knowledge for which
they were made, that which comes from taking their Creator's word. So as to
make this renunciation clear-cut, God has ensured that no single article of
faith should be demonstrable as, say, a geometrical theorem is, nor free from
unsolved mystery. Man must be content to know by faith, and to know, in this
world at any rate, in part. We must not, therefore, expect to find the doctrine of
biblical inspiration free from difficulties, any more than are the doctrines of
the Trinity, incarnation, or atonement. Nor must we expect to be able to solve
all its problems in this world. Nor must we wonder that Christians easily fall
into heresy over this doctrine, as over others. It is worth while, however, briefly
to indicate the right attitude for faith to adopt in face of some prevalent errors
concerning it.

First, the doctrine is sometimes diluted by those who profess to be its
friends. It is said that the Bible is the product of inspiration in some sense, but
not of verbal inspiration. God revealed truth to the writers, but it was
inevitable that, being sinful, fallible men, they should distort it in the course of
reporting it. We must expect, therefore, to find error in Scripture. This,
however, as we saw, was not the view of Christ and the apostles. It appears to be
a mistaken inference from the admitted fact that not all the biblical books are
on the same level of spiritual profundity and doctrinal finality; but it amounts
to a flat denial that God in his sovereign providence could do what it was
evidently desirable that he should do, and so prepare and control the human
instruments through whom he caused Scripture to be written that they put
down exactly what he intended, no more and no less. In other words, the Bible,
on this view, is neither what God intended it should be, nor what Christ

thought and taught that it was. Such a position is plainly intolerable.

Secondly, the doctrine is sometimes rejected on the grounds of the internal characteristics of the Bible. Such objections, however, invariably prove on examination to be grounded upon an *a priori*, man-made idea of what a verbally inspired Bible ought to be like, and the very act of bringing them forward as valid grounds for doubting what God says about his book is itself a sign of continued intellectual impenitence, unconscious, perhaps, but no less real for that. The believing method of approach is, rather, to start by accepting God's testimony that the Bible is verbally inspired and then to examine the internal characteristics of Scripture in order to find out what this verbally inspired Bible is in fact like. The most cursory inspection shows that inspiration has completely accommodated itself to the thought-forms, literary methods, stylistic conventions and characteristic vocabulary of the writers. These are the media through which the inspired truth-content is conveyed, and unless we take pains to acquire a sympathetic understanding of them we shall be in danger of misinterpreting what God has said in terms of them, and thus manufacturing errors where none exist. We must be guided in biblical study by the principle – which is a certainty of faith – that Scripture nowhere misrepresents the truths it was inspired to teach and that every biblical fact has been recorded in the way best adapted for the communication of what the church is meant to learn from it. What that is, however, can be determined in each case only by examining the passage in the context of Scripture as a whole. This is a principle of fundamental importance for biblical interpretation. We must not lose sight of it through controversial preoccupations, nor allow our confidence in its truth to be shaken by difficulties which may confront us when we try to apply it.

One example of its application may be given here. It has sometimes been asserted that the occasional appearance in the Old Testament of sub-Christian attitudes, actions and theological reflections is itself a refutation of the doctrine of an inspired Scripture. But this objection reveals a misunderstanding of the nature of the Bible. We stressed earlier that the Bible is not an aggregate of isolated texts, but an organism, no part of which can be rightly interpreted except in terms of its place and function in the whole. Now God has included in his Word much exemplary material; and some of the examples he has recorded are bad examples. All is for our learning; but we must learn from different parts of Scripture in different ways. We learn from records of theological and practical error, not by supposing that, because they are included in Scripture, the words and deeds in question must have met with divine approval, but by detecting the mistakes in the light of Bible doctrine and taking warning. Principles of biblical theology must interpret, as they are in their turn illustrated by, facts of biblical history and biography. Scripture must interpret scripture. Once it is grasped that the Bible is an organic unity, that the Word of God is its doctrine as a whole, and that each passage must be understood in the light of, even as it throws light upon, the truth as it is in Jesus, the grounds for this kind of objection vanish.

Lack of space forbids any further development of these principles here. We would conclude by reiterating our fundamental contention, that faith's attitude to the doctrine of biblical inspiration, as to all other doctrines, is one of acceptance on God's testimony. Nothing, therefore, will shake faith's certainty here, for nothing can shake the testimony on which it rests. When faced by difficulties in and objections to the doctrine as he understands it, the believer will infer that the cause is his own failure to comprehend God's testimony rather than God's failure to make the truth plain, and will accordingly be driven back to a closer re-thinking of the matter in the light of a closer study of the biblical evidence. This is how all doctrinal advance has been made throughout the history of the church. And this is how a truer and fuller understanding of the doctrine of Holy Scripture as the inspired, and therefore infallible and inerrant, Word of God, can be reached in our own day.

Questions for study

1. Try to identify the key biblical passages on which Packer rests his case for biblical authority.
2. Packer clearly regards the notion of Scripture as *theopneustos* as being of major importance for his argument. Set out, in your own words, what Packer understands by this term, and the use which he makes of it.
3. 'We must be guided in biblical study by the principle – which is a certainty of faith – that Scripture nowhere misrepresents the truths it was inspired to teach and that every biblical fact has been recorded in the way best adapted for the communication of what the church is meant to learn from it. What that is, however, can be determined in each case only by examining the passage in the context of Scripture as a whole.' Locate this statement. What does Packer mean by it? Why is it so important? Whom do you think Packer has in mind in making it?
4. 'The Bible is not an aggregate of isolated texts, but an organism, no part of which can be rightly interpreted except in terms of its place and function in the whole.' Locate this text, and study it in its context. What does Packer mean by this statement? What are its implications for the practice of citing 'proof texts' – generally out of context – to prove controversial points?

5. 'A text taken out of context is simply a con.' From your study of this passage, would Packer endorse this witticism?

Notes

1. John R. W. Stott, *Fundamentalism and Evangelicalism*, London: Crusade Booklets, 1956. North American edition published by Eerdmans in 1959.

2. 'Christianity and non-Christian religions' (1959)

Evangelism has been a perennial concern of J. I. Packer's. Even though he may have felt that he lacked the personal gifts for an evangelistic ministry, Packer believed that it was important to lay sound theological foundations for evangelism. This concern can be seen as underlying his book *Evangelism and the Sovereignty of God* (1961), which can be seen as a response both to those who argued on the one hand that divine sovereignty made evangelism redundant, and to those who, on the other, argued that evangelism was simply a matter of human technique.

Yet another issue of importance underlies evangelism in modern western culture – namely, the question of the relationship of Christianity to non-Christian religions. This has become of particular importance within the modern western world, which is acutely aware of a plurality of cultures within its midst. As the British theologian Lesslie Newbigin remarks: 'It has become a commonplace to say that we live in a pluralist society – not merely a society which is in fact plural in the variety of cultures, religions and lifestyles which it embraces, but pluralist in the sense that this plurality is celebrated as a thing to be approved and cherished.'[1]

Given the importance of this question, it is clearly of interest to consider what Packer has to say on the matter.

Two main approaches to this question can be identified, within both mainline and evangelical theology: 'particularism' or 'exclusivism', which holds that only those who hear and respond to the Christian gospel may be saved; and 'inclusivism', which argues that, although Christianity represents the normative revelation of God, salvation is none the less possible for those who belong to other religious traditions. A third approach, usually referred to as 'pluralism', holds that all the religious traditions of humanity are equally valid paths to the same core of religious reality. This position is not representative of mainline Christianity, and is often regarded as a culturally accommodated response to western pluralist culture.

The most significant exponent of a pluralist approach to religious traditions is John Hick (b. 1922). In his *God and the Universe of Faiths* (1973), Hick argued for a need to move away from a Christ-centred to a God-centred approach. Describing this change as a 'Copernican Revolution', Hick declared that it was necessary to move away from 'the dogma that Christianity is at the centre to the realization that it is God who is at the centre, and that all religions ... including our own, serve and revolve around him'. Developing this approach, Hick suggests that the aspect of God's nature of central importance to the question of other faiths was his universal saving will. If God wishes everyone to be saved, it is inconceivable that God should be revealed in such a way that only a small portion of humanity could be saved. In fact, as we shall see, this is not a necessary feature of either particularist or inclusivist approaches. However, Hick draws the conclusion that it is necessary to recognize that all religions lead to the same God. Christians have no special access to God, who is universally available through all religious traditions.

This suggestion has major problems. For example, it is fairly clear that the religious traditions of the world are radically different in their beliefs and practices. Hick deals with this point by suggesting that such differences must be interpreted in terms of a 'both-and' rather than an 'either-or'. They should be understood as complementary, rather than contradictory, insights into the one divine reality. This reality lies at the heart of all the religions; yet 'their differing experiences of that reality, interacting over the centuries with the different thought-forms of different cultures, have led to increasing differentiation and contrasting elaboration'. (This idea is very similar to the 'universal rational religion of nature', propounded by Deist writers, which became corrupted through time.) Equally, Hick has difficulties with those non-theistic religious traditions, such as Advaitin Hinduism or Theravada Buddhism, which have no place for a god.

These difficulties relate to observed features of religious traditions. In other words, the beliefs of non-Christian religions make it difficult to accept that they are all speaking of the same God. But a more fundamental theological worry remains: is Hick actually talking about the Christian God at all? A central Christian conviction – that God is revealed definitively in Jesus Christ

– has to be set to one side to allow Hick to proceed. Hick argues that he is merely adopting a theocentric, rather than a Christocentric, approach. Yet the Christian insistence that God is known normatively through Christ implies that authentically Christian knowledge of God is derived through Christ. For a number of critics, Hick's desertion of Christ as a reference point means abandoning any claim to speak from a Christian perspective.

Traditional Christianity is strongly resistant to the homogenizing agenda of religious pluralists, not least on account of its high Christology. The suggestion that all religions are more or less talking about vaguely the same 'God' finds itself in difficulty in relation to certain essentially Christian ideas – most notably, the doctrines of the incarnation and the Trinity. For example, if God is Christ-like, as the doctrine of the divinity of Christ affirms in uncompromising terms, then the historical figure of Jesus, along with the witness to him in Scripture, becomes of foundational importance to Christianity. Many pluralists thus find themselves rejecting a series of central Christian teachings – such as that of the divinity and the resurrection of Jesus, and the doctrine of the Trinity. This strongly reductionist approach to Christianity is regarded with distaste by many Christians, who feel that serious liberties are being taken with their faith to serve the notion that all religions are saying the same thing.

We shall thus explore the two main lines of approach found within the Christian tradition in relation to other religions, before looking at Packer's defence of the 'exclusivist' position.

The particularist or exclusivist approach

Perhaps the most influential statement of this position may be found in the writings of Hendrik Kraemer (1888–1965), especially his *Christian Message in a Non-Christian World* (1938). Kraemer emphasized that 'God has revealed the Way and the Truth and the Life in Jesus Christ, and wills this to be known throughout the world'. This revelation is absolutely distinctive, and exists in a category of its own, and cannot be set alongside the ideas of revelation found in other religious traditions.

What, then, of those who have not heard the gospel of Christ? What happens to them? Are not particularists denying salvation to those who have not heard of Christ – or, who having heard of him, choose to reject him? This criticism is frequently levelled against particularism by its critics, especially from a pluralist perspective. Thus John Hick, arguing from a pluralist perspective, suggests that the doctrine that salvation is possible only through Christ is inconsistent with belief in the universal saving will of God. That this is not, in fact, the case is easily demonstrated by considering the view of Karl

Barth, easily the most sophisticated of twentieth-century defenders of the particularist position.

Barth declares that salvation is possible only through Christ. He nevertheless insists on the ultimate eschatological victory of grace over unbelief – that is, at the end of history. Eventually, God's grace will triumph completely, and all will come to faith in Christ. This is the only way to salvation – but it is a way that, through the grace of God, is effective for all. For Barth, the particularity of God's revelation through Christ is not contradicted by the universality of salvation.

In closing this brief discussion of particularism, it should be noted that a number of works published in the 1980s termed this type of approach as 'exclusivism'. This term has now been generally abandoned, mainly because it is considered to be polemical. The approach is now generally described as 'particularism', on account of its affirmation of the particular and distinctive features of the Christian faith.

The inclusivist approach

The most significant advocate of this model is the leading Jesuit writer Karl Rahner (1904–84). In the fifth volume of his *Theological Investigations*, Rahner develops four theses, setting out the view, not merely that individual non-Christians may be saved, but that the non-Christian religious traditions in general may have access to the saving grace of God in Christ.

1. Christianity is the absolute religion, founded on the unique event of the self-revelation of God in Christ. But this revelation took place at a specific point in history. Those who lived before this point, or who have yet to hear about this event, would thus seem to be excluded from salvation – which is contrary to the saving will of God.

2. For this reason, despite their errors and shortcomings, non-Christian religious traditions are valid and capable of mediating the saving grace of God, until the gospel is made known to their members. After the gospel has been proclaimed to the adherents of such non-Christian religious traditions, they are no longer legitimate, from the standpoint of Christian theology.

3. The faithful adherent of a non-Christian religious tradition is thus to be regarded as an 'anonymous Christian'.

4. Other religious traditions will not be displaced by Christianity. Religious pluralism will continue to be a feature of human existence.

We may explore the first three theses in more detail. It will be clear that Rahner strongly affirms the principle that salvation may only be had through Jesus, as he is interpreted by the Christian tradition. 'Christianity understands itself as the absolute religion, intended for all people, which cannot recognize any other religion beside itself as of equal right.' Yet Rahner supplements this with an emphasis upon the universal saving will of God: God wishes that all shall be saved, even though not all know Christ. 'Somehow all people must be able to be members of the church.'

For this reason, Rahner argues that saving grace must be available outside the bounds of the church – and hence in other religious traditions. He vigorously opposes those who adopt too-neat solutions, insisting that either a religious tradition comes from God or that it is an unauthentic and purely human invention. Where Kraemer argues that non-Christian religious traditions were little more than self-justifying human constructions, Rahner argues that such traditions may well include elements of truth.

Rahner justifies this suggestion by considering the relation between the Old and New Testaments. Although the Old Testament, strictly speaking, represents the outlook of a non-Christian religion (Judaism), Christians are able to read it and discern within it elements which continue to be valid. The Old Testament is evaluated in the light of the New, and as a result, certain practices (such as food laws) are discarded as unacceptable, while others are retained (such as the moral law). The same approach can and should, Rahner argues, be adopted in the case of other religions.

The saving grace of God is thus available through non-Christian religious traditions, despite their shortcomings. Many of their adherents, Rahner argues, have thus accepted that grace, without being fully aware of what it is. It is for this reason that Rahner introduces the term 'anonymous Christians', to refer to those who have experienced divine grace without necessarily knowing it. This term has been heavily criticized. For example, John Hick has suggested that it is paternalist, offering 'honorary status granted unilaterally to people who have not expressed any desire for it'. Nevertheless, Rahner's intention is to allow for the real effects of divine grace in the lives of those who belong to non-Christian traditions. Full access to truth about God (as it is understood within the Christian tradition) is not a necessary precondition for access to the saving grace of God. A related approach has been developed by the Canadian evangelical writer Clark Pinnock, in his *Wideness in God's Mercy* (1992). Many evangelicals are very uneasy about Pinnock's approach, which they regard as calling into question the uniqueness of the gospel and the sufficiency of the death of Christ.

For this reason, Packer's contribution to this debate continues to be of considerable importance. We shall consider it in what follows.

Related works by Packer

Evangelism and the Sovereignty of God, London: Inter-Varsity Fellowship; Chicago: InterVarsity Press, 1961.

'Isn't One Religion as Good as Another?', in F. Colquhoun (ed.), *Hard Questions*. London: Falcon Press, 1967), pp. 16–19.

'The Problem of Universalism Today', *Theolog Review: Australian Journal of the Theological Students Fellowship* 5/3 (November, 1969), pp. 16–24. (Essay 6 in this collection.)

'The Way of Salvation: I. What is Salvation? II. What is Faith? III. The Problem of Universalism. IV: Are Non-Christian Faiths Ways of Salvation?' *Bibliotheca Sacra* 129 (1972), pp. 105–125; 291–306; 130 (1973), pp. 3–10; 110–116.

'What is Evangelism?', in H. Conn (ed.), *Theological Perspectives on Church Growth*, Nutley, NJ: Presbyterian and Reformed, 1976, pp. 91–105.

'The Uniqueness of Jesus Christ', *Churchman* 92 (1978), pp. 101–111.

'Good Pagans and God's Kingdom', *Christianity Today*, 17 January 1986, pp. 27–31.

'Evangelicals and the Way of Salvation: New Challenges to the Gospel', in C. F. H. Henry and K. Kantzer (eds.), *Evangelical Affirmations*, Grand Rapids, MI: Zondervan, 1990, pp. 107–136.

Christianity and non-Christian religions

Christianity has always been a missionary religion. At the close of his earthly ministry, our Lord commissioned his followers to go and make disciples of all nations (Matt. 28:19), and it is generally admitted today that the church of later generations has no right to call herself apostolic unless she acknowledges this missionary obligation to be her own. Now, the universal missionary imperative implies an exclusive claim, a claim made by our Lord himself: 'I am the way, the truth, and the life: no man cometh unto the Father, but by me' (John 14:6). To deny that men can know the Father apart from Christ is to affirm that non-Christian religion is powerless to bring them to God and effective only to keep them from him.

Only one saving religion

Accordingly, the summons to put faith in Christ must involve a demand for the endorsement of this adverse verdict, and for the avowed renunciation of non-Christian faith as empty and, indeed, demonic falsehood. 'Turn from these vanities to the living God' (Acts 14:15) – that was what the gospel meant for those who worshipped the Greek pantheon at Lystra in Paul's day, and that is what it means for the adherents of non-Christian religions now. The gospel calls their worship idolatry (1 Thess. 1:9) and their deities demons (1 Cor. 10:20), and asks them to accept this evaluation as part of their repentance and faith.

And this point must be constantly and obtrusively made; for to play down the impotence of non-Christian religion would obscure the glory of Christ as the only Saviour of men. 'There is none other name under heaven ... whereby we must be saved' (Acts 4:12). If Christless religion can save, the incarnation and atonement were superfluous. Only, therefore, as the church insists that Christless religion, of whatever shape or form, is soteriologically bankrupt can it avoid seeming to countenance the suspicion that for some people, at any rate, our Lord's death was really needless.

What of other religions?

It is beyond dispute that this is the biblical position but naturally it raises questions. How does the gospel evaluate the religions which it seeks to displace? How, in view of its condemnation of them, does it account for the moral and intellectual achievements of their piety and theology? And how does it propose to set about commending Christ to the sincere and convinced adherents of the religions it denounces, without giving an impression of ignorance, intolerance, patronage, or conceit?

These questions press more acutely today than at any time since the Reformation, and there are three reasons for this.

In the first place, a century's intensive study of comparative religion has made available more knowledge than the church ever had before about the non-Christian faiths of the world, and in particular of the intellectual and mystical strength of the highest forms of eastern religion. This makes it necessary at least to qualify the sweeping dismissal of these faiths as ugly superstitions which to earlier missionary thinkers, who knew only the seamy side of eastern popular piety, seemed almost axiomatic. Fair dealing is a Christian duty, and every body of opinion has a right to be assessed by its best representatives as well as its worst. (How would historic Christianity fare if measured solely by popular piety down the ages?)

In the second place, the great Asian faiths are reviving and gaining ground partly, no doubt, through the impetus given them by upsurging nationalism. It is no longer possible naïvely to assume, as our evangelical grandfathers often did, that these religions must soon wither and die as the gospel advances. As we meet them today, they are not moribund, but confident, aggressive, and forward-looking, critical of Christian ideas and convinced of their own superiority. How are we to speak to their present condition?

In the third place, Christian evangelism has been accused, and to some extent convicted, by eastern spokesmen in particular, of having in the past formed part of a larger cultural, and sometimes imperialistic, programme of 'westernization'. These thinkers now tend to dismiss Christianity as a distinctively western faith and its exclusive claim as one more case of western cultural arrogance, and to insist that the present aspirations of the East are compatible only with indigenous eastern forms of religion. There seems no doubt that Protestant missionary policy during the last hundred years really has invited this tragic misunderstanding. Too often it did in fact proceed on the unquestioned assumption that to export the outward forms of western civilization was part of the missionary's task, and that indigenous churches should be given no more than colonial status in relation to the mother church from which the missionaries had come. It is not surprising that such a policy has been both misunderstood and resented. The Protestant missionary enterprise needs urgently to learn to explain itself to the new nations in a way that makes clear it is not part of a cunning plan for exporting the British or American way of life, but is something quite different. This necessitates a reappraisal on our part of non-Christian religions which will be, if not less critical in conclusions, more sympathetic, respectful, and theologically discriminating in method than was the case in earlier days. Christian missionary enterprise inevitably gives offence to those of other faiths simply by existing; but the church must watch to see that the offence given is always that of the cross and never of fancied cultural snobbery and imperialism of the missionaries.

It seems that the need for a deepening of accuracy and respect in the evangelistic dialogue with other religions is more pressing than evangelical Christians generally realize. This, perhaps, is because evangelical missionary effort during the past fifty years has been channelled largely through small inter- (or un-)denominational societies which have concentrated on pioneer and village work, whereas it is in the towns that resentment and suspicion of the missionary movement are strongest. But it is very desirable that evangelicals should appreciate the situation and labour to give the necessary lead. They are uniquely qualified to do this, having been preserved from the confusion about the relation of Christianity to other religions which has clouded the greater part of Protestant thinking since the heyday of liberalism fifty years ago. Though liberalism is now generally disavowed, its ideas still have influence; and its ideas on this particular subject are the reverse of helpful, as we shall now see.

Liberal bias lingers

The liberal philosophy (you could not call it a theology) of religion was built on two connected principles, both of which have a pedigree going back to the philosophical idealism of Hegel and the religious romanticism of Schleiermacher. The first principle was that the essence of religion is the same everywhere: that religion is a genus wherein each particular religion is a more or less highly developed species. This idea was usually linked with the reading of man's religious history as a record of ascent from animistic magical rites through ritualistic polytheism to the heights of ethical monotheism – a specious speculative schematization, the evolutionary shape of which gave it a vogue much greater than the evidence for it warrants. (In fact, the evidence for primitive monotheism, and for cyclic degeneration as the real pattern of mankind's religious history, seems a good deal stronger. Romans 1:18–32 cannot now be dismissed as scientifically groundless fantasy.)

The second principle, following from the first, was that creeds and dogmas are no more than the epiphenomena of moral and mystical experience, attempts to express religious intuitions verbally in order to induce similar experiences in others. Theological differences between religions, or within a single religion, therefore, can have no ultimate significance. All religion grows out of an intuition, more or less pure and deep, of the same infinite. All religions are climbing the same mountain to the seat of the same transcendent Being. The most that can be said of their differences is that they are going up by different routes, some of which appear less direct and may not reach quite to the top.

If these ideas are accepted, the only question that can be asked when two religions meet is: which of these is the higher and more perfect specimen of its kind? And this question is to be answered by comparing, not their doctrines, but their piety and the characteristic religious experiences which their piety enshrines. For religions are not the sort of things that are true or false, nor are their doctrines more than their by-products. Nor, indeed, has any existing form of religion more than a relative validity; the best religion yet may still be superseded by a worthier. Accordingly, the only possible justification for Christian missions is that Christians, whose piety and ethics represent the highest in religion that has emerged to date, are bound by the rule of charity to share their possessions with men of other faiths, not in order to displace those faiths, but to enrich them and (doubtless) to be enriched by them. And from this pooling of religious experience a still higher form of religion may well be developed. This position was expounded at the academic level by Troeltsch and on the popular level in such a document as the American laymen's enquiry, *Rethinking Missions* (1931), which Hendrik Kraemer has described as 'devoid of real theological sense ... a total distortion of the Christian message', involving 'a suicide of missions and an annulment of the Christian faith' (*Religion and the Christian Faith*, 1956, p. 224). (This is just what J. Gresham Machen said when the report came out, but with less acceptance than Kraemer's words command today.)

A change for the better

Since 1931, however, the theological atmosphere has changed for the better. The liberal philosophy of religions has been demolished by the broadsides of such writers as Barth, Brunner, and Kraemer himself, and attention is being given once again to the theology of religions found in the Bible.

What is theology? It can be summed up in the following antithesis: Christianity is a religion of revelation received; all other faiths are religions of revelations denied. This we must briefly explain.

Christianity is a religion of revelation received. It is a religion of faith in a special revelation, given through specific historical events, of salvation for sinners. The object of Christian faith is the Creator's disclosure of himself as triune Saviour of his guilty creatures through the mediation of Jesus Christ, the Father's Word and Son. This is a disclosure authoritatively reported and interpreted in the God-inspired pages of Holy Scripture. Faith is trust in the Christ of history who is the Christ of the Bible. The revelation which the gospel declares and faith receives is God's gracious answer to the question of human sin. Its purpose is to restore guilty rebels to fellowship with their Maker. Faith in Christ is no less God's gift than is the Christ of faith; the faith which receives Christ is created in fallen men by the sovereign work of the Spirit, restoring spiritual sight to their blind minds. Thus true Christian faith is an adoring acknowledgment of the omnipotent mercy of God both in providing a perfect Saviour for hopeless, helpless sinners and in drawing them to him.

Non-Christian religions, however, are religions of revelation denied. They are religions which spring from the suppression and distortion of a general revelation given through man's knowledge of God's world concerning the being and law of the Creator. The *locus classicus* on this is Romans 1:18–32;

2:12–15. Paul tells us that 'the invisible things' of God – his deity and creative power – are not merely discernible but actually discerned ('God manifested' them; they 'are clearly seen', 1:19–20, Revised Version) by mankind; and this discernment brings knowledge of the obligation of worship and thanksgiving (verses 20–21), the duties of the moral law (2:14–15), God's wrath against ungodliness (1:18), and death as the penalty of sin (1:32). General revelation is adapted only to the needs of man in innocence and answers only the question: what does God require of his rational creatures? It speaks of wrath against sin but not of mercy for sinners. Hence it can bring nothing but disquiet to fallen man. But man prefers not to face it, labours to falsify it, and wilfully perverts its truth into the lie of idolatry (1:25) by habitual lawlessness (1:18). Man is a worshipping being who has refused in his pride to worship his Maker; so he turns the light of divine revelation into the darkness of man-made religion, and enslaves himself to unworthy deities of his own devising, made in his own image or that of creatures inferior to himself (1:23). This is the biblical aetiology of non-biblical religion, from the crudest to the most refined.

Flashes of common grace

Yet common grace prevents the truth from being utterly suppressed. Flashes of light break through which we should watch for and gratefully recognize (as did Paul at Athens when he quoted Aratus, Acts 17:28), and no part of general revelation is universally obscured. Despite all attempts to smother them, these truths keep seeping through the back of man's mind, creating uneasiness and prompting fresh efforts to blanket the obtrusive light. Hence we may expect to find in all non-Christian religions certain characteristic recurring tensions, never really resolved. These are a restless sense of the hostility of the powers of the universe; an undefined feeling of guilt, and all sorts of merit-making techniques designed to get rid of it; a dread of death, and a consuming anxiety to feel that one has conquered it; forms of worship aimed at once to placate, bribe, and control the gods, and to make them keep their distance except when wanted; an alarming readiness to call moral evil good, and good evil, in the name of religion; an ambivalent attitude of mind which seems both to seek God and to seek to evade him in the same act.

Therefore, in our evangelistic dialogue with non-Christian religions, our task must be to present the biblical revelation of God in Christ not as supplementing them but as explaining their existence, exposing their errors, and judging their inadequacy. We shall measure them exclusively by what they say, or omit to say, about God and man's relation to him. We shall labour to show the real problem of religion to which the gospel gives the answer, namely, how a sinner may get right with his Maker. We shall diligently look for the hints and fragments of truth which these religions contain, and appeal to them (set in their proper theological perspective) as pointers to the true knowledge of God. And we shall do all this under a sense of compulsion (for Christ has sent us), in love (for non-Christians are our fellow-creatures, and without Christ they cannot be saved), and with all humility (for we are sinners ourselves, and there is nothing, no part of our message, not even our faith, which we have not received). So, with help from on high, we shall both honour God and bear testimony of him before men.

Questions for study

1. Of the three positions outlined in the introduction to this section – namely, 'exclusivism', 'inclusivism' and 'pluralism' – which corresponds most closely to Packer's position?
2. What form would the main lines of Packer's criticisms of the two rival positions take?
3. What reasons does Packer offer for the new concern for religious pluralism? How does he evaluate them?
4. 'Non-Christian religions ... are religions of revelation denied.' Locate this quotation within the text, and study it carefully in its context. What does Packer mean by this? And what are the implications of this assertion?
5. 'We shall diligently look for the hints and fragments of truth which these religions contain, and appeal to them (set in their proper theological perspective) as pointers to the true knowledge of God.' Locate this quotation. What biblical passage plays a major role in Packer's thinking at this point? What evangelistic approaches towards other religions does Packer's statement suggest?

Notes

1. Lesslie Newbigin, *The Gospel in a Pluralist Society*, Grand Rapids, MI: Eerdmans, 1989, p. 1.

3. 'The nature of the church' (1962)

The question of the nature of the church was of central importance to evangelicals in the twentieth century. The evangelical debate within England during the 1960s often focused on which model of the church was appropriate for evangelicals. Two main models emerged during those debates, each of which had excellent historical and biblical credentials. John Calvin had stated the case for a 'mixed body' understanding of the church, and some Puritan writers – including John Owen – the case for a 'gathered community'. The 'mixed body' approach recognized that the visible church (that is, the church as seen in real, everyday life) consisted of both the regenerate and the unregenerate, in much the same way as wheat and 'tares' (or weeds) grew together in the same field in the parable of Matthew 13. Separation would take place at the final judgment; in the meantime, the converted and the unconverted mingled in the same church. This concept of the church was typical of Protestant churches which traced their history back though the great Reformers Luther and Calvin, and include Anglicans, Lutherans, and Presbyterians.

The second model argued that the church was, by definition, a body of saints, not of sinners, so that only those who were publicly recognized as regenerate could be considered to be church members. This 'pure body' approach became especially influential within the more radical wing of the sixteenth-century Reformation, and became established in England in various separatist groups, including Baptists and Puritans. The model continues to find wide acceptance within North American evangelicalism, particularly within Baptist circles.

The crisis of 1966 led to intense division arising within British evangelicalism over the doctrine of the church (see Introduction, p. 13). For Martyn Lloyd-Jones, it was inevitable that there would be 'a crisis on what is to me the fundamental issue, namely, do we believe in a territorial church or a gathered community of saints?' While there is a danger of simplification at this point, Packer and John Stott argued for a 'mixed body' doctrine of the church, which allowed evangelicals to see themselves as an *ecclesiola in ecclesia* – in other words, a reforming body within a state church. Lloyd-Jones and his colleagues argued for a 'pure body' doctrine of the church, in which only those with explicitly evangelical convictions were to be accepted for membership.

Packer developed and justified his views still further in the course of the next decade. His fullest statement of his approach was set out in two pamphlets published by Latimer House, of which Packer had once been Warden.[1] In these pamphlets, Packer notes the difficulties which face evangelicals in doctrinally mixed churches, such as the Church of England. The arguments which Packer counters in these works are primarily those deriving from the circles around Lloyd-Jones, particularly the demand that evangelicals withdraw from such mixed churches to form 'pure' denominations:

> Some have urged evangelicals in 'doctrinally mixed' churches to withdraw into a tighter fellowship where the pre-critical, pre-liberal view of Scripture is rigorously upheld and sceptical revisionism in theology is debarred. It has been said that failure to do this is as unprincipled as it is foolish. It is unprincipled, the argument runs, because by staying in churches which tolerate heretics you become constructively guilty of their heresies, by your association with them; and it is foolish because you have not the least hope of cleaning up the Augean stables while liberals remain there. Withdrawal is the conscientious man's only option.[2]

Both these arguments can be discerned within Lloyd-Jones's writings from 1965 onwards, including his address at the 1965 Puritan Studies Conference.

Packer's response involved a number of observations. First, he noted that all mainline churches are, as a matter of historical fact, founded on a set of beliefs (embodied in the Christian creeds, and sets of confessional documents) which commit those churches to theological orthodoxy. Some may depart from this; evangelicals within those churches have a duty to recall them to faithfulness. They cannot be regarded as 'guilty by association' if they protest in this way. The idea of 'guilt by association' was, for Packer, 'a nonsense notion, which has been given an unhappy airing during the last two decades'.[3] If trends towards liberalism are not resisted, a denomination will slide into heresy. And who will protest and argue against this, unless evangelicals remain within those mainline churches for as long as possible?

Packer also offered a criticism against those who argued that their own congregations or denominations were theologically correct. He noted that smaller doctrinally pure bodies, such as the Federation of Independent Evangelical Churches, are open to the charge that they might 'purchase doctrinal purity at the price of theological stagnation, and are cultural backwaters out of touch with society around'. Underlying this point is Packer's conviction that cultural engagement – of such importance to effective evangelism – is not assisted by a total withdrawal from the society which is to be evangelized.

From this brief analysis, it will be clear that the question of the *identity and limits of the church* is of major importance to modern evangelicalism. The passage selected for study dates from 1962, before the outbreak of serious controversy within British evangelical circles over the issue. As a result, the essay lacks any polemical tone or content, and can be seen as a careful and responsible statement of an evangelical ecclesiology – to use the technical theological term for the 'doctrine of the church' – for a wide evangelical readership. The collection of essays was edited by Carl Henry, himself a leading Baptist evangelical writer.

Related works by Packer

'Fellowship: The Theological Basis', *Christian Graduate* 16/3 (September 1963), pp. 7–11.

'The Holy Spirit and the Local Congregation', *Churchman* 78 (1964), pp. 98–108.

'One Body in Christ: The Doctrine and Expression of Christian Unity', *Churchman* 80 (1966), pp. 16–26.

The nature of the church

The church of God, 'that wonderful and sacred mystery',[1] is a subject that stands at the very heart of the Bible. For the church is the object of the redemption which the Bible proclaims. It was to save the church that the Son of God became man and died;[2] God purchased his church at the cost of Christ's blood.[3] It is through the church that God makes known his redeeming wisdom to the hosts of heaven.[4] It is within the church that the individual Christian finds the ministries of grace, the means of growth, and his primary sphere for service.[5] We cannot properly understand the purpose of God, nor the method of grace, nor the kingdom of Christ, nor the work of the Holy Spirit, nor the meaning of world history without studying the doctrine of the church.

But what is the church? The fact that we all first meet the church as an organized society must not mislead us into thinking that it is essentially, or even primarily, that. There is a sense in which the outward form of the church disguises its true nature rather than reveals it. Essentially the church is not a human organization as such, but a divinely created fellowship of sinners who trust a common Saviour, and are one with each other because they are all one with him in a union realized by the Holy Spirit. Thus the church's real life, like that of its individual members, is for the present 'hid in Christ with God',[6] and will not be manifested to the world until he appears. Meanwhile, what we need, if we are to understand the church's nature, is insight into the person and work of Christ and of the Spirit and into the meaning of the life of faith.

The covenant people of God

The church is not simply a New Testament phenomenon. An ecclesiology which started with the New Testament would be out of the way at the first step. The New Testament church is the historical continuation of Old Testament Israel. The New Testament word for 'church', *ekklēsia* (in secular Greek a public gathering), is regularly used in the Greek Old Testament for the 'congregation' of Israel. Paul pictured the church in history, from its beginning to his own day, as a single olive tree, from which some natural (Israelite) branches had been broken off through unbelief, to be replaced by some wild (Gentile) branches.[7] Elsewhere, he tells Gentile believers that in Christ they have become 'Abraham's seed', 'the Israel of God'.[8]

The basis of the church's life in both Testaments is the covenant which God made with Abraham. The fundamental idea of biblical ecclesiology is of the church as the covenant people of God.

What is a covenant? It is a defined relationship of promise and commitment which binds the parties concerned to perform whatever duties toward each other their relationship may involve. The two main biblical analogies for God's covenant with sinners are the royal covenant between overlord and vassal and the marriage covenant between husband and wife, the former speaking of God's sovereignty and lordship, the latter of his love and saviourhood. By his covenant, God demands acceptance of his rule and promises enjoyment of his blessing. Both thoughts are contained in the covenant 'slogan', 'I will be your God, and ye shall be my people';[9] both are implied whenever a believer says 'my [our] God'.

God expounded his covenant to Abraham in Genesis 17, a chapter of crucial importance for the doctrine of the church. Four points should be noticed here. First, the covenant relationship was announced as a *corporate* one, extending to Abraham's seed 'throughout their generations'.[10] Thus, the covenant created a permanent community. Second, the relationship was one of *pledged beneficence* on God's part: he undertook to give Abraham's seed the land of Canaan.[11] This, as he had already told Abraham, would involve redeeming them from captivity in Egypt.[12] Third, the end of the relationship was fellowship between God and his people: that they should 'walk before' him, knowing him as they were known by him.[13] Fourth, the covenant was confirmed by the institution of a 'token',[14] the *initiatory rite* of circumcision.

Later, through Moses, God gave his people a *law* for their lives and authorized forms of *worship* (feasts, exhibiting his fellowship with them, and sacrifices, pointing to the bloodshedding for sin which alone could provide a basis for this fellowship). Also, he spoke to them repeatedly, through his prophets, of their glorious *hope* which was to be realized when the Messiah came.

Thus emerged the basic biblical notion of the church as the covenant people of God, the redeemed family, marked out as his by the covenant sign which they had received, worshipping and serving him according to his revealed will, living in fellowship with him and with each other, walking by faith in his promises, and looking for the coming glory of the messianic kingdom.

New Testament fulfilment

When Christ came, this Old Testament conception was not destroyed, but fulfilled. Christ, the Mediator of the covenant, was himself the link between the

Mosaic and the Christian dispensations of it.[15] The New Testament depicts him as the true Israel, the servant of God in whom the nation's God-guided history is recapitulated and brought to completion,[16] and also as the seed of Abraham in whom all nations of the earth find blessing.[17] Through his atoning death, which did away with the typical sacrificial services for ever, believing Jews and Gentiles become in him the people of God on earth. Baptism, the New Testament initiatory sign corresponding to circumcision, represents primarily union with Christ in his death and resurrection, which is the sole way of entry into the church.[18]

Thus, the New Testament church has Abraham as its father,[19] Jerusalem as its mother[20] and place of worship,[21] and the Old Testament as its Bible.[22] Echoing Exodus 19:5–6 and Hosea 2:23, Peter describes the Christian church in thorough-going Old Testament fashion as 'a chosen generation, a royal priesthood, an holy nation, a peculiar people; ... Which in time past were not a people, but are now the people of God'.[23]

A new creation in Christ

The New Testament idea of the church is reached by superimposing upon the notion of the covenant people of God the further thought that the church is the company of those who share in the redemptive renewal of a sin-spoiled creation, which began when Christ rose from the dead.[24] As the individual believer is a new creation in Christ,[25] raised with him out of death into life,[26] possessed of and led by the life-giving Holy Spirit,[27] so also is the church as a whole. Its life springs from its union with Christ, crucified and risen. Paul, in Ephesians, pictures the church successively as Christ's *building*, now growing unto 'an holy temple in the Lord';[28] his *body*, now growing toward a state of full edification;[29] and his *bride*, now being sanctified and cleansed in readiness for 'the marriage supper of the Lamb'.[30]

Some modern writers in the 'catholic' tradition treat Paul's body metaphor as having a special 'ontological' significance, and indicating that the church is 'really' (in a sense in which it is not 'really' anything else) an extension of the manhood and incarnate life of Christ. But, according to Paul, the church's union with Christ is symbolically exhibited in baptism; and what baptism symbolizes is not incorporation into Christ's manhood simply, but sharing with him in his death to sin, with all its saving fruits, and in the power and life of his resurrection. When Paul says that the Spirit *baptizes* men into one body, he means that the Spirit makes us members of the body by bringing us into that union with Christ which baptism signifies.[31] Scripture would lead us to call the church an extension of the resurrection rather than of the incarnation!

In any case, Paul uses the body metaphor only to illustrate the authority of the Head and his ministry to his members, and the various ministries that they must fulfil to each other; and we have no warrant for extrapolating it in other theological directions.

Ministry in the church

The New Testament conceives of all ministry in the church as Christ's ministry to and through the church. As the church is a priestly people, all its members having direct access to God through Christ's mediation, so it is a ministering people, all its members holding in trust from Christ gifts of ministry (i.e., service) for the edifying of the one body.[32] Within the context of this universal ministry, Christ calls some specifically to minister the gospel,[33] giving them strength and skill for their task[34] and blessing their labours.[35] As spokesmen and representatives of Christ, teaching and applying his Word, church officers exercise his authority; yet they need to remember that, as individuals, they belong to the church as its servants, not the church to them as their empire. The church is Christ's kingdom, not theirs.[36] This is a basic point which Luther accused the papacy of forgetting.

Universal and local

Paul speaks not merely of the whole body but also of local groups in an area, and even of a Christian household, as '*the* church'. No local group is ever called 'a church'. For Paul does not regard the church universal as an aggregate of local churches (let alone denominations!); his thought is rather that whenever a group of believers, even Christ's statutory two or three,[37] meet in his name, they *are* the church in the place where they meet. Each particular gathering, however small, is the local manifestation of the church universal embodying and displaying the spiritual realities of the church's supernatural life. So Paul can apply the body metaphor, with only slight alteration, both to the local church (one body in Christ)[38] and to the universal church (one body *under* Christ).[39]

Visible and invisible

The Reformers drew a necessary distinction between the church visible and invisible; that is, between the one church of Christ on earth as God sees it and as man sees it; in other words, as it is and as it seems to be. Man sees the church as an organized society, with a fixed structure and roll of members. But (the Reformers argued) this society can never be simply identified with the one holy catholic church of which the Bible speaks. The identity between the two is at best partial, indirect, and constantly varying in degree. The point is important. The church as God sees it, the company of believers in communion with Christ and in him with each other, is necessarily invisible to men, since Christ and the Holy Spirit and faith, the realities which make the church, are themselves invisible. The church becomes visible as its members meet together in Christ's name to worship and hear God's Word. But the church visible is a mixed body. Some who belong, though orthodox, are not true believers – not, that is, true members of the church as God knows it – and need to be converted.[40] The Reformers' distinction thus safeguards the vital truth that visible church membership saves no man apart from faith in Christ.

Another matter on which this distinction throws light is the question of church unity. If a visible organization, as such, were or could be the one church of God, then any organizational separation would be a breach of unity, and the only way to reunite a divided Christendom would be to work for a single international super-church. Also, on this hypothesis, it would be open to argue that some institutional feature is of the essence of the church and is therefore a *sine qua non* of reunion. Rome, for instance, actually defines the church as the society of the faithful *under the Pope's headship*; some Anglicans make episcopacy in the apostolic succession similarly essential. But, in fact, the church invisible, the true church, is one already. Its unity is given to it in Christ.[41] The proper ecumenical task is not to create church unity by denominational coalescence, but to recognize the unity that already exists and to give it worthy expression on the local level.

In the purposes of God, the church, we have seen, is glorious; yet on earth it remains a little flock in a largely hostile environment. Often, its state and prospects seem to us precarious. But we need not fear. Christ himself, the King who reigns on Zion's hill, is its Saviour, its Head, its Builder, its Keeper. He has given his promise: 'the gates of hell shall not prevail against it'.[42] And he is not accustomed to break his word.

Questions for study

1. 'We cannot properly understand the purpose of God, nor the method of grace, nor the kingdom of Christ, nor the work of the Holy Spirit, nor the meaning of world history without studying the doctrine of the church.' Locate this citation within the text, and consider its position within Packer's argument. How does Packer justify this very strong statement?

Can you trace the trajectory of the argument which leads him to this conclusion?

2. Which biblical texts does Packer appear to consider to be of particular importance in formulating his understanding of the church?

3. Packer draws a clear distinction between the local and universal church. How does he defend this distinction? Can you identify biblical passages which Packer gives as illustrations of each?

4. 'The proper ecumenical task is not to create church unity by denominational coalescence, but to recognize the unity that already exists and to give it worthy expression on the local level.' What does Packer mean by this? How does he justify it? And if he is right, what are its implications for the way in which Christians should relate to each other?

Notes

Preamble

1. *The Evangelical Anglican Identity Problem*, Latimer Study No. 1, Oxford: Latimer House, 1978; *A Kind of Noah's Ark? The Anglican Commitment to Comprehensiveness*, Latimer Study No. 10, Oxford: Latimer House, 1981.
2. *A Kind of Noah's Ark?*, p. 10.
3. Ibid., p. 36.

Essay

1. Thomas Aquinas.
2. Eph. 5:25.
3. Acts 20:28.
4. Eph. 3:10.
5. Eph. 4:11–16.
6. Col. 3:3.
7. Rom. 11:16–24.
8. Gal. 3:29; cf. Rom. 4:11–18; Gal. 6:16.
9. Cf. Exod. 29:45; Lev. 26:12; Jer. 31:33; 2 Cor. 6:16; Rev. 21:3; etc.
10. Gen. 17:7.
11. Gen. 17:8, a type of heaven; cf. Heb. 11:8–16.
12. Gen. 15:13–21; cf. Exod. 2:24.
13. Gen. 17:1.
14. Gen. 17:11.
15. I.e., the 'old' and the 'new' covenants of Heb. 8 – 10, chapters which build upon Jer. 31:31ff.
16. Cf. Matt. 2:15; etc.
17. Gal. 3:8–9, 14–29.
18. Rom. 6:3ff.; Gal. 3:27ff.; Col. 2:11ff.
19. Rom. 4:11, 16.
20. Gal. 4:26.
21. Heb. 12:22.

22. Rom. 15:4.
23. 1 Pet. 2:9–10.
24. Cf. 1 Cor. 15:20; Col. 1:18.
25. 2 Cor. 5:17.
26. Eph. 2:1ff.
27. Rom. 8:9–14.
28. Eph. 2:21.
29. Found, as well as in Eph. 4, in Rom. 12; 1 Cor. 12 and Col. 1.
30. Eph. 5:25ff., cf. Rev. 19:7ff.
31. 1 Cor. 12:13.
32. 1 Cor. 12:4–28; Rom. 12:6–8; cf. 1 Cor. 16:15; 2 Cor. 9:1.
33. Eph. 4:11; cf. Rom.1:1, 5, 9; 15:16.
34. 1 Cor. 3:10; 15:10.
35. 1 Cor. 3:6–7.
36. Cf. 2 Cor. 4:5.
37. Matt. 18:20.
38. Rom. 12; 1 Cor. 12.
39. Eph. 4.
40. Cf. Matt. 13:24ff., 47ff.; 2 Cor. 13:5; 1 Cor. 15:34.
41. Eph. 4:3.
42. Matt. 16:18.

4. 'Keep yourselves from idols' (1963)

On 19 March 1963, John A. T. Robinson, the Anglican Bishop of Woolwich, published a book with the title *Honest to God*. It attracted particular attention on account of the simple fact that its author was a bishop in the Church of England. Shortly before the publication of the book, Robinson had contributed an article to *The Observer*, a leading English Sunday newspaper, with the provocative title: 'Our image of God must go'. When the book appeared, it became a bestseller in England, and earned the nickname 'Honest John' for its author.[1] The initial print run ordered by the publishers was a mere 8,000 copies, of which 2,000 were intended for export to the United States. The print run was sold out on the first day of publication. The demand for the book took everyone by surprise. It is estimated that the book sold 350,000 copies during its first seven months.

The work gave the impression that Robinson regarded traditional Christian beliefs as outdated, meaningless relics of a bygone era. Evangelicals were outraged; yet their responses failed to penetrate to the heart of the issues. Most evangelical responses could be summarized as simple variations on one or two themes. First, a bishop should not be allowed to write books of this kind and remain in office. Second, what the bishop described is not Christian orthodoxy.

It is widely agreed that by far the best evangelical critique of Robinson was Packer's *Keep Yourselves from Idols*. This twenty-page pamphlet was produced in some haste in order to be available as quickly as possible. Its title derives from John's warning to his readers to keep themselves from idols (1 John

5:21). At this stage, Packer was Warden of Latimer House, an evangelical theological think-tank in Oxford. Packer saw this as precisely the kind of public debate in which both he and Latimer House should become involved. The issues involved were crucial, and there was an urgent need for an evangelical voice to be heard in this debate.

For Packer, the choice was not between two different ways of thinking about God; it was about two different Gods, two different Christs – and ultimately, about two different religions. Robinson had not 'updated' the gospel; he had 'changed the truth about God into a lie'. Packer was particularly critical of the way in which Robinson had behaved in his role as a bishop. 'No doubt the church needs its gadflies ... But it is not to the office and work of a gadfly that a bishop is consecrated.' Robinson had, perhaps in effect rather than intention, used 'a position of trust as a vantage-point from which to torpedo the deepest convictions of those who trust him'.

In making these points, Packer can be seen to have repeated the two themes which we noted above. But Packer's response penetrated far more deeply than this. He went on to argue that Robinson's work lacked theological rigour, and rested on gross misunderstandings or simple misreadings of other writers. For Packer, Robinson's work represented a very superficial reading and application of the work of three leading modern Protestant theologians: Dietrich Bonhoeffer, Rudolf Bultmann, and Paul Tillich. Robinson applauded Bonhoeffer for his idea of a 'religionless Christianity', Bultmann for his attempt to 'demythologize' the gospel, and Tillich for his concern to relate Christianity to human 'ultimate concerns'. Indeed, Robinson felt that the time had come to abandon traditional Christian language about a God who was 'out there' or 'up there', and pick up on the insights of depth psychology, which spoke of God (if it spoke of God at all) in terms of the 'ground of our being' – a term much favoured by Tillich.

Packer declared that the work was little more than 'a plateful of mashed up Tillich fried in Bultmann and garnished with Bonhoeffer'. Every page, he argued, bore the unmistakable 'marks of unfinished thinking'. The fundamental flaws of the work were thus theological. While recognizing that Robinson was clearly concerned with relating Christianity to the needs of modern men and women, Packer declared that the entire project was misconceived. It was not Christianity which was being presented in a new manner, but a new religion, which made no reference to the incarnation, the atoning death of Christ, or the resurrection of Jesus. How could this legitimately be described as 'Christianity'? Far from rescuing people, Robinson was merely sinking their lifeboat.

Packer relentlessly pointed out the consequences of Robinson's position.

Robinson's Jesus cannot in any meaningful sense be termed 'Saviour' or 'Lord'. Robinson had eliminated anything distinctively Christian from his conception of God, ending up with a vague form of theism to which any religious person could give at least some degree of assent. Perhaps most tellingly, Packer stressed the serious tension which Robinson generated between theology and worship. On the basis of Robinson's theology, no meaningful account can be given of Christian worship. Robinson's God 'has done nothing to be praised for. He did not make us; we do not depend on him for our existence; he has not ransomed us from hell, nor has he promised to bring us to glory'. Robinson's theology had no place for the concepts of God as creator or redeemer; what, therefore, can he be praised for? Perhaps it was no cause for surprise that Robinson redefined worship in terms of some kind of preparation for service of other people, rather than a response to God's being and deeds. In the end, he sets out a view of religion 'which will be either devoid of devotion to God, or filled with adoration of oneself; and one fears that in practice this either-or would become a both-and'. The work can be seen as a classic evangelical response to the liberalism of many mainline denominations during the 1960s, and remains of importance today.

Related works by Packer

'Atheism', *Inter-Varsity*, Special Introductory Issue (1964), pp. 4–6.
'A Broad Church Reformation?' *London Quarterly and Holborn Review* 189 (October 1964), pp. 270–275.
'Must We Demythologize?', *Theological Students Fellowship Bulletin* 50 (Spring 1968), pp. 1–5.
'A Secular Way to Go', *Third Way* 1/7 (April 1977), pp. 3–5.

Keep yourselves from idols

The bishop's book

The reformed Church of England is founded on the Bible, and its bishops are under orders to maintain its biblical creed. No bishop is consecrated till he has given an affirmative answer to the question, 'Will you ... faithfully exercise yourself in the ... holy Scriptures, and call upon God by prayer, for the true understanding of the same; so as you may be able by them to teach and exhort with wholesome Doctrine, and to withstand and convince the gainsayers?'[1] The English church, like the church of the early centuries, means its bishops to be guardians of 'the faith which was once for all delivered to the saints'.[2]

It is, therefore, a grave matter when a bishop appears to be driving a coach and four through the plain and acknowledged sense of Scripture, the teaching of the Thirty-nine Articles, and the beliefs of the mass of English churchmen. It distresses clergy and layfolk that one of their constitutional leaders should be thus undermining Anglican faith. It disgusts the uncommitted, who feel that no man should use a position of trust as a vantage-point from which to torpedo the deepest convictions of those who trust him.

Also, it brings unholy comfort to those many whose consciences are uneasy about their unbelief, and who, therefore, seek excuses with which to prop it up. 'Look,' they say, 'he doesn't believe this stuff; why should we?'

These consequences are natural and predictable. One would suppose that only a stupid man could fail to foresee them, and only an irresponsible man would go out of his way to court them. One would have expected, therefore, that a bishop who found himself developing what he knew were disruptive views would hesitate to voice them while he was in office.

But it does not always happen that way. One recalls the late Bishop Barnes' book, *The Rise of Christianity*. And now there lies before us another episcopal essay in iconoclasm, this time from the Bishop of Woolwich, under the title – catchy, disarming, cocky, testy, priggish, take it how you will – *Honest to God*.

Not that Dr Robinson's honesty is in any doubt; on the contrary, *Honest to God* is a most frank and, for that reason, a most engaging book. But one wishes that it had not come from a bishop. No doubt the church needs its gadflies and even its heretics ('dissensions are necessary, if only to show which of your members are sound'[3]). But it is not to the office and ministry of a gadfly that a bishop is consecrated.

Still, *Honest to God* has come into print, the Sunday press has given it a boost, and it is now being widely read and discussed. We need, therefore, to examine it carefully, so that we may know what to say when the anxious enquire of us about it and the disgruntled throw it in our teeth.

Three questions

The book assumes from the start that we are moving rapidly and inexorably into an age of secularism in depth, an age for which the gospel as traditionally preached had, and can have, no relevance. This prospect, as he sees it, prompts Dr Robinson to raise three questions.

The first concerns evangelism. How, he asks, can we make Christian faith seem significant to the children of the space age, the men of today and tomorrow for whom the biblical picture of God, man, and the world, rings no bell?

The second question concerns the practice of Christianity. This question was forced on him, the bishop tells us, by his inability to 'get with' devotional routines worked out in a more stable Christian past, plus, against that background, Bonhoeffer's enigmatic vision of 'religionless Christianity' and the ideal for the future. How, he asks, should Christians live out their faith in a world like ours?

The third question concerns the revealed content of Christian belief itself. Is the traditional understanding of the faith true for today? One's answer to this third question will obviously repercuss on one's approach to the first two. For if – like Dr Robinson – one adopts what is in effect a new gospel, that is bound to issue in new conceptions of evangelism and Christian living; conceptions determined, however, less by changed conditions than by one's own changed convictions.

Such, then, are the bishop's questions. None should blame him for raising them; in this era of rapid cultural change, they are urgent questions for us all, and if we reject his answers, it is up to us to find better ones. *Honest to God* may yet do us service if it stimulates us to this task.

How does Dr Robinson tackle his three questions?

Honest to God is confessedly a tentative book. Indeed, for one of such an original mind as Dr Robinson, its ideas are surprisingly secondhand; it is just a plateful of mashed-up Tillich fried in Bultmann and garnished with Bonhoeffer. It bears the marks of unfinished thinking on page after page. But its main thrust is fairly clear. The bishop thinks we must accept the de-Christianized non-theistic frame of reference within which 'modern man' is supposed to do his thinking, and remodel Christianity to make it fit that frame. Accordingly, he answers his questions (taking them now in the reverse order) as follows:

God

(1) We must stop thinking of God as a person separate from ourselves, and give the name 'God' to the 'ground of our being', the deepest reality within us ('ground' is used, apparently, as in 'ground-floor', 'ground-level', 'ground-work', 'ground-bass'), which makes its presence felt in (a) the 'transcendent' experiences of life (mystical, aesthetic, numinous) and (b) the 'unconditional' moral claims of which we are periodically conscious. The idea of 'a self-

existent subject of infinite goodness and power, who enters into a relationship with us comparable with that of one human personality to another' should be ditched; the statement 'God is personal', if made, should be construed as an assertion about the world and man, to the effect that 'personality is of ultimate significance in the constitution of the universe, that in personal relationships we touch the final meaning of existence as nowhere else'.[4] In other words: 'God' is simply a name for that in our apprehension of things which strikes us as supremely worthwhile and significant, the end to which all else should be a means, the value in terms of which alone our ideals and conduct can be justified. 'God' is a quality of certain items in my own self-awareness, the quality, namely, of 'mattering'. So the sole subject of theology is man. 'A statement is called "theological" not because it relates to a particular Being called "God", but because it asks ultimate questions about the meaning of existence.'[5]

This is confessedly pure Tillich. The bishop cites the passage from Tillich which inspired it: we quote its main sentences. 'The name of this infinite and inexhaustible depth and ground of all being is God. That depth is what the word God means. And if that word has not much meaning for you, translate it, and speak of the depths of your life, of the source of your being, of your ultimate concern, of what you take seriously without any reservation ... For if you know that God means depth, you know much about him. You cannot then call yourself an atheist or unbeliever ... He who knows about depth knows about God.'[6]

In America it is disputed whether it is more correct to call Tillich a theist or an atheist. Clearly, the same question arises with regard to Bishop Robinson.

What, then, is the Christian faith? The bishop would have us boil it down to the following three convictions: (a) the 'ultimate reality' disclosed in our experience of transcendent things and unconditional claims is love; (b) this love was mirrored perfectly in Jesus (which, says the bishop, is what is meant, or ought to be meant, when we call him divine); (c) we know, and are reconciled to, the ground of our being, as we respond to the actual claims of love which we encounter in our fellow-men. 'Belief in God is the trust ... that to give ourselves to the uttermost in love is not to be confounded but to be "accepted", that Love is the ground of our being, to which ultimately we "come home".'[7]

Three comments suggest themselves. First: it is clear that this 'God' cannot meaningfully be called 'Father'. Second: it is equally clear that the bishop is really saying what he blames another writer for saying – not that God is love, but that love is God. Third: it is clear, too, that the bishop's Jesus (whose pre-existence and virgin birth he certainly denies, and apparently his bodily resurrection, present dominion, and future return also) cannot meaningfully be called either 'Saviour' or 'Lord'. When the bishop speaks (quoting Tillich again) of our being reconciled to God, he does so without referring either to the blood of Christ as the ground of it, or to faith in Christ as the means of it; it was no wonder that the Moslems of Woking welcomed his book! All that is distinctive of the Christian faith in God, as opposed to that of a Moslem or Hindu, seems to have gone from the bishop's theology.

The Christian life

(2) It is in the light of this concept of 'God' as no more than a dimension of depth in human experience that Dr Robinson attempts to bring the Christian life up to date. Henceforth, he says, we must drop the idea that in prayer and worship we draw aside to deal with God directly and personally. Instead, we must learn to equate loving openness and responsiveness to others with prayer, and to see the deepening of this disposition as the true purpose and criterion of worship. Prayer and worship, in their nature, can be nothing but exercises in the love of man.

This, of course, is all one can say on the basis of Tillich's teaching. If 'God' is not personal, he cannot speak words to us, nor we to him, and the old idea of communion with God is, quite simply, no go. So the real Christian life, whatever else it is, is precisely not the life of faith in the living Lord, of believing his promises and obeying his orders, which Abraham and Moses and David and Elijah and Jeremiah and Paul and Augustine and Luther and Tyndale and Wesley and Hudson Taylor and George Müller and the Auca martyrs of our own day lived. Here, then, is a dilemma; either those in the heroes' gallery of Hebrews 11, and the millions more who have lived and died by 'faith' as there defined, were really deluded, and the knowledge of God, which they thought they had, was unreal, or else the Tillich–Robinson 'theology' is not theology, and their 'God' is not God, and their 'prayer' is not prayer, and their 'worship' is not worship. Perhaps, on reflection, the dilemma will not prove too hard to resolve.

A further inconvenience arises. Not being a person in any sense, Dr Robinson's 'God' cannot speak; he cannot, therefore, give laws, any more than he can give promises. So there can be no guiding principles for Christian behaviour at all other than the demand that the spirit of love be expressed on every occasion. 'Nothing can of itself be labelled as "wrong"' – not even (we are told) sex relations before marriage,[8] nor (as follows by parity of reasoning) homosexual relations. Nothing is intrinsically evil except failure of love, and love can in principle warrant a breach of any moral 'rule' (the 'rules' are only provisional rules of thumb based on experience, anyway). Thus, in a novel sense, the end (the will to love) justifies the means (anything I feel will express the depth of my love at the moment). The baby of law vanishes with the bath-water of legalism; love is the moral plug-hole down which both go.

It seems to follow that the ten commandments are not, and never were, words from God; that Christ should not have endorsed them as if they were (was it love in him to deceive us so?); and that in Romans 13:10, Paul should have said that love is the abolishing rather than the fulfilling (*plērōma*) of the law, since love shows that the commandments, as such, were never really law in any divinely binding sense at all. This is a far cry from the ethics of the Bible. Also, if it is true (as I think it is) that law is love's eyes, and without law to give it vision love is blind, the practical effect of Dr Robinson's 'new morality' could be disastrous for the lives of many well-meaning people.

Evangelism

(3) What about evangelism? Dr Robinson's programme seems to be that Christians should (i) agree with modern man that historic Christianity is irrelevant to him, but (ii) tell him that he is not, and cannot be, an atheist, since his 'ultimate concern' (whatever that may be) is 'God'. A non-Tillichite may be forgiven for feeling that this is more of a policy for calling worldlings Christians than for making them such.

Critique

The saddest thing about *Honest to God* is that it was written with genuine pastoral and evangelistic intent, to meet genuine pastoral and evangelistic needs. The bishop is rightly unhappy about the arrogant and unsympathetic theological formalism with which the orthodox are inclined to rough-house doubters and questioners ('God is in heaven, and you can't catch him – now open your mouth and swallow the creed'). He rightly deplores the prevalence in our churches of ethical legalism ('these are the rules – mind you keep them') and religious isolationism ('what goes on in the world is none of our business'). He feels acutely the lethargy, the conventionality, the put-on religiosity, in which many Christians today are bogged down. Rightly, he wants to shake us out of all this. Also, he wants a starting-point for evangelizing intellectuals, who in their superior way have written off the Christian creeds as crude myth. His sense of what is wrong is admirable. But his attempt to put things right is unhelpful and inept to the last degree. The cure is far worse than the disease.

For what does the bishop do? To counter atheism, and restore a deeper sense of God's nearness and relevance, he offers us the thought of God as the deepest thing within us, no less – but also no more. The God of creation, providence, and revelation, the God in whose image we were made, the Lord of history, self-existent and tri-personal, vanishes from the scene. Nor is there any place in the picture for the incarnation, the atoning sacrifice of Christ, the resurrection, and the second coming, nor for the law and the promises. A gospel for intellectuals (or anyone else) that is bought at the price of such a loss is not worth having. By mutilating the Christian message in this fashion, the bishop is not, as he thinks, rescuing the perishing; he is merely sinking the lifeboat.

On the bishop's position as a whole, four comments may be made.

(i) This teaching does not stand up; it is not meaningful unless it leans on something else. At each point it invokes the category of love to one's neighbour as the ultimate principle of explanation. Love, it says, is God, the ground of our being; love was God in Jesus; and we are one with God when and as love is God in us. Everything reduces to love. But what is love? The New Testament has a special word for it (*agapē*), to distinguish it from all merely natural passions and affections; *agapē* is a new, divine thing, that came into the world with Jesus. But what essentially is it? The meaning of the word is not self-evident; it has to be defined. And how can we define it? Only in terms of the gospel of grace that Dr Robinson has abandoned. Nobody ever learns what *agapē* is from any other source.

What is love to my neighbour? It is my endeavour to imitate, on the human level, the love which God, my Maker and the Lawgiver against whom I had rebelled, showed to me when he 'spared not his own Son, but delivered him up'[9] on the cross to pay the price of my wrongdoing, and then freely forgave me and took me into his family and became my heavenly Father. From seeing how he has loved me, I see how I must love others – how I must seek to share with them what God has shared with me, and how I must count no cost too great to do them service, following in the footsteps of 'the Son of God, who loved me, and gave himself for me'.[10]

But I could never learn what love is from contemplating the non-personal, non-redeeming 'God' of Tillichite theology. Nor could I learn it from Dr Robinson's Jesus, who, it seems, neither came down from heaven, nor put away anyone's sins by his death. Dr Robinson talks glowingly about love being perfectly revealed in Jesus, but it is not clear what that can mean when the biblical meaning of the cross is denied.

It thus appears that Robinsonianism is a parasite which lives off the very thing it professes to reject – a theological bankrupt, that can only keep in business by illegitimately transferring orthodox Christian capital to its own account. The most appealing thing about *Honest to God* is the genuine warmth with which the bishop speaks of love as the ultimate imperative in all our relationships. He is right to speak so. But if ever Robinsonianism displaces orthodoxy, its bottom will fall out forthwith, for nobody will know any more what 'love' means.

(ii) This teaching makes true worship impossible. Neither the 'God' nor the Jesus of Robinsonianism can be adored. The bishop's transmutation of worship into a limbering-up for love towards men reflects the basic fact that on his principles no such thing as an exercise of love towards God in himself, and for himself alone, can exist. For, firstly, the bishop's 'God' is not a person. Secondly, this 'God' has done nothing to be praised for. He did not make us; we do not depend on him for our existence; he has not ransomed us from hell, nor has he promised to bring us to glory. We cannot say to him, 'Thou art worthy, O Lord, to receive glory, and honour, and power; for thou hast created all things …', nor can we say to him, 'Salvation to our God, which sitteth upon the throne, and unto the Lamb.'[11] What sort of worship can there be, when the themes of creation and redemption are both struck out?

Thirdly, if God's being is an aspect of my own, 'the depth in me', all attempts to worship him become self-worship. G. K. Chesterton thought the doctrine of the 'inner light' the worst of religious perversions, since if Jones starts worshipping the God within Jones he cannot but end up worshipping – Jones. Similarly, it is not clear from *Honest to God* how, if the Bishop of Woolwich sought to love and worship God as God, he could do anything other than love and worship the noble qualities – the love and sympathy – of the Bishop of Woolwich.

Nor may we worship the bishop's Jesus, for, though God was seen in and through him, he was not God in any personal sense. Dr Robinson stresses this. It would seem to follow that Thomas had no business to say, 'My Lord and my God',[12] nor had Jesus any business to let his words stand uncorrected, nor have we any business to echo Thomas' false Christology. These are odd conclusions: but they seem inescapably to follow from what Dr Robinson says in his chapter, 'The Man for Others'. If Jesus is not in a personal sense God, then obviously he should not be worshipped.

So the bishop shuts us up to a religion which will be either devoid of devotion to God, or filled with adoration of oneself: and one fears that in practice this either-or would become a both-and.

(iii) This teaching is not a reaffirmation of Christianity, but a denial of it. It is amazing as it is alarming that the bishop does not see this. Repeatedly he speaks as if the issue were simply an open choice between two 'images of God', an old, much-loved, but now broken-down and out-of-date one, and a modern product of revolutionary design which admittedly will take some getting used to, but will do the job that the old one did far more efficiently. But in fact this is not the issue at all.

The choice that the bishop really offers us, whether intentionally or not, is not between two images of the same God, but between two Gods, two Christs, two histories, and ultimately two religions. The choice is between a God who is personal and a Father, and a God who is neither, but simply an aspect of ourselves; between a God who rules history, and speaks and acts in it, and a God who does not; between a pre-existent Saviour who was born of a virgin, bore a world's sin, rose from death, and will come again in glory, and a man named Jesus of whom none of these things was true; between a life of faith and fellowship with God, and a new sort of yoga. 'The faith which was once for all delivered unto the saints' is one thing, and Robinsonianism, as here expounded, is another. And if Robinsonianism is accepted, the faith of the Apostles' Creed is rejected. No good can come of obscuring this. This is simply saying that Robinsonianism is, in effect, not a brand of Christianity at all, but a sort of idolatry – a new paganism. There is a point in theological and religious degeneration at which one ceases to be talking and thinking inadequately about the real God, and takes up instead with a God who is unreal – a point, that is, at which the God in whom one believes is no longer recognizable as 'the God and Father of our Lord Jesus Christ'. When one reaches this point, one had changed the truth of God into a lie[13] and started to worship a false God. In this book, at any rate, the bishop has undoubtedly passed that point, and John's admonition, 'little children, keep yourselves from idols,'[14] becomes very relevant.

The bishop tells us that he seeks to be 'honest to God' in his speculations. It is not clear what that means if God is as Dr Robinson describes him, but there is no doubt what it means for orthodox Christians. The man who is 'honest to God' is the man who listens to God's Word and lets it have its way with him, not evading its substance, nor deflecting its application one iota. It ought to be said that Dr Robinson is not the only one in this generation who tries to be 'honest to God', and that by publishing this book he has created acute problems of conscience for many such people. How, for instance, can an incumbent who was 'honest to God' when he took his ordination vows and subscribed the Articles and Prayer Book, henceforth allow the bishop in his pulpit? How can a layman who is 'honest to God' in holding the faith of the New Testament consent any more to listen to him preach?

(iv) This teaching misconceives both the nature of the Word of God and its relation to the world of men. The source from which the bishop's mishandling of Scripture, his eroding of the substance of the faith, and his disastrous pastoral and evangelistic suggestions, all spring, is his mistaken view of the relations between the Bible, that of which it speaks, and the world which it addresses. This is the real root of all the trouble.

Dr Robinson has broken with the historic Christian view of the Bible: he neither venerates it as divinely inspired, nor interprets it as written revelation. He seems to think, with Bultmann and Tillich, that the New Testament writings do not inform us directly about God and divine things at all, but only about the writers' own experience of being touched by God: an experience which, like poets and novelists, they have sought to express in terms of objectifying symbols – historical narratives, and cosmic mythology. Though the narratives may be false as history (e.g., the virgin birth and the resurrection), and the cosmology false as science (e.g., the three-decker universe, with heaven up above and hell down under), yet both may do good service as symbols for articulating, and conveying the 'feel' of, the challenge-response experience which is the reality that they clothe. But in our age, scientific and historical criticism has discredited them, and it is necessary to fish new symbols out of the flowing streams of contemporary thought in order to re-clothe the experience and make it intelligible and inescapable for modern men. This is what the bishop is at. His key thought is that essential Christianity is responding to an authoritative summons to love one's neighbour uncon-ditionally, a summons which arises from the depths of one's being ('God'), and is crystallized and reinforced within one through contemplating the stories told and things said in Scripture about Jesus, which convince one that he who loves cannot ultimately lose out. This is all (according to *Honest to God* anyway) that historic Christianity amounts to, and the book is simply an attempt to find a way of saying it that modern intellectuals cannot side-step.

But what if there is more to Christianity than this? What if God really has spoken through the mouths of prophets and apostles? What if faith means, not just trusting that by loving one's neighbour one fits into the universe, but also believing truths from God which prophetic and apostolic men wrote down for us? What if the things they tell us about God as creator, Lord, and redeemer, and about the Son of God who came down from heaven to save us, and returned thither to prepare a place for us, and will come again to take us there, are not dispensable myths, but literal truths – metaphysical and analogical in form, no doubt, as human language about divine things has to be, but none the less 'literal' in the sense that they give a factual account, as plain as the situation allows, of an objective state of affairs? What if the biblical books of history and theology are themselves divine witness in the form of human witness, God himself telling us, in terms that we can understand, what is true about himself – what he has done, and why, and what he will do, and what he wants us to do – and so giving us a standard of reference for all our own thinking about him?

What if the law and the prophets, and the apostolic books of the New Testament, really had the double authorship claimed for them ('men spake from God, being moved by the Holy Ghost')?[15] What if the images and thought-forms of Scripture, from the human point of view mere relics of a long-gone ancient civilization, are in reality not quasi-poetic symbols expressing a sense of the significance of an experience, but God-given analogies and ways of thinking, valid and indeed essential in every age for grasping his truth? What if the mass of biblical testimony has the nature, not so much of poetry and emotional symbol, expressing personal religious awareness, as of propositions and logical analyses, factual assertions, and deductions, embodying direct teaching from God? What if God has ordained that the way to know his mind in every age is to learn to think the thoughts of the inspired biblical writers after them? What if Holy Scripture really is 'God's word written', revelation in the indicative mood as well as the imperative, as till recently almost the whole church supposed?

If we believe this, or anything like it, we shall say that Christianity has a revealed doctrinal content; that the teaching of Holy Scripture is a standard of faith for all generations; that the only permissible thoughts about God are such as would have commended themselves to the apostles; and that no form of faith or religion that parts company with the basic positions of biblical theism can properly be called Christian. And in that case we shall be forced to say that the bishop, through mistaking the nature of Scripture, is working with a shockingly inadequate conception of what Christianity is, a conception so inadequate that we are forced to dismiss it as a new idolatry.

Also, if we accept this estimate of the Bible, we shall approach the problem of a world drifting into post-Christian unbelief in a different way from that taken by Dr Robinson. For we shall not find ourselves free to jettison the thought-forms and assertions of Scripture as lightly as he does, even if 'modern men' for the moment show little interest in them.

It is not, of course, a new thing for 'modern men', children of a culture partly or wholly pagan, to write off the biblical gospel as incredible and irrelevant; they have been doing that in one way or another ever since Paul went to Greece. 'The preaching of the cross is to them that perish foolishness'[16] – yesterday, today, and as long as the world shall stand.

But what is the right reaction to the world's censure? Bishop Robinson's reaction, as we have seen, is to accept it, and then in effect to try to make the gospel relevant for unbelievers by turning it into a form of unbelief itself. For him, the world's judgment on the Word is evidently decisive.

But what should be decisive here is the Word's judgment on the world. For the world, even the 'modern', post-Christian world, is there in the Bible, and it is judged in the Bible. Just as the Bible shows us God, so it shows us man – even twentieth-century, space-age man. Cultural changes are important, and we should not be insensitive to them, but the Bible enables us to see that they do not decisively affect man's nature and state at all. God stays the same; so, at bottom, does man; so do man's problems – the problems of getting right with himself, with others, and (the root problem) with God; and so does the God-given solution to these problems – 'the old, old story of Jesus and his love'.

So the true evangelistic task is not to amend the Bible view of things, but to explain and apply it – to go out and tell the world what its own real problems are (it won't know, until we do), to set forth Christ crucified and risen, and to rely on the sovereign Holy Spirit to demonstrate the truth with power in men's consciences.

The bishop's fear that if we stick to preaching 'the old, old story' nobody will believe it, makes one wonder whether he still believes in the Holy Spirit (a topic on which, perhaps significantly, *Honest to God* has little to say).

It is indeed true that there is a wide and probably widening gulf between the presuppositions of the average modern westerner, child as he is of scientifically dominated culture, and those of Christians. Hence evangelism today requires much challenging of things people take for granted, and much conceptual bridge-building, by image, analogy, and illustration, to help scientifically conditioned minds to grasp the meaning and application of God's truth. But all forging of attractive contemporary forms of speech is labour lost if they are then to be used to put over something not recognizable as the gospel. To accept the anti-theistic presuppositions of humanism, and then to disembowel the Christian story in order to be able to tell it to humanists more arrestingly, is evangelistic hara-kiri, and the poorest of ambassadorship for Christ.

Thus we see that the truly radical approach to the post-Christian world is not that of those who change the gospel, under the shallow delusion that man has changed, but the far profounder radicalism of those who, in face of the shibboleth that 'modern man' is entirely different from any man before him, are bold enough to maintain that the Bible is still right, that God is still on the throne, that the risen Christ is still mighty to save, that man remains the sinner he always was, that the apostolic gospel is still 'the power of God unto salvation',[17] and that not even such great mistakes as these we have been examining can finally stop its course, or thwart its triumph.

Conclusion

It is not pleasant to write of a book, or of a bishop, in terms of such strong censure as *Honest to God* seems to call for. We would end, therefore, by expressing the hope that the bishop's mistakes will turn out to be errors of inadvertence rather than tokens of apostasy. *Honest to God*, we know, was written in haste during a sick spell, and invalids writing at speed do not always do themselves justice. The book abounds in sweeping generalizations of a kind which suggest superficiality of study, and it is written in a warm and hazy rhetorical style which betokens more of sentiment than of thought. The bishop says at the start, 'nothing that I go on to say should be taken to deny [the] indispensable vocation' of those who give themselves to 'the firm reiteration, in fresh and intelligent contemporary language, of "the faith once delivered to the saints"'[18] – such people as Dorothy Sayers, C. S. Lewis, and J. B. Phillips.[19] Yet his exposition proceeds in antithetical relation to that faith, and involves, as we have seen, a decisive rejection of it at its most crucial points, compelling us to choose between two different Christs, and two different religions. You cannot eat your cake and have it. However, the bishop's lack of intention to do what he actually has done allows us to hope that on reflection he may find, after all, that he neither said what he meant, nor meant what he said. We would not wish to rule out this possibility.

Questions for study

1. How would you summarize the general approach that Packer adopts in criticizing Robinson's book?
2. Packer singles out three areas for special comment. Make sure that you can summarize his arguments in each of these areas in your own words. How persuasive do you find the points which he makes?
3. 'The choice that the bishop really offers us, whether intentionally or not, is not between two images of the same God, but between two Gods, two Christs, two histories, and ultimately two religions.' Locate this citation, and study it in context. What does Packer mean by this? And how does he arrive at this conclusion?
4. 'The true evangelistic task is not to amend the Bible view of things, but to explain and apply it.' Locate this quotation, and consider it in its context. What is the point that Packer is making? How does he lead up to it? And what conclusions does he draw from it, especially in regard to apologetics and evangelism?

5. Packer commends Dorothy L. Sayers and C. S. Lewis at one point. Why does he do this? And what criticism of Robinson does he imply in doing so?

Notes

Preamble

1. For background, see Eric James, *A Life of Bishop John A. T. Robinson*, London: Collins, 1987. For an analysis of the reaction, see David L. Edwards, *The Honest to God Debate*, London: SCM Press, 1963.

Essay

1. Quoted from the form of ordaining or consecrating of an Archbishop or Bishop.
2. Jude 3 (Revised Version).
3. 1 Cor. 11:19 (New English Bible).
4. John A. T. Robinson, *Honest to God*. London: SCM Press, 1963, pp. 48–49.
5. Op. cit., p. 49.
6. Op. cit., p. 22, cited from Paul Tillich, *The Shaking of the Foundations*, Harmondsworth: Penguin, 1962, pp. 63–64.
7. Op. cit., p. 49.
8. Op. cit., p. 118.
9. Rom. 8:32.
10. Gal. 2:20.
11. Rev. 4:11; 7:10.
12. John 20:28.
13. Rom. 1:25.
14. 1 John 5:21.
15. 2 Peter 1:21 (Revised Version).
16. 1 Cor. 1:18.
17. 1 Rom. 1:16.
18. Op. cit., p. 7, citing Jude 3.
19. Op. cit., p. 15.

5. 'What is revival?' (1963)

The theme of revival was much discussed in English evangelical circles during the 1950s and early 1960s, partly in reaction to the very significant response to the Billy Graham crusades. As Packer observed developments, he gradually came to share Benjamin B. Warfield's view that aggressive evangelistic campaigns were ultimately based on a Pelagian foundation. They saw evangelism as a human activity, the success of which depended upon the techniques being used. Somehow, God seemed to have been eliminated from the picture altogether. Yet was not God the supreme evangelist? It seemed to Packer that some serious distortions were emerging which required correction at the theological level.

Packer developed this point in a paper on 'Puritan Evangelism', delivered at the 1955 Puritan Studies Conference, in which he set out a theological corrective to an implicit Pelagianism in the tactics and approaches which seemed to lie behind the new evangelistic campaigns. Packer pointed out that the origins of the modern evangelistic campaign – including some of the methods still being used in the 1950s – lay with Charles Finney in the 1820s. Packer's article is also significant on account of his critique of the evangelistic methods of Charles G. Finney, such as the 'altar call', which had become widely accepted within evangelistic crusade movements in the United States. Packer's concern here, which was echoed in the 1961 work *Evangelism and the Sovereignty of God*, was that an emphasis on evangelistic technique and the personality of the evangelist seriously obscured the fact that 'God himself is the true evangelist'. From a Calvinist perspective, Packer was alarmed that the approaches associated with Finney and his successors ended up by making evangelism a human achievement, primarily concerned with technique, method and atmosphere, and thus neglected the vital role of God in the conversion of individuals.

Packer developed this point further at the 1960 Puritan and Reformed Studies Conference. On the afternoon of Tuesday 20 December 1960, Packer spoke on 'Jonathan Edwards and the Theology of Revival'. It was an important address, in that Edwards was directly linked with the origins of the 'Great Awakening' in New England during the eighteenth century. Packer's point was simple: revival is something which has its origins and instigation with God, not with human effort or planning. The very idea of an evangelist 'planning' a revival was therefore theologically ridiculous. Packer explored this theme further in a major address on the theme of 'revival' given to the London Meeting of the Graduates' Fellowship in November 1966.[1] This address remains of major importance, and we shall summarize its main points below.

'Revival is widely thought of as a work of man, something that man can and should organize.' With these words, Packer summarized what seemed to him to be the theological misperception which lay behind so much evangelistic entrepreneurship, especially in North America. 'But the truth is exactly opposite. Revival cannot be organized or planned by man.' It is a work of God, which must be recognized to lie under his sovereign control. A failure or refusal to accept this point seemed to Packer to be typical of many major North American evangelistic campaigns, which traced their history back to Charles Finney, and especially his work *Revivals of Religion*.

> I once saw in an American journal an advertisement which began, in large letters, DON'T PLAN A REVIVAL – and I thought, how remarkably right minded! But alas, the ad. went on, in smaller type, – until you have these free samples of color advertising planned especially for the church which wants something different but must operate on a conservative budget.

Against this idea of revival as something that churches or evangelists can engineer or contrive by the use of suitable techniques, Packer argued for the recovery of a biblical understanding of revival as 'a gracious work of God, restoring spiritual vitality'. For Packer, three major principles could be discerned lying behind the biblical witness to revival within the church. First, we need to recognize the need for revival. Second, 'we must be clear that we cannot create or work up revival. We can remove hindrances to revival, but we cannot restore life'. While we can humble ourselves before God, exaltation is something which God alone can do. The corollary of this was clear: just 'as we cannot ensure revival by our preparations, so we cannot preclude it by our lack of preparation'. This, for Packer, was a particularly encouraging thought. Third, we should be praying for revival. For Packer, the theological analysis he had just presented should lead directly to prayer. If revival is a work of God, we should be crying out to God to do what he alone can do, and we cannot do – revive his church.

The question of revival remains important, not least in relation to debates over 'Church Growth' techniques and the role that Christians should take in relation to evangelism. The essay selected for inclusion in this collection is widely regarded as one of Packer's most thoughtful contributions to this debate, and merits close study.

Related works by Packer

Evangelism and the Sovereignty of God, London: Inter-Varsity Fellowship; Chicago: InterVarsity Press, 1961.
'Revival', *Christian Graduate* 24/4 (December 1971), pp. 97–100.
'Puritanism as a Movement of Revival', *Evangelical Quarterly* 52 (1980), pp. 2–16.
'Lord, Send Revival', *The Bulletin*, Winter 1983, pp. 4–5.
'Jonathan Edwards and Revival', in *Among God's Giants: Aspects of Puritan Christianity*, Eastbourne: Kingsway, 1991, pp. 408–432. North American edition published as *A Quest for Godliness: The Puritan Vision of the Christian Life*, Westchester, IL: Crossway, 1991.
'The Spirit with the Word: The Reformational Revivalism of George Whitefield', in W. P. Stephens (ed.), *The Bible, the Reformation and the Church*, Sheffield: Sheffield Academic Press, 1995, pp. 166–189.

What is revival?

The way to find out what a group of people are really like is to see what they habitually talk about. And the most revealing commentary on the state of British evangelicalism over the past forty years is a list of the topics which have occupied evangelical minds during that time. Thus, in the twenties the great talking-point was evolution and the truth of the Bible, for evangelicals had their backs to the wall. In the thirties, the talking-points were guidance and prophecy, for evangelicals felt adrift, and unsure as to where they were going. In the forties and early fifties, evangelicals recovered vigour, and the chief subject of discussion was ways and means of evangelism. Now, at the start of the sixties, it seems that evangelicals are recovering vision; the impotence of our churches and our evangelism in face of the entrenched ungodliness of today is becoming a burden to us, and the recurring theme of our talk is coming more and more to be revival. One thanks God for this; it means that evangelicalism is putting down roots again, and seeking, after a century in the wilderness, to re-enter the world of spiritual realities in which our forefathers lived. May God look in mercy on our blindness, and lead us further in this direction.

The really odd thing in all this is not that the topic of revival is concerning evangelicals now, but that it has for so long failed to concern them, so much so that some find this renewed interest in it disconcerting and distasteful. The strange truth is that for the past hundred years, although the churches, and evangelicalism within the churches, have been continuously losing ground, Christian people have not been longing for revival. Interest in the subject, where it has existed at all, has been guarded and a little patronizing: the news of what God did in Wales in 1904–5, and in Manchuria in 1906–8, does not seem to have stirred English evangelical hearts as did the news of the much smaller awakening in the Hebrides in 1949. On the whole, the faithful have been preoccupied throughout this period with other things.

This comparative unconcern about revival marks a break with the earlier evangelical outlook. For a century after the days of Whitefield and Jonathan Edwards, the immediate reaction of evangelicals when the fires of life burned low in the churches was to appoint times for self-humbling and confession of sin and special prayer that God would visit them again. They regarded revivals as the chief means by which the gospel advanced; they believed, and often declared in print, that without revivals churches could not stay alive. But after about 1860 evangelicals ceased to think in these terms. We may well ask, why? The deepest reason seems to be that their minds were possessed by two thoughts which, taken together, made any desire for revival seem positively improper. The one was an optimistic belief that the mounting number of organized evangelical activities – missions, campaigns, conventions, Christian Unions and interdenominational doings of all sorts – would suffice of themselves to meet the situation. The other was a pessimistic notion, born of J. N. Darby's esoteric dispensationalism, that the great final apostasy had begun and there was, therefore, no possibility of any real recovery of the churches' fortunes. The first thought implied that revival was not really needed; the second, that it was in any case out of the question.

It is worth pointing out that, even if Darbyite suspicions were justified (and non-Darbyites have their doubts), they could not justify Christians in ceasing to pray for revival. Christ taught his disciples to pray, 'Hallowed be thy name.' God's 'name' means God himself as he has made himself known. That which dishonours and profanes God's name is lukewarmness and deadness in the churches, the gospel belied by the lives of its adherents, and paganism triumphant in the world. That which hallows God's name is the reversal of these conditions – strong faith and victorious holiness in the churches, and the winning of lost souls to the Saviour (see Ezek. 36:20–23). To pray 'Hallowed be thy name' with understanding in days of spiritual decline therefore involves praying for revival. If, then, it is right to think that the Lord will return at a time of great apostasy, does it not follow that when he comes he should find the faithful on their knees praying for revival? And does it not follow too that whenever churches find themselves weak and ineffective, whenever their defeats reveal that the judgment of God is upon them for their past unfaithfulness, the saints should begin to pray for revival? Such circumstances should bring to their lips Habakkuk's prayer: 'O Lord, revive thy work in the midst of the years ... in wrath remember mercy' (Hab. 3:2). And the worse things are, the more earnestly should the cry for revival go up, as it did in Israel of old. (See the great Bible prayers for revival in the Old Testament: Pss. 44; 74; 79; 80; 85:4–7; Is. 63:15 – 64:12; Lam. 5.) In these days of growing apostasy and secularism, we should be inexcusable if we were prepared to be content with anything less than revival, and did not make the cry for revival our own: 'Wilt thou not revive us again; that thy people may rejoice in thee?' (Ps. 85:6).

But what exactly is revival?

There are two factors in our situation which obstruct right thinking about this question. The first is a matter of language; the second is a mistake in theology.

The first obstructing factor is a restricted usage. In the eighteenth century, the word 'revival' took its place in the evangelical vocabulary as a description of the kind of spiritual movements which were taking place on both sides of the Atlantic. But since then the word has come to be used in two narrower senses. Some (especially in America) give the name 'revival' to what we would call an evangelistic campaign, and designate its leader as a 'revivalist'. Others speak of 'personal revival' and 'continuous revival', meaning the restoration of individual backsliders and cold-hearted Christians to a state of spiritual health, and the maintaining of that state once it is recovered. The very existence of these narrower usages encourages the idea that successful evangelism and the quickening of believers is all that revival really amounts to. But this is not so. Both these things happen in revivals; but both happen also apart from revivals. Neither can be equated with revival, for revival includes both, and much more. It would make for clarity, therefore, if we could drop these narrower usages entirely.

The second obstructing factor I call the antiquarian fallacy. It consists of building up a mental blueprint of revival from the history of revivals, or of one particular revival, in the past, and treating this as a norm to which all revivals in the future must correspond. In fact, what we have to look into is not the outward forms that revival has taken in history, but the inward pattern of God's reviving work as presented in the Bible.

The biblical evidence falls into three main categories. First there are prayers for revival (the main passages under this head were mentioned earlier). Second, there are prophetic pictures of revival, given in Old Testament terms with immediate reference to Old Testament situations, but disclosing the permanent principles of God's action whenever he restores a church in decline (see especially Is. 35:3–10; 40 – 46; Jer. 31; Ezek. 34; 36:16–38; Joel 2:12–32; Zech. 1 – 8). Third, there are narratives of revival (under Asa, 2 Chr. 15; Hezekiah, 2 Chr. 29 – 31; Josiah, 2 Chr. 34, 35; Ezra, Ezra 9 – 10; Nehemiah, Neh. 8 – 10; and – foremost in importance – the revival that began with Pentecost, Acts 2 – 12).

The main points in the biblical presentation of revival are these:

1. Revival is God renewing the church. Revival is a work of restoring life (that is what the word 'revive' means), and it is the people of God who are the subjects of it. It is a social, corporate thing. Every Bible prayer for revival implores God to quicken, not me, but us. Every Bible prophecy of revival depicts God visiting and enlivening, not one or two individual Israelites, but Israel, the whole people. Every record of revival, in biblical and later Christian history, tells of an entire community being affected. Revival reaches Christians individually, no doubt, but it is not an individualistic affair; God revives, not just the Christian, but the church, and then the new life overflows from the church for the conversion of outsiders and the renovation of society.

2. Revival is God turning away his anger from the church. For God's people to be impotent against their enemies is a sign that God is judging them for their sins. The cry for revival springs from the sense of judgment (Pss. 79:4–9; 80:12–14; 85:4–7; Hab. 3:2); the coming of revival is God's comforting of his people and restoring them after judgment.

Revival is God manifesting himself to his people; visiting them (Ps. 80:14; Jer. 29:10–14), coming to dwell with them (Zech. 2:10ff.), pouring out his Spirit on them (Joel 2:28; Acts 2:17ff.), quickening their consciences, showing them their sins and exalting Christ in their eyes in his saving glory. In times of revival, there is a deep awareness of God's presence and an inescapable sense of being under his eye; spiritual things become overwhelmingly real and the truth of God becomes overwhelmingly powerful, both to wound and to heal. Conviction of sin becomes intolerable; repentance goes very deep; faith springs up strong and assured; spiritual understanding grows quick and keen, and converts mature in an amazingly short time; joy overflows (Ps. 85:6; 2 Chr. 30:26; Neh. 8:12, 17; Acts 2:46f.; 8:8), and loving generosity abounds (Acts 4:32); Christians become fearless in witness and tireless in labour for their Saviour's glory. The manifesting of God's gracious presence in revival awakens them out of sleep and energizes them to serve their Lord in a quite unprecedented way. Indeed, they recognize their new experience as a real foretaste of the life of heaven, where God will disclose himself to them so fully that they will never be able to rest day or night from singing his praises and doing his will.

3. Revival, lastly, is God making known the sovereignty of his grace. Revival is entirely a work of grace, for it comes to churches that deserve only judgment; and God brings it about in such a way as to show that his grace is entirely sovereign in it, and human plans and schemes have had nothing to do with it. We can organize conventions and campaigns, but the only organizer of revival is God the Holy Ghost. Revival, when it comes, comes suddenly, unexpectedly, as at Pentecost, breaking out often in obscure places through the ministry of obscure people; God sends revival in a way that shows that he is its only source, and all the praise and glory of it must be given to him alone.

God is our sovereign in revival, and men cannot extort it from him by any endeavour or technique. What, then, should those who long for revival do?

Two things: First, preach and teach God's truth; second, pray. Preach and teach because it is his truth, and the blessing of revival cannot reach further than the gospel has gone. Pray, because God has told us that we need not expect to receive unless we ask, and, in the words of Jonathan Edwards, the classic theologian of revival, 'When God has something very great to accomplish for his Church, it is his will that there should precede it, the extraordinary prayers of his people; as is manifest by Ezek. 36:37 [see the context]. And it is revealed that, when God is about to accomplish great things for his Church, he will begin by remarkably pouring out the spirit of grace and supplication (Zech. 12:10)' (*Thoughts on the Revival in New England*, chap. 5:3). God help us, then, to seek his face till he come and rain righteousness upon us; and to him shall be all the glory and the praise.

Questions for study

1. J. I. Packer suggests that different eras in history debate different questions. Why, according to Packer, did evangelicals discuss revival in the early 1960s?
2. How does Packer define 'revival'? And how does this definition help him to clarify the extent to which God is involved in this process?
3. Why does Packer make such use of Jonathan Edwards? You will find it useful to learn something about the 'Great Awakening' to answer this question fully.
4. 'We can organize conventions and campaigns, but the only organizer of revival is God the Holy Ghost.' Locate this citation, and note its context. What point is Packer making? And who are the intended targets of this criticism?

Notes

1. Published in a slightly shortened form as 'Revival', *Christian Graduate* 24/4 (December 1971), pp. 97–100.

6. 'The problem of universalism today' (1969)

'Universalism' may be conveniently defined as the religious teaching that it is God's purpose to save every individual from sin or damnation through grace. Although universalism has been a significant viewpoint throughout the history of western culture, it became institutionalized in 1779, when John Murray became pastor of the first Universalist church in the United States. The basic beliefs of universalism are conveniently set out in The Winchester Profession (1803), which takes the form of three articles:

Article I. We believe that the Holy Scriptures of the Old and New Testament contain a revelation of the character of God, and of the duty, interest and final destination of mankind.

Article II. We believe that there is one God, whose nature is Love, revealed in one Lord Jesus Christ, by one Holy Spirit of Grace, who will finally restore the whole family of mankind to holiness and happiness.

Article III. We believe that holiness and true happiness are inseparably connected, and that believers ought to be careful to maintain order and practice good works; for these things are good and profitable unto men.

It is the second of these three articles of belief which is of particular importance in relation to the present discussion. If God is loving, why are some not saved? Is not the very idea that some will not be saved a denial of the love of God? These ideas are of considerable importance, and are reflected at many points in modern western culture. In the face of such a widespread assumption that all will be saved, how can Christians argue that only some will be saved?

It is these questions which Packer set out to address in his major address 'The Problem of Universalism Today', which took the form of a paper originally published in the *Australian Journal of the Theological Students Fellowship*. Packer had already given some considerable thought to this issue. In 1965, he delivered the Payton Lectures at Fuller Theological Seminary in Pasadena, California, on 'The Problem of Universalism Today'. The four lectures on this theme were never published; some of their themes, however, are incorporated in the article with the same title.

In this article, Packer drew a sharp distinction between two senses of the term 'universalism': the 'universal Christian claim' on humanity, grounded in Jesus Christ as the one and only Saviour, and the universal need for redemption; and as the universal restoration of humanity 'to the fellowship with God for which Adam was made, and from which he fell'. Packer notes that it is the first form of universalism which establishes the credentials of Christianity as a world religion, and establishes its missionary credentials; the second, however, threatens to erode the distinctiveness, authenticity and integrity of the Christian faith, and rob it of its evangelistic thrust.

Packer's discussion of the matter set out to achieve two major objectives. First, it aims to offer an explanation of why universalism has become so pervasive in modern western Christianity. Packer sets out four main considerations, which be believes cast light on the rapid advances made by this doctrine in recent years. Second, it aims to offer orthodox Christianity arguments which may be used to counter the rise of universalism. Packer remains one of the most solid evangelical defenders of the view that salvation depends on an explicit response to Christ in this life, and this article may be regarded as a brief yet precise statement of the classic evangelical position on this matter.

Related works by Packer

'Isn't One Religion as Good as Another?', in F. Colquhoun (ed.), *Hard Questions*, London: Falcon Press, 1967, pp. 16–19.
'The Way of Salvation: I. What is Salvation. II. What is Faith? III. The Problem of Universalism. IV: Are Non-Christian Faiths Ways of Salvation?' *Bibliotheca Sacra* 129 (1972), pp. 105–125; 291–306; 130 (1973), pp. 3–10; 110–116.

'What is evangelism?', in H. Conn (ed.), *Theological Perspectives on Church Growth*, Nutley, NJ: Presbyterian and Reformed, 1976, pp. 91–105.

'The Uniqueness of Jesus Christ', *Churchman* 92 (1978), pp. 101–111.

'Good Pagans and God's Kingdom', *Christianity Today*, 17 January 1986, pp. 27–31.

'Evangelicals and the Way of Salvation: New Challenges to the Gospel', in C. F. H. Henry and K. Kantzer (eds.), *Evangelical Affirmations*, Grand Rapids, MI: Zondervan, 1990, pp. 107–136.

The problem of universalism today

By universalism I mean the expressed hope, the professed certainty, that all men, past, present and future, from Adam right up to the end of time, will be found at the last in the kingdom and the enjoyment of God. It is the doctrine of which the Greek name is *apokatastasis* – 'the restoration'. It's based upon another sort of universalism about which there is no dispute, and which we all of us will take as our starting-point for thinking about this *apokatastasis* doctrine. The universalism which we all accept is the sum total of those qualities which make New Testament Christianity a faith for the whole world, i.e. the universal claim that is essential to Christianity, based upon proclaiming one Creator, one humanity, and one Redeemer. You remember how Paul at Athens affirmed the reality of the one God, and the one humanity, and the one destiny for the whole world, namely, to stand before God to be judged – 'he has appointed a day in which he will judge the world by that man whom he has ordained'. Many scriptures could be added to this to show how the universal Christian claim upon mankind is based on redemption – on the doctrine, that is, that there was one Saviour of the whole world, and one atoning transaction in virtue of which forgiveness is freely offered to the world. One thinks of Romans 5, the Adam–Christ parallel; one thinks of 2 Corinthians 5:19, 'God in Christ was reconciling the world to himself', or John 1:29, 'Behold the Lamb of God who takes away the sin of the world.' From this the New Testament writers draw the conclusion, the corollary conclusion, that there is in fact only one people of God – the seed of Abram has become a world-wide community; Gentiles are invited to join, as it were, by receiving Jesus Christ, and becoming Abram's heirs in him. And the Christian claim is that no other faith can stand beside it: by being an inclusive claim demanding response from all men in the world it becomes an exclusive claim insisting that all other faiths must be abandoned in order to worship God as we should and honour Christ as we ought.

'The gospel', says Paul in Romans 1:16, 'is the power of God unto salvation to everyone that believeth.' There is universalism for you. But to respond to it means as he said to the Thessalonians, 'to turn from idols to serve the living and true God'. There is a universal mission committed to the church to take the gospel to the ends of the earth. 'Go and make disciples of all nations,' said our Lord in Matthew 28:18. The message preached is the call of God for the whole earth and by virtue of creation and redemption (those basic facts) God claims a response from every man to whom the message comes.

Now this sort of universalism which makes Christianity into a world religion is not in dispute; and we take it as our starting-point. The question for us is whether any of this implies a doctrine of universal salvation, the restoration, literally, of all men to the fellowship with God for which Adam was made and from which he fell.

Now the title of this paper speaks of universalism as a problem today. Why is it especially a problem? There are four reasons:

Reason 1

Universalism is rapidly advancing throughout Protestantism. This is a new situation. Universalism was first broached by the Greek Father Origen: and it was condemned, and he was condemned for teaching it – this of course subsequent to his death in the fifth century. That condemnation repercussed in Christendom for centuries: universalism was regarded as a condemned minority eccentricity. In the days of the Reformation, the Anabaptists took it up (some of them), and the Reformers repeated the patristic condemnation against the Anabaptists. And this is how things were in Protestantism until the nineteenth century. Then in the nineteenth century the status of universalism began to change. The father of German liberalism, Schleiermacher, and many liberals following him, and English divines like the Anglican Andrew Jukes and the Baptist Samuel Cox, and various North American divines, the Scotsman Erskine and others, began seriously to argue universalism. The poets of Britain began to express it in their verses; Browning and Tennyson, Coventry Patmore, and in North America in poets like Whittier and Walt Whitman. And by the twentieth century universalism had established itself as an undoubtedly respectable position and in our time we see it literally carrying all before it. I think it would be true to say that the majority of theologians and missionary leaders active today are at least sympathetic, and in many cases actually committed, to universalist teaching. I quote Bishop John Robinson, 'It is impossible to ignore a consensus of contemporary names such as Nicholas Berdyaev, the Russian Orthodox; William Temple, Anglican; John Baillie, Church of Scotland; C. H. Dodd, Congregationalist; Charles Raven, another Anglican; Herbert Farmer, an English Presbyterian, all of whom have come out more or less in favour of this doctrine.' And Robinson's own name can be added to the list; so can that of the Swiss theologians Michaelis and Karl Barth, who if he did not actually commit himself to universalism, was clearly very sympathetic towards it, and the American Nels Ferré and John Hick. Universalism it seems has come to stay. It is going to be advocated during our lifetime by very able men. We cannot ignore this. What are we going to think about it? What are we going to say?

Reason 2

The theological claim of universalism is momentous. The claim is that this teaching alone does justice to the love of God and the victory of the cross and the thrust of the Bible. Whereas, so it is claimed, any belief in the eternal loss, eternal torment, of any of God's rational creatures makes God out to be at the least a failure and perhaps even a devil. This is the kind of thing that is constantly said by universalist theologians. It is a tremendously far-reaching claim and one that we cannot ignore. Is this really true? If not, why not?

Reason 3

The pastoral implications of universalism are far-reaching. If all men are, in the title of the nineteenth-century tract, 'Doomed to be Saved', then it follows that the decisiveness of decisions made in this life, and the urgency of evangelism here in this life, immediately, are undermined. Other ways of loving your neighbour here in this life may now be considered as perhaps more important than seeking to win him to Christ. And it is no accident that keenness on the social gospel, so-called, and universalist theology, have gone hand in hand, viz. G. Müller wrote, 'almost all leading religious socialists have appeared as universalists in their theology'. This is true, from F. D. Maurice – a wishful universalist of the last century, to J. A. T. Robinson, who is a thorough-going socialist and a thorough-going universalist at the present time. You can see what the missionary implications of this teaching are going to be at this point. What is the main job of Christian missionary witness? To win men to

Christian faith? Or to do something else for them? In evangelical history there have been repeated movements of the Spirit, movements of missionary and evangelistic advance which have had at their heart earnest prayer offered by many good Christian souls, prayer that was made in terms of the belief that without Christ men and women were lost. This is not a question now of how they preached; it is a question of how they prayed. Were they right to pray that way? Such prayer was, literally, the powerhouse of the evangelical awakening in the eighteenth century and many spiritual movements since. Was it off the beam? – Uninstructed prayer? – Foolish and stupid prayer? Or did it reflect a true insight into how things were?

Reason 4

Its personal appeal is strong. I know that the historic evangelical attitude has been to regard universalism with what one book speaks of as 'something akin to hatred': evangelicals have said how morally weakening this doctrine is and how spiritually deadening it is. They have equated it with the first lie, the devil's lie in the garden of Eden, 'you shall not surely die'. They have seen it as a modern version of the first piece of armour the devil puts on Mansoul in Bunyan's *Holy War*, viz., 'the hope of doing well at the last what life soever you have lived'. This is what universalism is in practice, evangelicals have said, and it is a deadly thing. It is false hope. And yet in these days of our expanding world population when there are literally millions who have never heard of Christ and great political forces are now ranged in battle array to ensure that they never will hear of Christ, it is difficult for a person to be glib about a rejection of universalism. We would, all of us, in our hearts, like to be universalists; we find that the doctrine of eternal punishment for some is a very uncomfortable truth to live with and sometimes we find ourselves wishing that it was not there. Many pastors have, I think, succumbed to the temptation to live and preach and act as if it were not there. We ourselves will be exposed to the same temptation. Is it the ostrich temptation? Simply to hide your head in the light of God's facts? Or might it be that, after all, we are allowed in this day and age to jettison the doctrine of eternal punishment and take up universalism after all? Will the Bible let us?

The case for universalism

1. The biblical picture

Universalism is a thesis about human destiny argued, at least by its modern exponents, from the Bible itself. Now what the Bible has to say about the destiny of the believer is not in question at all. The Bible is very clear and emphatic on this. You know the glorious doctrine of Christian hope which the New Testament proclaims:

'No condemnation to them that are in Christ Jesus.'
'Neither life nor death nor anything in creation can separate us from the love that is in Christ Jesus our Lord.'
'Where I am, there shall my servant be.'

> My knowledge of that life is small, my faith is dim,
> But it's enough that Christ knows all,
> And I shall be with him.

That is the Christian hope in a nutshell, as Richard Baxter formulated it 300 years ago.

The question is not about the destiny of believers, it is about those who go through life and leave the world as unbelievers: those who in this world (cf. Paul, Eph. 2:12) 'are without God and without hope in the world'. The New Testament seems very clear at first sight about the hopelessness both in this world and in the world to come of unbelievers. Remember how in Romans, Paul draws out and dwells on the wretchedness of the unbeliever at this point, how he is under the law, obliged to keep God's requirements perfectly, and is exposed to judgment if he breaks the law: And he is also under sin. So that he lacks in him the power to keep the law; all men, Jews and Gentiles, are under sin (Rom. 3:9). And says Paul, 'Therefore all men are under God's wrath' – for disobedience. This is worked out in Romans 1 – 2 (cf. 2 Cor. 5:10 – 'receives the things done in the body' – the past comes straight back at us in the form of retribution. 'Whether those things be good or whether they be evil'). This is the meaning of the wrath of God: it stands for the first retributive judgment of the Lord upon those who have transgressed his law. This means that unbelievers are subjected to death; under law, under sin, under wrath, under death. Death had reigned over all men who have lived without Christ. 'The wages of sin is death' (Rom. 3:23), and death in the New Testament does not mean annihilation or extinction, but rather what indeed it means in the Old Testament, too, separation from that which makes for true and complete life, the loss, that is, of something that is essential to your fulfilling your own destiny. That is how it is that you can have a living death; the thought is not biological, but the thought is of a spiritual relationship that has gone wrong. 'And she that liveth in sin is dead while she lives' (Paul, in the Pastorals). 'You were dead in trespasses and sin' – the death in this case is the death of a broken and spoiled relationship with God, which means that something essential for which you were made is missing from you – you are separated from your own true and complete life. That is death here, and that will be the essence of death hereafter. In Romans 8, Paul says, 'to be carnally minded is death' (that is in the present) and he says, 'Then if you live after the flesh you shall die' (that is future). But the essence of death in both texts is the same. Here is a non-relationship with God where it should be a positive relationship. Consequently loss of true life, something essential for which you were made, missing – continued unhealthy existence. Under law, under sin, under wrath, under death. This is all that the New Testament seems to be saying about unbelievers. And we might add to this the fact that there are two texts (quoting Oliver Quick, the Anglican divine) which seem to be quite explicit for continued existence in the experience of retribution beyond this life. The one that he quotes is Matthew 25:46 at the end of the parable of the sheep and the goats. The one group, those hailed as blessed by the Father, go away into eternal life (*zoē aiōnios*), and the others go away into *kolasin aiōnios*, translated in our Bibles 'eternal punishment', 'chastisement'. What does *aiōnios* mean here? Well, we know the basic meaning of *aiōnios* in the New Testament is 'that which relates to this world to come as contrasted with that which relates to this aeon. Thus it stands for fixity and finality', and so comes by that root of meaning to denote endlessness, just because the age to come is the last age. And thus it must be held to mean 'eternal' in the old naïve sense of 'endless-continuous'.

The second text that Quick quotes is the picture text at the end of Revelation 20:10, 15 which refers to the lake of fire, where the beast and the false prophet are, and where those who are rejected at the great white throne at the judgment will also be. The torment there goes on for ever and ever, says the writer of Revelation. The torment presumably being the knowledge of one's own ill desert and God's displeasure, and of the good that one has lost. This is the witness of the New Testament. This was the doctrine of the synagogue and the apocalyptic writings in the days of the New Testament and for a century before. This doctrine appears to have been enforced by Jesus Christ throughout his ministry. W. G. T. Shedd, the last-century Presbyterian divine, says very forthrightly, 'Jesus Christ is the person who is responsible for the doctrine of eternal perdition.' And you remember some of the fearsome pictorial language which he used and which, *prima facie*, is expressing precisely this idea: the weeping and gnashing teeth, the outer darkness, the worm dying not and the fire not being quenched. His use of the picture of Gehenna, the valley of Hinnom, outside of Jerusalem where they burn the rubbish, as a picture of the final destiny of some; the reference to the great gulf fixed between the place where Dives is and the place where Lazarus is. And this text we have quoted from Matthew 25 takes its place among a whole group of texts. E.g. that text in which he says, 'depart from me, you cursed, into the place of eternal fire prepared for the devil and his angels'. One has to say, soberly I hope, and reverently, how could the Lord have made the fact of eternal punishment for the impenitent clearer than he did? What more could he have said to make it clear if passages like this do not make it clear? It is, to be sure, a fearful doctrine but it is there in the Gospels, and we must take it as seriously as we take any other elements of our Lord's teaching. This is the consistent teaching of the New Testament to the destiny of those who live and die without faith. It is observable that the New Testament is not in the least troubled about this. Rather the insistence all the way through is that the final punishment of the impenitent is right, and is a manifestation of God's glorious justice and something for which the people of God should praise him. It is a bit breathtaking, this, in the New Testament. Read the exposition of the principle in Romans 2:5-6, 'the righteous judgment of God'; and the way in which the judgment on Babylon is regarded (in Rev. 18:20 and 19:2) as a matter for which God should be praised. Compare also the Old Testament where 'saints' or 'the Psalmist' rejoice at the righteous judgment of God. The thing that seems to be uppermost in their mind is the knowledge that God is vindicated, and his righteousness has triumphed at last. If we find it hard to attain to that, we must ask ourselves why and where the difficulty comes. Certainly this is the Bible view.

2. The universalist response

Now what does the universalist say in the face of all this? There were some in the last century who based their universalist belief on a flat denial – a flat wiping out of their Bibles – and all this teaching as some sort of mistake and the substituting in its place the belief that all men would be restored to fellowship with God immediately upon death. But that is not the way in which universalists, I think, put it; not one, from Origen on, has ever put it this way. The way they have put it, rather, is in the form of a speculation about what happens after death. They say that for all those who die out of Christ, there is a second chance. Universalism is one of the many types of 'second chance' speculation. And, say the universalists, hereby setting themselves apart from other exponents of the 'second chance' idea, our conviction is that the second chance is going to be accepted in every single case; that God's confrontation of the impenitent after death with the issues of the gospel, which either they did not hear or rejected in this life, is going to be successful: there is going to be a positive response.

Hell, say the universalists, is real, but they say it is temporary. It is not the ultimate state for anyone, it is only the penultimate state. E. Brunner, expounding this doctrine (he never finally committed himself to it), speaks of hell as a pedagogic cleansing process. Hell on this view is a means of grace: it is a rough place, a place of correction, a place where people come to their senses. It is a kind of purgatory for those whom the church of Rome would not allow into purgatory. This doctrine is a doctrine of salvation through, and out of, the state which the New Testament refers to in one place as 'perdition', in another place as 'eternal destruction', and in another 'eternal punishment'. It is an unqualified and unlimited optimism of grace. Sin is a reality, hell is a reality: but God's grace is going to triumph in the end!

3. Arguments justifying this thesis

The positive arguments put forward fall into two classes: first, exegetical; secondly, theological. Taking the exegetical argument first, there are, universalists say, three classes of text in the New Testament which point this way. (1) Those which predict the actual salvation of all men: John 12:32; Acts 3:21; Ephesians 1:10; Romans 5:18; Philippians 2:9–11; 1 Corinthians 15:22–28, 'God shall be all things in all.' (2) Those texts announcing God's will to save all men: 2 Peter 3:9; 1 Timothy 2:4. (3) Those that assert that God stands here and now in such a relation to men that salvation must come to them eventually: 2 Corinthians 5:19; 1 John 2:2; Hebrews 2:9; Titus 2:11; Colossians 1:20, 'God reconciled all things to himself through the cross of Christ.'

Are these texts conclusive as props of the position they are produced to prove? One cannot say so for the following three reasons.

(1) Do these texts admit of another explanation more germane to the context? (2) All these texts are juxtaposed with texts in the documents from which they are drawn which refer specifically to the prospect of some perishing through unbelief. And unless we assume that the writers did not know their own minds, we have to conclude that they cannot, in the texts quoted, really have meant to confirm universal final salvation. (3) Let us note the fact that there is no scripture for the form of the second probation theory. You certainly cannot argue it from that mysterious text 1 Peter 3:19, telling us how, quickened in the spirit, Christ went and preached to the spirits in prison 'who were disobedient in the days of Noah'. Whatever that means, it is a reference to a message taken to a particular limited group of spirits in prison. And the fact that the group is so limited is a strong argument against there being any suggestion of a universal publishing of the gospel to people beyond the grave in Peter's mind.

The attempt to establish the doctrine of universalism by exegetical means must be held to have failed, and as long ago as 1908, Robert McIntosh, whose position might be regarded as wishful universalism, wrote, 'The question is generally argued as one of New Testament interpretation, but the present writer does not think that hopeful. He sees no ground for challenging the old doctrine on exegetical lines.' And most of the modern universalists would agree with that. Therefore they base their universalist speculation on a different foundation. They seek to present it as an irresistible theological inference from certain things in the New Testament; an inference so irresistible and certain as to warrant our discounting certain other things in the New Testament. It is, in other words, a hermeneutical speculation, bound up with the belief that you are allowed to handle the Bible like this. Let us see how they argue this line of thinking in theological terms.

God, they say, is love. This is the real centre of the New Testament revelation, and love must have the last word, and love in the Scriptures is sovereign love, therefore the love of God must imply an effective intention in saving all the rational creatures he has made. Nels Ferré, the American, expounds this in terms of the old liberal thought of the universal fatherhood of God – 'God has no permanent problem children.' Bishop Robinson, in his pre-*Honest to God* days, argued that the only way of holding to the Bible–New Testament insistence that love is the last word to be spoken of God, is to be quite frank in seeing what the Scriptures say about his retributive justice as a function of his redeeming love. He rejects the idea that God's loving purpose could triumph if any were lost on the grounds that it 'cannot preserve the absolute identity of divine love and justice'. For Robinson, you have to assert the absolute identity of divine love and justice, so that you have to understand God's justice as a function and activity of his love preserving the purpose of love, i.e. of correction leading to the response of repentance and the final enjoyment of heaven. But, does the New Testament anywhere lead us to believe that the doctrines of justice and love are identical? I would not have thought so. But Robinson says you must say this.

The second line of theological arguing is to argue from the fact that the cross was a decisive victory. The very essence of the victory, so they say, consists in the fact that the cross effectively saved all men. And they understand faith as simply a matter of coming to acknowledge the fact that you were saved; faith is the opening of men's blind eyes so that they acknowledge what they already are – men are in a state of salvation and grace. But is this New Testament? The New Testament, to me, seems to be saying that no-one is actually saved, no-one is actually in Christ, until he has actually believed into Christ. This is the doctrine of Ephesians 2:12–13, 'Before you came to Christ, you were without hope.' The New Testament seems to be very clear that where there is no actual belief there is no actual salvation, no state of grace in any sense at all. Compare John 3:16 and 36, which make this very explicit. Likewise, 'Whosoever calls upon the name of the Lord shall be saved' sounds a very different doctrine from the universalists' awakening to faith. Again compare Hebrews 10:39: 'We are not of them that draw back but have faith unto the saving of the same.'

Now there is a positive cogent and conclusive argument against universalism. I simply ask, does not the New Testament actually insist on the decisiveness of this life? What did our Lord mean when he threatened the Jews with the prospect of dying in their sins (John 8:21 and 24) as being the ultimate disaster? What did he mean in the parable of Dives and Lazarus where he included the detail about the great gulf fixed between the two men?

What did he mean when he spoke of one group going away into eternal life and the other group going away into eternal punishment, the judgment being passed in each case on the basis of what they had done in this life? What did he mean when he spoke of Judas in this way: Matthew 26:24, '… good it were for that man if he had not been born'? Universalism is a doctrine of the salvation of Judas. Could our Lord have said this if he had expected the salvation of Judas? And what does the rest of the New Testament mean when it speaks in similar terms: Galatians 6:7, Hebrews 9:27, etc? What are we going to make of these passages? And there are many more like them. Are they not pressing for the decisiveness of this life?

The conclusion of the matter must be that of James Denney writing on this subject sixty years ago: 'I dare not say to myself that if I forfeit the opportunity this life offers I shall ever have another, and therefore I dare not say so to another man.'

Preachers, can you get around that? It would simply be dishonest to encourage in others a hope I dare not rely on myself.

So I don't find myself able to be a universalist. Though it is uncomfortable, though is a doctrine that troubles and grieves the heart, I find myself obliged to stick to the old view that the choices of this life are decisive, and to evangelize and to preach the gospel in these terms and as an expression of this conviction.

This is where the argument leads me and these are my reasons for judging that universalist speculation at the present time is a very great evil, calculated to blight a man's ministry, and, as the older evangelicals used to think, 'calculated to ruin souls'.

Questions for study

1. Packer sets out four reasons why universalism has become increasingly common within modern western Protestantism. Summarize each in your own words. Which do you think is the most important?
2. Which biblical texts does Packer regard as being of especial importance in relation to this question?
3. To what extent is Packer's argument motivated by a desire to ensure a continuing passion for evangelism?

7. 'What did the cross achieve? The logic of penal substitution' (1974)

The cross is central to Christian faith, and is of decisive importance for evangelicalism. For Packer, a defining characteristic of evangelicalism is its concern to retain the atoning death of Christ as central to both its spirituality and its theology. Evangelicalism had traditionally regarded the doctrine of penal substitution as the only valid means of interpreting the cross of Christ. However, the doctrine came under mounting criticism during the later nineteenth century, and subsequently during the twentieth. Works such as John McLeod Campbell's *The Nature of the Atonement* (1856) and R. C. Moberly's *Atonement and Personality* (1901) placed an emphasis on the re-creative impact of Christ's sufferings on all of humanity, rather than adopting a penal or substitutionary approach. A particularly severe criticism of the concept of penal substitution was launched by Geoffrey W. H. Lampe in 1962, who argued that it should be discarded as outdated and offensive.[1] It is clear that by 1970, many evangelicals had concluded that the traditional (and closely related) concepts of 'substitutionary atonement' and 'penal substitution' were being seen as one approach to the cross, among others. The cumulative impact of such criticisms on evangelicals was significant.[2] The second National Evangelical Anglican Congress, held at Nottingham in April 1977, can be seen as a telling witness to this increasing reluctance on the part of many evangelicals to commit themselves exclusively to this traditional understanding of the atonement. The final statement of the congress made reference to this diversity amongst evangelicals in the following terms:

Regarding the Atonement, we all gladly affirm that the death and resurrection of Jesus is the heart of the gospel of salvation: 'Christ died for our sins in accordance with the Scriptures, and was raised on the third day.' Nevertheless, we give different emphasis to the various biblical expressions of the Atonement. Some see the truth that Christ died in our place as the central explanation of the cross, while others, who also give this truth a position of great importance, lay greater stress on the relative significance of the other biblical pictures.[3]

In 1973, Packer was invited to deliver the Tyndale Biblical Theology Lecture for that year. Packer chose as the topic for this lecture, which was delivered at Tyndale House on 17 July, the theme of penal substitution. He used the occasion to defend the traditional view of penal substitution, knowing that the lecture would receive wide attention within the evangelical constituency. In view of the significance of Tyndale House and its associated Tyndale Fellowship, we may spend a little while ensuring that their importance is appreciated, before going on to consider the substance of the lecture itself.

The origins of Tyndale House, Cambridge, can be traced back to the Second World War. There was a widespread feeling within evangelical circles that the movement was being dismissed as 'anti-intellectual' or hostile to scholarship. It was widely accepted that there was a need to counter these objections by establishing an evangelical research centre, which would be dedicated to the fostering of good scholarship. It was eventually decided to acquire a residential centre in the English university town of Cambridge, to ensure that an evangelical presence would be secured in this university environment. The stimulus for this choice appears to have been the fact that Oliver Barclay, a rising young evangelical scholar who was then serving as chairman of the Universities Executive Committee of the IVF, reported that a relative was about to offer a suitable property in Cambridge at a very advantageous price. John Laing provided most of the necessary capital, allowing the purchase of the property in Selwyn Gardens to proceed. By 1945, Tyndale House – as it was named – was operational.

As subsequent events proved, the vision of the original committee was more than amply fulfilled. In addition to establishing a major residential study and research centre in Cambridge, a number of study groups were brought into being, each concerned with fostering evangelical scholarship and reflection in areas of importance. Packer had become involved with the work of the Tyndale Fellowship from an early stage. The Puritan Studies Conference, founded in 1950 by Packer and O. R. Johnston, was originally constituted as a study group of the Tyndale Fellowship, and was known simply as the 'Puritan Studies

Group'. Packer subsequently remained a contributing member of the Tyndale Fellowship, and chaired the Biblical Theology Group for several years.

Packer's lecture, entitled 'What did the Cross Achieve? The Logic of Penal Substitution', is to be seen as a vigorous defence of the centrality of the concept of 'penal substitution' against some of the criticisms offered against it. The lecture is a remarkable piece of constructive theology, showing a deep awareness of the development of Christian theology, along with a shrewd and critical awareness of the theological trends of the 1960s. Many regard it as one of Packer's finest essays. Packer opened the lecture by noting the importance of his theme. 'The task which I have set myself in this lecture is to focus and explicate a belief which, by and large, is a distinguishing mark of the world-wide evangelical fraternity; namely, the belief that Christ's death on the cross had the character of penal substitution, and that it was in virtue of this fact that it brought salvation to mankind.' In affirming its importance, Packer noted the need to defend it against both misunderstandings and criticisms.

One such misunderstanding concerns the status of the approach. Many loosely refer to it as the 'doctrine of penal substitution'. As Packer points out, this is not strictly correct; the approach is better defined as a model, or way of picturing, what God achieved on the cross, showing some parallels with the ideas developed by the Swedish writer Gustaf Aulén in the 1930s:

> It is a Christian theological model, based on biblical exegesis, formed to focus a particular awareness of what Jesus did at Calvary to bring us to God. If we wish to speak of the 'doctrine' of penal substitution, we should remember that this model is a dramatic, kerygmatic picturing of divine action, much more like Aulén's 'classic idea' of divine victory (though Aulén never saw this) than it is like the defensive formula-models which we call the Nicene 'doctrine' of the Trinity and the Chalcedonian 'doctrine' of the person of Christ.

Having clarified the status of this approach, or way of picturing God's action on the cross, Packer moved to clarify the precise meaning of the term 'substitution', arguing that many of the criticisms directed against the approach rest on misunderstandings at this point.

> Substitution is, in fact, a broad idea that applies whenever one person acts to supply another's need, or to discharge his obligation, so that the other no longer has to carry the load himself ... In this broad sense, nobody who wishes to say with Paul that there is a true sense in which 'Christ died for us' (once, on our behalf, for our benefit), and 'Christ

redeemed us from the curse of the law, having become a curse for us'
... and who accepts Christ's assurance that he came 'to give his life a
ransom for many' ... should hesitate to say that Christ's death was
substitutionary.

Packer then proceeded to show how the notion of substitution was of
fundamental importance to responsible Christian approaches to an understanding of the meaning of the death of Christ. Packer set out three broad
approaches to the atonement, along the following lines: (1) A *subjective*
approach, which identifies the locus of the effect of the cross in terms of the
effects of Christ upon us, particularly in engendering a response of human love
to the divine love made known in the death of Christ. (2) An *objective*
approach, which sees the impact of the cross in terms of the defeat of satanic
or demonic forces, which hold humanity in captivity. (3) A *substitutionary*
approach, which affirms that Christ's death on the cross is to be understood as
a satisfaction for human sins, by which their guilt may be expunged and we
may be accepted by God.

Packer's approach is that the third approach combines all the authentic
elements of the first two. 'The third type of account denies nothing asserted by
the other two views save their assumption that they are complete. It agrees that
there is biblical support for all they say, but it goes further.' Packer also pointed
out how the second approach implicitly assumes that Christ is our substitute,
even though this is not brought out explicitly in most treatments of the matter.
On the basis of this analysis, Packer points out how the theme of 'substitution'
can be seen as being fundamental to all proper Christian thinking concerning
the atonement. Having explored the development of Christian thinking on the
atonement, Packer concludes that the theme of substitution is of foundational
importance, whether this is explicitly recognized or not. This then raises the
question of how this can be understood in 'penal' terms.

'Penal substitution', according to Packer, 'presupposes a penalty (*poena*)
due to us from God the judge for wrong done and failure to meet his claims.'
Noting that the *locus classicus* for this view is Romans 1:18 – 3:20, Packer
argues that four central biblical insights may be distilled into this approach:
(1) God, in his holiness, justice and goodness, has announced a rightful
sentence against sinful humanity. This verdict includes death, both spiritual
and physical. (2) Sinful humanity lacks the ability to undo the past or break
free from sin in the present. In consequence, we are unable to avert the
righteous judgment of God. (3) Jesus Christ, as God-man, took our place under
judgment, and 'received in his own personal experience all the dimensions of
the death that was our sentence', thus laying the foundation for our pardon

and immunity. (4) Faith recognizes that God's righteous demands remain as they were, and that God's retributive justice does not and will not cease to operate. Nevertheless, those demands have been met in Christ. 'All our sins, past, present and even future, have been covered by Calvary ... Our sins have already been judged and punished, however strange the statement may sound, in the person and death of another.'

To talk about 'penal substitution' is thus not to become involved in muddled argument about the propriety of the transference of guilt (which Packer argues to rest on rationalist assumptions, typical of sixteenth-century humanistic Socinian rationalism, and, later, the Enlightenment), but to articulate the insights of believers who recognize that Jesus bore whatever punishment, penalty and judgment was due to us. For Packer, this is the essential meaning of Paul's declaration that Christ 'loved me, and gave himself for me' (Gal. 2:20).

Packer's defence of this doctrine confirmed his reputation as a competent and vigorous defender of classic evangelical orthodoxy. There were many, particularly among former students at Tyndale Hall and subsequently at Trinity College, who hoped that he might expand the lecture into a book, given the growing misgivings within evangelicalism over the traditional teaching. The published form of the lecture, however, remains the most substantial piece of writing by Packer on the meaning of the cross. In view of its importance, and the fact that there are no other points at which Packer addresses this issue in great detail, this long article is here reprinted in full.

What did the cross achieve?
The logic of penal substitution

The task which I have set myself in this lecture is to focus and explicate a belief which, by and large, is a distinguishing mark of the worldwide evangelical fraternity: namely, the belief that Christ's death on the cross had the character of penal substitution, and that it was in virtue of this fact that it brought salvation to mankind. Two considerations prompt my attempt. First, the significance of penal substitution is not always stated as exactly as is desirable, so that the idea often gets misunderstood and caricatured by its critics; and I should like, if I can, to make such misunderstanding more difficult. Second, I am one of those who believe that this notion takes us to the very heart of the Christian gospel, and I welcome the opportunity of commending my conviction by analysis and argument.

My plan is this: first, to clear up some questions of method, so that there will be no doubt as to what I am doing; second, to explore what it means to call Christ's death substitutionary; third, to see what further meaning is added when Christ's substitutionary suffering is called penal; fourth, to note in closing that the analysis offered is not out of harmony with learned exegetical opinion. These are, I believe, needful preliminaries to any serious theological estimate of this view.

I. Mystery and model

Every theological question had behind it a history of study, and narrow eccentricity in handling it is unavoidable unless the history is taken into account. Adverse comment on the concept of penal substitution often betrays narrow eccentricity of this kind. The two main historical points relating to this idea are, first, that Luther, Calvin, Zwingli, Melanchthon and their reforming contemporaries were the pioneers in stating it and, second, that the arguments brought against it in 1578 by the Unitarian Pelagian, Faustus Socinus, in his brilliant polemic *De Jesu Christo Servatore* (*Of Jesus Christ the Saviour*)[1] have been central in discussion of it ever since. What the Reformers did was to redefine *satisfactio* (satisfaction), the main medieval category for thought about the cross. Anselm's *Cur Deus Homo?*, which largely determined the medieval development, saw Christ's *satisfactio* for our sins as the offering of compensation or damages for dishonour done, but the Reformers saw it as the undergoing of vicarious punishment (*poena*) to meet the claims on us of God's holy law and wrath (i.e. his punitive justice). What Socinus did was to arraign this idea as irrational, incoherent, immoral and impossible. Giving pardon, he argued, does not square with taking satisfaction, nor does the transferring of punishment from the guilty to the innocent square with justice; nor is the temporary death of one a true substitute for the eternal death of many; and a perfect substitutionary satisfaction, could such a thing be, would necessarily confer on us unlimited permission to continue in sin. Socinus' alternative account of New Testament soteriology, based on the axiom that God forgives without requiring any satisfaction save the repentance which makes us forgivable, was evasive and unconvincing, and had little influence. But his classic critique proved momentous: it held the attention of all exponents of the Reformation view for more than a century, and created a tradition of rationalistic prejudice against that view which has effectively shaped debate about it right down to our own day.

The almost mesmeric effect of Socinus' critique on Reformed scholastics in particular was on the whole unhappy. It forced them to develop rational strength in stating and connecting up the various parts of their position, which was good, but it also led them to fight back on the challenger's own ground, using the Socinian technique of arguing *a priori* about God as if he were a man – to be precise, a sixteenth- or seventeenth-century monarch, head of both the legislature and the judiciary in his own realm but bound none the less to respect existing law and judicial practice at every point. So the God of Calvary came to be presented in a whole series of expositions right down to that of Louis Berkhof (1938) as successfully avoiding all the moral and legal lapses which Socinus claimed to find in the Reformation view.[2] But these demonstrations, however skilfully done (and demonstrators like François Turretin and A. A. Hodge, to name but two,[3] were very skilful indeed), had built-in weaknesses. Their stance was defensive rather than declaratory, analytical and apologetic rather than doxological and kerygmatic. They made the word of the cross sound more like a conundrum than a confession of faith – more like a puzzle, we might say, than a gospel. What was happening? Just this: that in trying to beat Socinian rationalism at its own game, Reformed theologians were conceding the Socinian assumption that every aspect of God's work of reconciliation will be exhaustively explicable in terms of a natural theology of divine government, drawn from the world of contemporary legal and political thought. Thus, in their zeal to show themselves rational, they became rationalistic.[4] Here as elsewhere, methodological rationalism became in the seventeenth century a worm in the Reformed bud, leading in the next two centuries to a large-scale withering of its theological flower.

Now I do not query the substantial rightness of the Reformed view of the atonement; on the contrary, I hope to confirm it, as will appear; but I think it is vital that we should unambiguously renounce any such intellectual method as that which I have described, and look for a better one. I shall now try to commend what seems to me a sounder method by offering answers to two questions: (1) What sort of knowledge of Christ's achievement on the cross is open to us? (2) From what source and by what means do we gain it?

(1) What sort of knowledge of God's action in Christ's death may we have? That a man named Jesus was crucified under Pontius Pilate about AD 30 is common historical knowledge, but Christian beliefs about his divine identity and the significance of his dying cannot be deduced from that fact alone. What further sort of knowledge about the cross, then, may Christians enjoy?

The answer, we may say, is faith-knowledge: by faith we know that God was in Christ reconciling the world to himself. Yes, indeed; but what sort of knowledge is faith-knowledge? It is a kind of knowledge of which God is both giver and content. It is a Spirit-given acquaintance with divine realities, given through acquaintance with God's word. It is a kind of knowledge which makes the knower say in one and the same breath both 'whereas I was blind, now I see' (John 9:25) and also 'now we see as in a mirror, darkly … now I know in part' (1 Cor. 13:12). For it is a unique kind of knowledge which, though real, is not full; it is knowledge of what is discernible within a circle of light against a background of a larger darkness; it is, in short, knowledge of a mystery, the mystery of the living God at work.

'Mystery' is used here as it was by Charles Wesley when he wrote:

> 'Tis mystery all! The immortal dies!
> Who can explore his strange design?
> In vain the first-born seraph tries
> To sound the depths of love divine!

'Mystery' in this sense (traditional in theology) means a reality distinct from us which in our very apprehending of it remains unfathomable to us: a reality which we acknowledge as actual without knowing how it is possible, and which we therefore describe as incomprehensible. Christian metaphysicians, moved by wonder at the world, speak of the created order as 'mystery', meaning that there is more to it, and more of God in it, than they can grasp; and similarly Christian theologians, taught by revelation, apply the same word for parallel reasons to the self-revealed and self-revealing God, and to his work of reconciliation and redemption through Christ. It will be seen that this definition of mystery corresponds less to Paul's use of the word *mysterion* (which he applied to the open secret of God's saving purpose, set forth in the gospel) than to his prayer that the Ephesians might 'know the love of Christ which passes knowledge' (Eph. 3:19). Knowing through divine enlightenment that which passes knowledge is precisely what it means to be acquainted with the mystery of God. The revealed 'mystery' (in Paul's sense) of Christ confronts us with the unfathomable 'mystery' (in the sense I defined) of the Creator who exceeds the comprehension of his creatures. Accordingly, Paul ends his full-dress, richest-ever exposition of the mystery of Christ by crying: 'O depth of wealth, wisdom, and knowledge in God! How unsearchable his judgments, how untraceable his ways! Who knows the mind of the Lord? … Source, Guide and Goal of all that is – to him be glory for ever! Amen' (Rom. 11:33ff., New English Bible). Here Paul shows, and shares, his awareness that the God of Jesus remains the God of Job, and that the highest wisdom of the theological theorist, even when working under divine inspiration as Paul did, is to recognize that he is, as it were, gazing into the sun, whose very brightness makes it impossible for him fully to see it; so that at the end of the day he has to admit that God has much more to him than theories can ever contain, and to humble himself in adoration before the one whom he can never fully analyse.

Now the atonement is a mystery in the defined sense, one aspect of the total mystery of God. But it does not stand alone in this. Every aspect of God's reality and work, without exception, is mystery. The eternal Trinity; God's sovereignty in creation, providence, and grace; the incarnation, exaltation, present reign and approaching return of Jesus Christ; the inspiring of the Holy Scriptures; and the ministry of the Spirit in the Christian and the church – each of these (to look no further) is a reality beyond our full fathoming, just as the cross is. And theories about any of these things which used human analogies to dispel the dimension of mystery would deserve our distrust, just as rationalistic theories about the cross do.

It must be stressed that the mystery is in each case the reality itself, as distinct from anything in our apprehension of it, and as distinct therefore from our theories, problems, affirmations and denials about it. What makes it a mystery is that creatures like ourselves can comprehend it only in part. To say this does not open the door to scepticism, for our knowledge of divine realities (like our knowledge of each other) is genuine knowledge expressed in notions which, so far as they go, are true. But it does close the door against rationalism, in the sense of theorizing that claims to explain with finality any aspect of God's way of existing and working. And with that, it alerts us to the fact that the presence in our theology of unsolved problems is not necessarily a reflection on the truth or adequacy of our thoughts. Inadequate and untrue theories do of course exist: a theory (the word comes from *theōrein*, to look at) is a 'view' or 'sight' of something, and if one's way of looking at it is perverse one's view will be distorted, and distorted views are always full of problems. But the mere presence of problems is not enough to prove a view distorted; true views in theology also entail unsolved problems, while any view that was problem-free would certainly be rationalistic and reductionist. True theories in theology, whether about the atonement or anything else, will suspect themselves of being inadequate to their object throughout. One thing that Christians know by faith is that they know only in part.

None of this, of course, is new or unfamiliar; it all belongs to the main historic stream of Christian thought. But I state it here, perhaps too laboriously, because it has not always been brought to bear rigorously enough on the doctrine of the atonement. Also, this position has linguistic implications which touch the doctrine of the atonement in ways which are not always fully grasped; and my next task is to show what these are.

Human knowledge and thoughts are expressed in words, and what we must note now is that all attempts to speak of the mystery of the unique and transcendent God involve many kinds of stretching of ordinary language. We say, for instance, that God is both plural and singular, being three in one; that he directs and determines the free acts of men; that he is wise, good and sovereign when he allows Christians to starve or die of cancer; that the divine Son has always upheld the universe, even when he was a human baby; and so forth. At first sight, such statements might appear nonsensical (either meaningless or false). But Christians say that, though they would be nonsensical if made of men, they are true as statements about God. If so, however, it is clear that the key words are not being used in an everyday way. Whatever our views on the origins of human language and inspiration of the Scriptures (both matters on which it seems that options are currently being broadened rather than reduced), there can be no dispute that the meaning of the nouns, adjectives and verbs that we use for stating facts and giving descriptions is anchored, at least in the first instance, in our experience of knowing things and people (ourselves included) in this world. Ordinary language is thus being adapted for an extraordinary purpose when we use it to speak of God. Christians have always made this adaptation easily in their prayers, praises and proclamations, as if it were a natural thing to do (as indeed I think it is), and the doubts articulated by living if somewhat old-fashioned philosophers like A. J. Ayer and Antony Flew as to whether such utterance expresses knowledge and conveys information about anything more than private attitudes seem curiously provincial as well as paradoxical.[5] Moreover, it is noticeable that the common Christian verbal forms for expressing divine mysteries have from the first shown remarkable consistency and steadiness in maintaining their built-in logical strangeness, as if the apprehended reality of God was itself sustaining them (as indeed I think it was). Language about the cross illustrates this clearly: liturgies, hymns and literature, homiletical, catechetical and apologetic, all show that Christians have from the start lived by faith in Christ's death as a sacrifice made to God in reparation for their sins, however uncouth and mythological such talk sounds (and must always have sounded), however varied the presentations of atonement which teachers tried out, and however little actual theologizing about the cross went on in particular periods, especially the early centuries.[6]

Christian language, with its peculiarities, has been much studied during the past twenty years, and two things about it have become clear. First, all its odd, 'stretched', contradictory- and incoherent-sounding features derive directly from the unique Christian notion of the transcendent, tri-personal Creator God. Christians regard God as free from the limits that bind creatures like ourselves, who bear God's image while not existing on his level, and Christian language, following biblical precedent, shakes free from ordinary limits in a way that reflects this fact. So, for instance, faced with John's declaration in 1 John 4:8–10, 'God is love. ... Herein is love, not that we loved God, but that he loved us, and sent his Son to be the propitiation for our sins,' Calvin can write without hesitation: 'The word propitiation (*placatio*; Greek, *hilasmos*) has great weight: for God, in a way that cannot be put into words (*ineffabili quodam modo*), at the very time when he loved us, was hostile (*infensus*) to us till he was reconciled in Christ.'[7] Calvin's phrase 'in a way that cannot be put into words' is his acknowledgment that the mystery of God is beyond our grasp. To Calvin, this duality of attitude, love and hostility, which in human psychological terms is inconceivable, is part of God's moral glory; a sentiment which might make rationalistic theologians shake their heads, but at which John certainly would have nodded his.

Second, Christian speech verbalizes the apprehended mystery of God by using a distinctive non-representational 'picture-language'. This consists of parables, analogies, metaphors and images piled up in balance with each other, as in the Bible itself (from which this language is first learned), and all pointing to the reality of God's presence and action in order to evoke awareness of it and response to it. Analysis of the functioning of this language is currently in full swing,[8] and no doubt much remains to be said. Already, however, the discussion has produced one firm result of major importance – the recognition that the verbal units of Christian speech are 'models', comparable to the thought-models of modern physics.[9] The significance of this appears from John MacIntyre's judgment 'that the theory of models succeeds in reinstating the doctrine of analogy in modern theological logic ... and that analogy is to be interpreted in term of a theory of models and not vice versa.'[10] The doctrine of analogy is the time-harboured account, going back to Aquinas, of how ordinary language is used to speak intelligibly of a God who is partly like us (because we bear his image) and partly unlike us (because he is the infinite Creator while we are finite creatures).[11] All theological models, like the non-descriptive models of the physical sciences, have an analogical character; they are, we might say, analogies with a purpose, thought-patterns which function in a particular way, teaching us to focus one area of reality (relationships with God) by conceiving of it in terms of another, better-known area of reality (relationships with each other). Thus they actually inform us about our relationship with God and through the Holy Spirit enable us to unify, clarify and intensify our experience in that relationship.

The last song in *Joseph and the Amazing Technicolor Dreamcoat* assures us that 'any dream will do' to wake the weary into joy. Will any model do to give knowledge of the living God? Historically, Christians have not thought so. Their characteristic theological method, whether practised clumsily or skilfully, consistently or inconsistently, has been to take biblical models as their God-given starting-point, to base their belief-system on what biblical writers use these models to say, and to let these models operate as 'controls', both suggesting and delimiting what further, secondary models may be developed in order to explicate these which are primary. As models in physics are hypotheses formed under the suggestive control of empirical evidence to correlate and predict phenomena, so Christian theological models are explanatory constructs formed to help us know, understand and deal with God, the ultimate reality. From this standpoint, the whole study of Christian theology, biblical, historical and systematic, is the exploring of a three-tier hierarchy of models: first, the 'control' models given in Scripture (God, Son of God, kingdom of God, word of God, love of God, glory of God, body of Christ, justification, adoption, redemption, new birth and so forth – in short, all the concepts analysed in Kittel's great *Wörterbuch* and its many epigoni); next, dogmatic models which the church crystallized out to define and defend the faith (*homoousion*, Trinity, nature, hypostatic union, double procession, sacrament, supernatural, etc. – in short, all the concepts usually dealt with in doctrinal textbooks); finally, interpretive models lying between Scripture and defined dogma which particular theologians and theological schools developed for stating the faith to contemporaries (penal substitution, verbal inspiration, divinization, Barth's 'Nihil' – *das Nichtige* – and many more).

It is helpful to think of theology in these terms, and of the atonement in particular. Socinus went wrong in this matter first by identifying the biblical model of God's kingship with his own sixteenth-century monarchy model (a mistake later repeated by Hugo Grotius), second by treating this not-wholly-biblical model as his 'control', and third by failing to acknowledge that the mystery of God is more than any one model, even the best, can express. We have already noticed that some orthodox writers answering Socinus tended to slip in a similar way. The passion to pack God into a conceptual box of our own making is always strong, but must be resisted. If we bear in mind that all the knowledge we can have of the atonement is of a mystery about which we can only think and speak by means of models, and which remain a mystery when all is said and done, it will keep us from rationalistic pitfalls and thus help our progress considerably.

II. Bible and model

(2) Now we come up to our second question, my answer to which has been hinted at already. By what means is knowledge of the mystery of the cross given us? I reply: through the didactic thought-models given in the Bible, which in truth are instruction from God. In other words, I proceed on the basis of the mainstream Christian belief in biblical inspiration, which I have sought to justify elsewhere.[12]

What this belief means, in formula terms, is that the Holy Scriptures of both Testaments have the dual character which the *viva voce* teaching of prophets, apostles and supremely Jesus had: in content, if not in grammatical form, it is both human witness to God and God's witness to himself. The true analogy for inspiration is incarnation, the personal Word of God becoming flesh. As a multiple confession of faith in the God who rules, judges and saves in the space-time continuum which we call world history, the Bible consists of occasional documents, historical, didactic and liturgical, all proclaiming in various ways what God has done, is doing and will do. Each document and each utterance within that document, like Jesus Christ and each of his utterances, is anchored in a particular historical situation – this particularity marks all the Christian revelation – and to discern within these particularities truths from God for universal application is the interpreter's major task. His guideline is the knowledge that God's word for today is found through understanding and reapplying the word that God spoke long ago in identity (substantial, not grammatical) with the message of the biblical authors. The way into God's mind remains *via* their minds, for their assertions about God embody in particularized form what he wants to tell us today about himself. In other words, God says in application to us the same things that he originally said in application to those to whom the biblical books were first addressed. The details of the second application differ from the first in a way that corresponds to the difference between our situation and that of the first addresses, but the truths of principle being applied are the same. Divine speech is itself, of course, a model, but it is a controlling one. It signifies the reality of mind-to-mind instruction from God to us by verbal means, and thus teaches us to categorize all other didactic models found in Scripture, not as hypothesis or hunch, but as revelation.

How do these revealed models become means of God's instruction? Here, it must regretfully be said, Ian Ramsey, the pioneer exponent of model-structure of biblical thinking, fails us. He describes vividly how these models trigger off religious disclosures and so evoke religious responses, but instead of equating the beliefs they express with divine teaching he leaves quite open, and therefore quite obscure, the relation between the 'disclosures' as intuitions of reality and the thoughts which the models convey. This means that he lacks criteria for distinguishing true from false intuitions. Sometimes he speaks as if all feelings of 'cosmic disclosure' convey insights that are true and self-authenticating, but one need only mention the Buddha, Muhammad, Mrs Mary Baker Eddy, the false prophets exposed by Jeremiah, Ezekiel and Micaiah in 1 Kings 22, and the visionaries of Colossians 2:18–19, to show that this is not so. Also Ramsey seems to be without criteria for relating models to each other and developing from them a coherent belief-system, and he nowhere considers what the divine-speech model implies.[13]

Must our understanding of how biblical models function be as limited or as loose as Ramsey's is? Not necessarily. Recognition that the biblical witness to God has the logic of models – not isolated, incidentally, but linked together, and qualifying each other in sizeable units of meaning – is compatible with all the views taken in the modern hermeneutical debate. Central to this debate are two questions. The first is whether the reference-point and subject-matter of biblical witness is just the transformed psyche, the 'new being' as such, or whether it does not also, and indeed primarily, refer to saving acts of God and a living divine Saviour that were originally 'there' as datable realities in the space-time continuum of world history, and that owe their transforming power 'here' in Christian lives now to the fact that they were 'there' on the stage of history then. To the extent that the former alternative is embraced, one has to say that the only factual information which the biblical writers communicate is that God's people felt and thought in certain ways at certain times in certain situations. Then one has to face the question whether the writers thought this was all the factual information they were communicating; if one says no, then one has to justify one's disagreement with them; if one says yes, one has to explain why so much of their witness to Christ has the form of factual narration about him – why, indeed, the 'gospel' as a literary form was ever invented. If, however, one takes the latter alternative, as all sober reason seems to counsel, then the second central question arises: how much distortion of fact is there in the narrating, and how much of guesswork, hunch, and fantasy is there in the interpreting, of the historical realities that were 'there'? I cannot discuss these massive and complex issues here; suffice it to declare, in relation to this debate, that I am proceeding on the basis that the biblical writers do indeed give true information about certain historical events, public and in principle datable, which have resulted in a Saviour and a salvation being 'there' for sinners to receive by faith; and that the biblical thought-models in terms of which these events are presented and explained are revealed models, ways of thought that God himself has taught us for the true understanding of what he has done for us and will do in us.

Also, I proceed on the basis that the Holy Spirit who inspired prophetic and apostolic testimony in its written as well as its oral form is now active to teach Christians through it, making them aware of its divine quality overall, its message to themselves, and the presence and potency of God in Christ to whom it points. Since the Spirit has been teaching the church in this way in every age, much of our listening to the Bible in the present will rightly take the form of reviewing theological constructions of the past, testing them by the written word from which they took their rise. When a particular theological view, professedly Bible-based, has over the centuries proved a mainspring of Christian devotion, faith and love, one approaches it, not indeed uncritically, but with respect, anticipating the discovery that it is substantially right. Our present task is to elucidate and evaluate one historic line of biblical inter-pretation which has had an incalculable impact on countless lives since it was clarified in the century of the Reformation; it will be strange if it proves to have been entirely wrong.[14]

So much, then, for methodological preliminaries, which have been tedious but necessary; now to our theme directly.

III. Substitution

The first thing to say about penal substitution has been said already. It is a Christian theological model, based on biblical exegesis, formed to focus a particular awareness of what Jesus did at Calvary to bring us to God. If we wish to speak of the 'doctrine' of penal substitution, we should remember that this model is a dramatic, kerygmatic picturing of divine action, much more like Aulén's 'classic idea' of divine victory (though Aulén never saw this) than it is like the defensive formula-models which we call the Nicene 'doctrine' of the Trinity and the Chalcedonian 'doctrine' of the person of Christ. Logically, the model is put together in two stages: first, the death of Christ is declared to have been substitutionary; then the substitution is characterized and given a specific frame of reference by adding the word penal. We shall examine the two stages separately.

Stage one is to declare Christ's death substitutionary. What does this mean? The *Oxford English Dictionary* defines substitution as 'the putting of one person or thing in the place of another'. One oddity of contemporary Christian talk is that many who affirm that Jesus' death was vicarious and representative deny that it was substitutionary; for the *Dictionary* defines both words in substitutionary terms! Representation is said to mean 'the fact of standing for, or in place of, some other thing or person, esp. with a right or authority to act on their account; substitution of one thing or person for another'. And vicarious is defined as 'that takes or supplies the place of another thing or person; substituted instead of the proper thing or person'. So here, it seems, is a distinction without a difference. Substitution is, in fact, a broad idea that applies whenever one person acts to supply another's need, or to discharge his obligation, so that the other no longer has to carry the load himself. As Pannenberg says, 'in social life, substitution is a universal phenomenon ... Even the structure of vocation, the division of labour, has substitutionary character. One who has a vocation performs this function for those whom he serves.' For 'every service has vicarious character by recognizing a need in the person served that apart from the service that person would have to satisfy for himself'.[15] In this broad sense, nobody who wishes to say with Paul that there is a true sense in which 'Christ died for us' (*hyper*, on our behalf, for our benefit), and 'Christ redeemed us from the curse of the law, having become a curse for us' (*hyper* again) (Rom. 5:8; Gal. 3:13), and who accepts Christ's assurance that he came 'to give his life a ransom for many' (*anti*, which means precisely 'in place of', 'in exchange for'[16]), should hesitate to say that Christ's death was substitutionary. Indeed, if he describes Christ's death as vicarious he is actually saying it.

It is, of course, no secret why people shy off this word. It is because they equate, and know that others equate, substitution in Christology with penal substitution. This explains the state of affairs which, writing in 1948, F. W. Camfield described as follows:

> If there is one conclusion which [has] come almost to be taken for granted in enlightened Christian quarters, it is that the idea of substitution has led theology on a wrong track; and that the word 'substitution' must now be dropped from the doctrine of the Atonement as too heavily laden with misleading and even false connotations. By 'liberal' or 'modernist' theology the idea of substitution is of course rejected out of hand. And even the theology which prides itself on being 'positive' and 'evangelical' and which seeks to maintain lines of communication with the great traditional doctrines of atonement is on the whole disposed to reject it. And this, not merely on the ground that it holds implications which are irrational and morally offensive, but even and specifically on the ground that it is unscriptural. Thus Dr Vincent Taylor as a result of exhaustive examination of the 'Idea of Atonement in the New Testament' gives it as his conclusion that the idea of substitution has no place in the New Testament writings; that in fact it is opposed to the

fundamental teaching of the New Testament; that even St Paul though he sometimes trembles on the edge of substitutionary conceptions nevertheless avoids them. It is difficult to escape the impression that Dr Vincent Taylor's anxiety to eliminate the idea of substitution from evangelical theology has coloured his interpretation of the New Testament witness. But his conclusions provide a striking indication of the tendency at work in modern evangelical circles. It is felt that nothing has done more to bring the evangelical doctrine of the Atonement into disrepute than the idea of substitution; and therefore, something like a sigh of relief makes itself heard when it is suggested that this idea rests on a misunderstanding of the teaching of Scripture.[17]

Today, more than a quarter of a century later, the picture Camfield draws would have to be qualified by reference to the vigorous vindication and use of the substitution idea by such as Pannenberg and Barth;[18] none the less, in British theology the overall situation remains very much as Camfield describes. It would, however, clarify discussion if all who hold that Jesus by dying did something for us which we needed to do but could not would agree that they are regarding Christ's death as substitutionary, and differing only on the nature of the action which Jesus performed in our place and also, perhaps, on the way we enter into the benefit that flows from it. Camfield himself goes on to spell out a non-penal view of substitution.

Broadly speaking, there have been three ways in which Christ's death has been explained in the church. Each reflects a particular view of the nature of God and our plight in sin, and of what is needed to bring us to God in the fellowship of acceptance on his side and faith and love on ours. It is worth glancing at them to see how the idea of substitution fits in with each.

There is, first, the type of account which sees the cross as having its effect entirely on men, whether by revealing God's love to us, or by bringing home to us how much God hates our sins, or by setting us a supreme example of godliness, or by blazing a trail to God which we may now follow, or by so involving mankind in his redemptive obedience that the life of God now flows into us, or by all these modes together. It is assumed that our basic need is lack of motivation Godward and of openness to the inflow of divine life; all that is needed to set us in a right relationship with God is a change in us at these two points, and this Christ's death brings about. The forgiveness of our sins is not a separate problem; as soon as we are changed we become forgivable, and are then forgiven at once. This view has little or no room for any thought of substitution, since it goes so far in equating what Christ did for us with what he does to us.

A second type of account sees Christ's death as having its effect primarily on hostile spiritual forces external to us which are held to be imprisoning us in a captivity of which our inveterate moral twistedness is one sign and symptom. The cross is seen as the work of God going forth to battle as our champion, just as David went forth as Israel's champion to fight Goliath. Through the cross these hostile forces, however conceived – whether as sin and death, Satan and his hosts, the demonic in society and its structures, the powers of God's wrath and curse, or anything else – are overcome and nullified, so that Christians are not in bondage to them, but share Christ's triumph over them. The assumption here is that man's plight is created entirely by hostile cosmic forces distinct from God; yet, seeing Jesus as our champion, exponents of this view could still properly call him our substitute, just as all the Israelites who declined Goliath's challenge in 1 Samuel 17:8–11 could properly call David their substitute. Just as a substitute who involves others in the consequences of his action as if they had done it themselves is their representative, so a representative discharging the obligations of those whom he represents is their substitute. What this type of account of the cross affirms (though it is not usually put in these terms) is that the conquering Christ, whose victory secured our release, was our representative substitute.

The third type of account denies nothing asserted by the other two views save their assumption that they are complete. It agrees that there is biblical support for all they say, but it goes further. It grounds man's plight as a victim of sin and Satan in the fact that, for all God's daily goodness to him, as a sinner he stands under divine judgment, and his bondage to evil is the start of his sentence, and unless God's rejection of him is turned into acceptance he is lost for ever. On this view, Christ's death had its effect first on God, who was hereby propitiated (or, better, who hereby propitiated himself), and only because it had this effect did it become an overthrowing of the powers of darkness and a revealing of God's seeking and saving love. The thought here is that by dying Christ offered to God what the West has called satisfaction for sins, satisfaction which God's own character dictated as the only means whereby his 'no' to us could become a 'yes'. Whether this Godward satisfaction is understood as the homage of death itself, or death as the perfecting of holy obedience, or an undergoing of the God-forsakenness of hell, which is God's final judgment on sin, or a perfect confession of man's sins combined with entry into their bitterness by sympathetic identification, or all these things together (and nothing stops us combining them together), the shape of this view remains the same – that by undergoing the cross Jesus expiated our sins, propitiated our Maker, turned God's 'no' to us into a 'yes', and so saved us. All forms of this view see Jesus as our representative substitute in fact, whether or not they call him that, but only certain versions of it represent his substitutions as penal.

This analysis prompts three comments.

First, it should be noted that though the two former views regularly set themselves in antithesis to the third, the third takes up into itself all the positive assertions that they make; which raises the question whether any more is at issue here than the impropriety of treating half-truths as the whole truth, and of rejecting a more comprehensive account on the basis of speculative negations about what God's holiness requires as a basis for forgiving sins. Were it allowed that the first two views might be misunderstanding and distorting themselves in this way, the much-disputed claim that a broadly substitutionary view of the cross has always been the mainstream Christian opinion might be seen to have substance after all. It is a pity that books on the atonement so often take it for granted that accounts of the cross which have appeared as rivals in historical debate must be treated as intrinsically exclusive. This is always arbitrary, and sometimes quite perverse.

Second, it should be noted that our analysis was simply of views about the death of Christ, so nothing was said about his resurrection. All three types of view usually agree in affirming that the resurrection is an integral part of the gospel; that the gospel proclaims a living, vindicated Saviour whose resurrection as the firstfruits of the new humanity is the basis as well as the pattern for ours is not a matter of dispute between them. It is sometimes pointed out that the second view represents the resurrection of Jesus as an organic element in his victory over the powers of death, whereas the third view does not, and hardly could, represent it as an organic element in the bearing of sin's penalty or the tasting and confessing of its vileness (however the work of Calvary is conceived); and on this basis the third view is sometimes criticized as making the resurrection unnecessary. But this criticism may be met in two ways. The first reply is that Christ's saving work has two parts, his dealing with his Father on our behalf by offering himself in substitutionary satisfaction for our sins and his dealing with us on his Father's behalf by bestowing on us through faith the forgiveness which his death secured, and it is as important to distinguish these two parts as it is to hold them together. For a demonstration that part two is now possible because part one is finished, and for the actual implementing of part two, Jesus' resurrection is indeed essential, and so appears as an organic element in his work as a whole. The second reply is that these two ways of viewing the cross should in any case by synthesized, following the example of Paul in Colossians 2:13–15, as being complementary models expressing different elements in the single complex reality which is the mystery of the cross.

Third, it should be noted that not all advocates of the third type of view have been happy to use the word 'substitution'. This has been partly through desire to evade the Socinian criticism that in the penal realm substitution is impossible, and partly for fear that to think of Christ dying for us as our substitute obscures his call to us to die and rise in him and with him, for the moral transforming of us into his holy image. P. T. Forsyth, for example, is one who stresses the vicariousness of Christ's action in his passion as he endured for man's salvation God's personal anger against man's sin;[19] yet he rejects 'substitution' in favour of 'representation' and replaces 'substitutionary expiation (which, as these words are commonly understood, leaves us too little committed)' by 'solidary reparation', 'solidary confession and praise', because he wants to stress that we enter into salvation only as we identify with Christ's death to sin and are re-created as the new humanity in him.[20] But, admirable as is Forsyth's wish to stress what is in Romans 6:1–11, avoiding the word substitution can only have the effect of obscuring what is in Romans 3:21–28, where Paul describes Christ as 'a propitiation[21] ... by his blood' (verse 25) in virtue of which God bestows 'the free gift of righteousness' (5:17) upon believing sinners and so 'justifies the ungodly' (4:5). As James Denney said, 'If Christ died the death in which sin had involved us – if in His death He took the responsibility of our sins on Himself – no word is equal to this which falls short of what is meant by calling Him our substitute.'[22] The correct reply to Forsyth would seem to be that before Christ's death can be representative, in Forsyth's sense of setting a pattern of 'confession and praise' to be reproduced in our own self-denial and cross-bearing, it has to be substitutionary in Denney's sense of absorbing God's wrath against our sins; otherwise, our 'confession and praise' in solidarity with Christ becomes itself a ploy for averting that wrath – in other words, a meritorious work, aimed at securing pardon, assuming that in Christ we save ourselves.

What Denney said about this in 1903 was in fact an answer by anticipation to Forsyth's formula of 1910. A reviewer of *The Death of Christ* had argued that 'if we place ourselves at Paul's point of view, we shall see that to the eye of God the death of Christ presents itself less as an act which Christ does for the race than as an act which the race does in Christ.' In *The Atonement and the Modern Mind* Denney quoted these words and commented on them thus:

> In plain English, Paul teaches less that Christ died for the ungodly, than that the ungodly in Christ died for themselves. This brings out the logic of what representative means when representative is opposed to substitute.[23] The representative is ours, we are in Him, and we are supposed to get over all the moral difficulties raised by the idea of

substitution just because He is ours, and because we are one with Him. But the fundamental fact of the situation is that, to begin with, Christ is not ours, and we are not one with Him ... we are 'without Christ' (*chōris Christou*) ... A representative not produced by us, but given to us – not chosen by us, but the elect of God – is not a representative at all in the first instance, but a substitute.[24]

So the true position, on the type of view we are exploring, may be put thus: we identify with Christ against the practice of sin because we have already identified him as the one who took our place under sentence for sin. We enter upon the life of repentance because we have learned that he first endured for us the death reparation. The Christ into whom we now accept incorporation is the Christ who previously on the cross became our propitiation – not, therefore, one in whom we achieve our reconciliation with God, but one through whom we receive it as free gift based on a finished work (cf. Rom. 5:10); and we love him, because he first loved us and gave himself for us. So substitution, on this view, really is the basic category; the thought of Christ as our representative, however construed in detail, cannot be made to mean what substitution means, and our solidarity with Christ in 'confession and praise', so far from being a concept alternative to that of substitution, is actually a response which presupposes it.

IV. Penal substitution

Now we move to the second stage in our model-building, and bring in the word 'penal' to characterize the substitution we have in view. To add this 'qualifier', as Ramsey would call it, is to anchor the model of substitution (not exclusively, but regulatively) within the world of moral law, guilty conscience, and retributive justice. Thus is forged a conceptual instrument for conveying the thought that God remits our sins and accepts our persons into favour not because of any amends we have attempted, but because the penalty which was our due was diverted on to Christ. The notion which the phrase 'penal substitution' expresses is that Jesus Christ our Lord, moved by a love that was determined to do everything necessary to save us, endured and exhausted the destructive divine judgment for which we were otherwise inescapably destined, and so won us forgiveness, adoption and glory. To affirm penal substitution is to say believers are in debt to Christ specifically for this, and that this is the mainspring of all their joy, peace and praise both now and for eternity.

The general thought is clear enough, but for our present purpose we need a fuller analysis of its meaning, and here a methodological choice must be made. Should we appeal to particular existing accounts of penal substitution, or construct a composite of our own? At the risk of seeming idiosyncratic (which is, I suppose, the gentleman's way of saying unsound) I plump for the latter course, for the following main reasons.

First, there is no denying that penal substitution sometimes has been, and still sometimes is, asserted in ways which merit the favourite adjective of its critics – 'crude'. As one would expect of that which for more than four centuries has been the mainspring of evangelical piety – 'popular piety', as Roman Catholics would call it – ways of presenting it have grown up which are devotionally evocative without always being theologically rigorous. Moreover, the more theological expositions of it since Socinus have tended to be one-track-minded; constricted in interest by the preoccupations of controversy, and absorbed in the task of proclaiming the one vital truth about the cross which others disregarded or denied, 'upholders of the penal theory have sometimes so stressed the thought that Christ bore our penalty that they have found room for nothing else. Rarely have they in theory denied the value of other theories, but sometimes they have in practice ignored them.'[25] Also, as we have seen, much of the more formative and influential discussing of penal substitution was done in the seventeenth century, at a time when Protestant exegesis of Scripture was coloured by an uncriticized and indeed unrecognized natural theology of law, and this has left its mark on many later statements. All this being so, it might be hard to find an account of penal substitution which could safely be taken as standard or as fully representative, and it will certainly be more straightforward if I venture an analysis of my own.

Second, I have already hinted that I think it important for the theory of penal substitution to be evaluated as a model setting forth the meaning of the atonement rather than its mechanics. One result of the work of rationalistic Protestant theologians over three centuries, from the Socinians to the Hegelians, was to nourish the now common assumption that the logical function of a 'theory' in theology is to resolve 'how'-problems within an established frame of thought about God and man. In other words, theological theories are like detectives' theories in whodunits; they are hypotheses relating puzzling facts together in such a way that all puzzlement is dispelled (for the convention of 'mystery stories' is that by the last page no mystery should be felt to remain). Now we have seen that, for discernible historical reasons, penal substitution has sometimes been explicated as a theory of this kind, telling us how divine love and justice could be, and were, 'reconciled' (whatever that means); but a doubt remains as to whether this way of understanding the theme is biblically right. Is the harmonization of God's attributes any part of the information, or is it even the kind of information, that the inspired writers are concerned to give? Gustaf Aulén characterized the '*Christus victor*' motif (he would not call it a theory) as a dramatic idea of the atonement rather than a rationale of its mechanics, and contrasted it in this respect with the 'Latin' view, of which penal substitution is one form;[26] but should not penal substitution equally be understood as a dramatic idea, declaring the fact of the atonement kergymatically, i.e. as gospel (good news), just as Aulén's conquest-motif is concerned to do? I believe it should. Surely the primary issue with which penal substitution is concerned is neither the morality nor the rationality of God's ways, but the remission of my sins; and the primary function of the concept is to correlate my knowledge of being guilty before God with my knowledge that, on the one hand, no question of my ever being judged for my sins can now arise, and, on the other hand, that the risen Christ whom I am called to accept as Lord is none other than Jesus, who secured my immunity from judgment by bearing on the cross the penalty which was my due. The effect of this correlation is not in any sense to 'solve' or dissipate the mystery of the work of God (it is not that sort of mystery!); the effect is simply to define that work with precision, and thus to evoke faith, hope, praise and responsive love to Jesus Christ. So, at least, I think, and therefore I wish my presentation of penal substitution to highlight its character as a kerygmatic model; and so I think it best to offer my own analytical definition which will aim to be both descriptive of what all who have held this view had had in common, and also prescriptive of how the term should be understood in any future discussion.

Third, if the present examination of penal substitution is to be worth while it must present this view in its best light, and I think an eclectic exposition will bring us closest to this goal. The typical modern criticism of older expositions of our theme is that, over and above their being less than fully moral (Socinus' criticism), they are less than fully personal. Thus, for instance, G. W. H. Lampe rejects penal substitution because it assumes that 'God inflicts retributive punishment', and 'retribution is impersonal; it considers offences in the abstract ... we ought not to ascribe purely retributive justice to God ... the Father of mankind does not deal with his children on the basis of deterrence and retribution ... to hang the criminal is to admit defeat at the level of love ... It is high time to discard the vestiges of a theory of Atonement that was geared to a conception of punishment which found nothing shocking in the idea that God should crucify sinners or the substitute who took their place. It is time, too, to stop the mouth of the blasphemer who calls it "sentimentality" to reject the idea of a God of retribution.'[27] Lampe's violent language shows the strength of his conviction that retribution belongs to a sub-personal, non-loving order of relationships, and that penal substitution dishonours the cross by anchoring it here.

James Denney's sense of the contrast between personal relations, which are moral, and legal relations, which tend to be impersonal, external and arbitrary, once drew from him an outburst which in isolation might seem parallel to Lampe's. 'Few things have astonished me more' (he wrote) 'than to be charged with teaching a "forensic" or "legal" or "judicial" doctrine of Atonement ... There is nothing that I should wish to reprobate more whole-heartedly than the conception which is expressed by these words. To say that the relations of God and man are forensic is to say that they are regulated by statute – that sin is a breach of statute – that the sinner is a criminal – and that God adjudicates on him by interpreting the statute in its application to his case. Everybody knows that this is a travesty of the truth.'[28] It is noticeable that Denney, the champion of the substitutionary idea, never calls Christ's substitution 'penal'; in his situation, the avoidance must have been deliberate. Yet Denney affirmed these four truths: first, that 'the relations of God and man ... are personal, but ... determined by (moral) law'; second, 'that there is in the nature of things a reaction against sin which when it has had its perfect work is fatal, that this reaction is the divine punishment of sin, and that its finally fatal character is what is meant by Scripture when it says that the wages of sin is death'; third, that 'the inevitable reactions of the divine order against evil ... are the sin itself coming back in another form and finding out the sinner. They are nothing if not retributive'; and fourth, 'that while the agony and the Passion were not penal in the sense of coming upon Jesus through a bad conscience, or making Him the personal object of divine wrath, they were penal in the sense that in that dark hour He had to realise to the full the divine reaction against sin in the race ... and that without doing so He could not have been the Redeemer of that race from sin'.[29] It seems to me that these affirmations point straight to a way of formulating the penal substitution model which is both moral and personal enough to evade all Lampe's strictures and also inclusive of all that the concept means to those who embrace it. But the formulation itself will have to be my own.

So I shall now attempt my analysis of penal substitution as a model of the atonement, under five heads: substitution and retribution; substitution and solidarity; substitution and mystery; substitution and salvation; substitution and divine love. Others who espouse this model must judge whether I analyse it accurately or not.

1. Substitution and retribution

Penal substitution, as an idea, presupposes a penalty (*poena*) due to us from God the Judge for wrong done and failure to meet his claims. The *locus classicus* on this is Romans 1:18 – 3:20, but the thought is everywhere in the New Testament. The judicial context is a moral context too; whereas human judicial systems are not always rooted in moral reality, the Bible treats the worlds of moral reality and of divine judgment as coinciding. Divine judgment means that retribution is entailed by our past upon our present and future existence, and God himself is in charge of this process, ensuring that the objective wrongness and guiltiness of what we have been is always 'there' to touch and wither what we are and shall be. In the words of Emil Brunner, 'Guilt means that our past – that which can never be made good – always constitutes one element in our present situation.'[30] When Lady Macbeth, walking and talking in her sleep, sees blood on her hand, and cannot clean or sweeten it, she witnesses to the order of retribution as all writers of tragedy and surely all reflective men – certainly, those who believe in penal substitution – have come to know it: wrongdoing may be forgotten for a time, as David forgot his sin over Bathsheba and Uriah, but sooner or later it comes back to mind, as David's sin did under Nathan's ministry, and at once our attention is absorbed, our peace and pleasure are gone, and something tells us that we ought to suffer for what we have done. When joined with inklings of God's displeasure, this sense of things is the start of hell. Now it is into this context of awareness that the model of penal substitution is introduced, to focus for us four insights about our situation.

Insight one concerns God: it is that the retributive principle has his sanction, and indeed expresses the holiness, justice and goodness reflected in his law, and that death, spiritual as well as physical, the loss of life of God as well as that of the body, is the rightful sentence which he has announced against us, and now prepares to inflict.

Insight two concerns ourselves: it is that, standing thus under sentence, we are helpless either to undo the past or to shake off sin in the present, and thus have no way of averting what threatens.

Insight three concerns Jesus Christ: it is that he, the God-man of John 1:1–18 and Hebrews 1 – 2, took our place under judgment and received in his own personal experience all the dimensions of the death that was our sentence, whatever these were, so laying the foundation for our pardon and immunity.

> We may not know, we cannot tell
> What pains he had to bear

> But we believe it was for us
> He hung and suffered there.

Insight four concerns faith: it is that faith is a matter first and foremost of looking outside and away from oneself to Christ and his cross as the sole ground of present forgiveness and future hope. Faith sees that God's demands remain what they were, and that God's law of retribution, which our conscience declares to be right, has not ceased to operate in his world, nor ever will; but that in our case the law has operated already, so that all our sins, past, present and even future, have been covered by Calvary. So our conscience is pacified by the knowledge that our sins have already been judged and punished, however strange the statement may sound, in the person and death of another. Bunyan's pilgrim before the cross loses his burden, and Toplady can assure himself that

> If thou my pardon hast secured,
> And freely in my room endured
> The whole of wrath divine,
> Payment God cannot twice demand,
> First from my bleeding surety's hand
> And then again from mine.

Reasoning thus, faith grasps the reality of God's free gift of righteousness, i.e. the 'rightness' with God that the righteous enjoy (cf. Rom. 5:16–17), and with it the justified man's obligation to live henceforth 'unto' the one who for his sake died and rose again (cf. 2 Cor. 5:14).

This analysis, if correct, shows what job the word 'penal' does in our model. It is there, not to prompt theoretical puzzlement about the transferring of guilt, but to articulate the insight of believers who, as they look at Calvary in the light of the New Testament, are constrained to say, 'Jesus was bearing the judgment I deserved (and deserve), the penalty for my sins, the punishment due to me' – 'he loved me, and gave himself for me' (Gal. 2:20). How it was possible for him to bear their penalty they do not claim to know, any more than they know how it was possible for him to be made man; but that he bore it is the certainty on which all their hopes rest.

2. Substitution and solidarity

Anticipating the rationalistic criticism that guilt is not transferable and the substitution described, if real, would be immoral, our model now invokes

Paul's description of the Lord Jesus Christ as the second man and last Adam, who involved us in his sin-bearing as truly as Adam involved us in his sinning (cf. 1 Cor. 15:45ff.; Rom. 5:12ff.). Penal substitution was seen by Luther, the pioneer in stating it, and by those who came after, as grounded in this ontological solidarity, and as being one 'moment' in the larger mystery of what Luther called 'a wonderful exchange'[31] and Dr Morna Hooker designates 'interchange in Christ'.[32] In this mystery there are four 'moments' to be distinguished. The first is the incarnation when the Son of God came into the human situation, 'born of a woman, under the law, that he might redeem them which were under the law' (Gal. 4:4–5). The second 'moment' was the cross, where Jesus, as Luther and Calvin put it, carried our identity[33] and effectively involved us all in his dying – as Paul says, 'one died for all, therefore all died' (2 Cor. 5:14). Nor is this sharing in Christ's death a legal fiction, a form of words to which no reality corresponds; it is part of the objective fact of Christ, the mystery that is 'there' whether we grasp it or not. So now Christ's substitution for us, which is exclusive in the sense of making the work of atonement wholly his and allowing us no share in performing it, is seen to be from another standpoint inclusive of us, inasmuch as ontologically and objectively, in a manner transcending bounds of space and time, Christ has taken us with him into his death and through his death into his resurrection. Thus knowledge of Christ's death for us as our sin-bearing substitute requires us to see ourselves as dead, risen and alive for evermore in him. We who believe have died – painlessly and invisibly, we might say – in solidarity with him because he died, painfully and publicly, in substitution for us. His death for us brought remission of sins committed 'in' Adam, so that 'in' him we might enjoy God's acceptance; our death 'in' him brings release from the existence we knew 'in' Adam, so that 'in' him we are raised to new life and become new creatures (cf. Rom. 5 – 6; 2 Cor. 5:17, 21; Col. 2:6 – 3:4). The third 'moment' in this interchange comes when, through faith and God's gift of the Spirit, we become 'the righteousness of God' and 'rich' – that is, justified from sin and accepted as heirs of God in and with Christ – by virtue of him who became 'poor' for us in the incarnation and was 'made sin' for us by penal substitution on the cross (cf. 2 Cor. 5:21; 8:9). And the fourth 'moment' will be when this same Jesus Christ, who was exalted to glory after being humbled to death for us, reappears to 'fashion anew the body of our humiliation, that it may be conformed to the body of his glory' (cf. Phil. 2:5–11; 3:21).

Sometimes it is urged that in relation to this comprehensive mystery of solidarity and interchange, viewed as a whole, Christ the 'pioneer' (*archēgos*: Heb. 2:10; 12:2) is best designated the 'representative' and 'first-fruits' of the new humanity, rather than be called our substitute.[34] Inasmuch as the interchange-theme centres upon our renewal in Christ's image, this point may be readily accepted, provided it is also seen that in relation to the particular mystery of sin-bearing, which is at the heart of the interchange, Christ as victim of the penal process has to be called our substitute, since the purpose and effect of his suffering was precisely to ensure that no such suffering – no Godforsakenness, no dereliction – should remain for us. In the light of earlier discussion[35] we are already entitled to dismiss the proposal to call Christ's death representative rather than substitutionary as both confusing and confused, since it suggests, first, that we chose Christ to act for us, second, that the death we die in him is of the same order as the death he died for us, and third, that by dying in Christ we atone for our sins – all of which are false. Here now is a further reason for rejecting the proposal – namely, that it misses or muffs the point that what Christ bore on the cross was the Godforsakenness of penal judgment, which we shall never have to bear because he accepted it in our place. The appropriate formulation is that on the cross Jesus' representative relation to us, as the last Adam whose image we are to bear, took the form of substituting for us under judgment, as the suffering servant of God on whom the Lord 'laid the iniquity of us all'.[36] The two ideas, representation and substitution, are complementary, not alternatives, and both are needed here.

3. Substitution and mystery

It will by now be clear that those who affirm penal substitution offer this model not as an explanatory analysis of what lay 'behind' Christ's atoning death in the way that the laws of heat provide an explanatory analysis of what lies 'behind' the boiling of a kettle, but rather as a pointer directing attention to various fundamental features of the mystery – that is, according to our earlier definition, the transcendent and not-wholly-comprehensible divine reality – of Christ's atoning death itself, as the New Testament writers declare it. Most prominent among these features are the mysterious divine love which was its source, and of which it is the measure (cf. Rom. 5:8; 1 John 4:8–10; John 15:13); the mysterious necessity for it, evident from Paul's witness in Romans 8:32 that God did not spare his Son, but gave him up to death for us, which shows that, he being he, he could not have saved us at any less cost to himself; the mysterious solidarity in virtue of which Christ could be 'made sin' by the imputing to him of our answerability, and could die for our sins in our place, and we could be 'made righteous' before God through faith by the virtue of his obedience (cf. Rom. 5:17–19; 3 Cor. 5:21); and the mysterious mode of union whereby, without any diminution of our individuality as persons, or his, Christ and we are 'in' each other in such a sense that already we have passed with him through death into risen life. Recognition of these mysteries causes no embarrassment, nor need it; since the cross is undeniably central in the New Testament witness to God's work, it was only to be expected that more dimensions of mystery would be found clustered here than anywhere. (Indeed, there are more than we listed; for a full statement, the tri-unity of the loving God, the incarnation itself, and God's predestining the free acts of his enemies, would also have to come in.) To the question, what does the cross mean in God's plan for man's good, a biblical answer is ready to hand, but when we ask how these things can be we find ourselves facing mystery at every point.

Rationalistic criticism since Socinus has persistently called in question both the solidarity on which substitution is based and the need for penal satisfaction as a basis for forgiveness. This, however, is 'naturalistic' criticism, which assumes that what man could not do or would not require God will not do or require either. Such criticism is profoundly perverse, for it shrinks God the Creator into the image of man the creature and loses sight of the paradoxical quality of the gospel of which the New Testament is so clearly aware. (When man justifies the wicked, it is a miscarriage of justice which God hates, but when God justifies the ungodly it is a miracle of grace for us to adore [Prov. 17:15; Rom. 4:5].) The way to stand against naturalistic theology is to keep in view its reductionist method which makes man the standard for God; to stress that according to Scripture the Creator and his work are of necessity mysterious to us, even as revealed (to make this point is the proper logical task of the word 'supernatural' in theology); and to remember that what is above reason is not necessarily against it. As regards the atonement, the appropriate response to the Socinian critique starts by laying down that all our understanding of the cross comes from attending to the biblical witnesses and learning to hear and echo what they say about it; speculative rationalism breeds only misunderstanding, nothing more.

4. Substitution and salvation

So far our analysis has, I think, expressed the beliefs of all who would say that penal substitution is the key to understanding the cross. But now comes a point of uncertainty and division. That Christ's penal substitution for us under divine judgment is the sole meritorious ground on which our relationship with God is restored, and is in this sense decisive for our salvation, is a Reformation point against Rome[37] to which all conservative Protestants hold. But in ordinary everyday contexts substitution is a definite and precise relationship whereby the specific obligations of one or more persons are taken over and discharged by someone else (as on the memorable occasion when I had to cry off a meeting at two days' notice due to an air strike and found afterwards that Billy Graham had consented to speak as my substitute). Should we not then think of Christ's substitution for us on the cross as a definite, one-to-one relationship between him and each individual sinner? This seems scriptural, for Paul says, 'He loved me and gave himself for me' (Gal. 2:20). But if Christ specifically took and discharged my penal obligation as a sinner, does it not follow that the cross was decisive for my salvation not only as its sole meritorious ground, but also as guaranteeing that I should be brought to faith, and through faith to eternal life? For is not the faith which receives salvation part of God's gift of salvation, according to what is affirmed in Philippians 1:29 and John 6:44f. and implied in what Paul says of God calling and John of new birth?[38] And if Christ by his death on my behalf secured reconciliation and righteousness as gifts for me to receive (Rom. 5:11, 17), did not this make it certain that the faith which receives these gifts would also be given me, as a direct consequence of Christ's dying for me? Once this is granted, however, we are shut up to a choice between universalism and some form of the view that Christ died to save only a part of the human race. But if we reject these options, what have we left? The only coherent alternative is to suppose that though God purposed to save every man through the cross, some thwart his purpose by persistent unbelief; which can only be said if one is ready to maintain that God, after all, does no more than make faith possible, and then in some sense that is decisive for him as well as us leaves it to us to make faith actual. Moreover, any who take this position must redefine substitution in imprecise terms, if indeed they do not drop the term altogether, for they are committing themselves to deny that Christ's vicarious sacrifice ensures anyone's salvation. Also, they have to give up Toplady's position, 'Payment God cannot twice demand, First from my bleeding surety's hand, And then again from mine' – for it is of the essence of their view that some whose sins Christ bore, with saving intent, will ultimately pay the penalty for those same sins in their own persons. So it seems that if we are going to affirm penal substitution for all without exception we must either infer universal salvation or else, to evade this inference, deny the saving efficacy of the substitution for anyone; and if we are going to affirm penal substitution as an effective saving act of God we must either infer universal salvation or else, to evade this inference, restrict the scope of the substitution, making it a substitution for some, not all.[39]

All this is familiar ground to students of the Arminian controversy of the first half of the seventeenth century and of the conservative Reformed tradition since that time;[40] only the presentation is novel, since I have ventured to point up the problem as one of defining Christ's substitution, taking this as the key word for the view we are exploring. In modern usage that indeed is what it is, but only during the past century has it become so; prior to that, all conservative Protestants, at least in the English-speaking world, preferred 'satisfaction' as the label and key word for their doctrine of the cross.[41]

As I pointed it up, the matter in debate might seem purely verbal, but there is more to it than that. The question is, whether the thought that substitution entails salvation does or does not belong to the convictional 'weave' of Scripture, to which 'penal substitution' as a theological model must conform. There seems little doubt as to the answer. Though the New Testament writers do not discuss the question in anything like this form, nor is their language about the cross always as guarded as language has to be once debate on the problem has begun, they do in fact constantly take for granted that the death of Christ is the act of God which has made certain the salvation of those who are saved. The use made of the categories of ransom, redemption, reconciliation, sacrifice and victory; the many declarations of God's purpose that Christ through the cross should save those given him, the church, his sheep and friends, God's people; the many statements viewing Christ's heavenly intercession and work in men as the outflow of what he did for them by his death; and the uniform view of faith as a means, not of meriting, but of receiving – all these features point unambiguously in one direction. Twice in Romans Paul makes explicit his conviction that Christ's having died 'for' (*hyper*) us – that is, us who now believe – guarantees final blessedness. In 5:8f. he says: 'While we were yet sinners, Christ died for us. Much more then, being now justified by his blood, shall we be saved from the wrath through him.' In 8:32 he asks: 'He that spared not his own Son, but delivered him up for us all, how shall he not also with him freely give us all things?' Moreover, Paul and John explicitly depict God's saving work as a unity in which Christ's death fulfils a purpose of election and leads on to what the Puritans called 'application of redemption' – God 'calling' and 'drawing' unbelievers to himself, justifying them from their sins and giving them life as they believe, and finally glorifying them with Christ in his own presence.[42] To be sure, Paul and John insist, as all the New Testament does, that God in the gospel promises life and salvation to everyone who believes and calls on Christ (cf. John 3:16; Rom. 10:13); this, indeed, is to them the primary truth, and when the plan of salvation appears in their writings (in John's case, on the lips of our Lord) its logical role is to account for, and give hope of, the phenomenon of sinners responding to God's promise. Thus, through the knowledge that God is resolved to evoke the response he commands, Christians are assured of being kept safe, and evangelists of not labouring in vain. It may be added: is there any good reason for finding difficulty with the notion that the cross both justifies the 'free offer' of Christ to all men and also guarantees the believing, the accepting and the glorifying of those who respond, when this was precisely what Paul and John affirmed?

At all events, if the use historically made of the penal substitution model is examined, there is no doubt, despite occasional confusions of thought, that part of the intention is to celebrate the decisiveness of the cross as in every sense the procuring cause of salvation.

5. Substitution and divine love

The penal substitution model has been criticized for depicting a kind Son placating a fierce Father in order to make him love men, which he did not do before. The criticism is, however, inept, for penal substitution is a trinitarian model, for which the motivational unity of Father and Son is axiomatic. The New Testament presents God's gift of his Son to die as the supreme expression of his love to men. 'God so loved the world that he gave his only-begotten Son' (John 3:16). 'God is love. ... Herein is love, not that we loved God, but that he loved us, and sent his Son to be the propitiation for our sins' (1 John 4:8–10). 'God shows his love for us in that while we were yet sinners Christ died for us' (Rom. 5:8). Similarly, the New Testament presents the Son's voluntary acceptance of death as the supreme expression of his love to men. 'He loved me, and gave himself for me' (Gal. 2:20). 'Greater love has no man than this, that a man lay down his life for his friends. You are my friends ...' (John 15:13–14). And the two loves, the love of Father and Son, are one: a point which the penal substitution model, as used, firmly grasps.

Furthermore, if the true measure of love is how low it stoops to help, and how much in its humility it is ready to do and bear, then it may fairly be claimed that the penal substitutionary model embodies a richer witness to divine love than any other model of atonement, for it sees the Son at his Father's will going lower than any other view ventures to suggest. That death on the cross was a criminal's death, physically as painful as, if not more painful than, any mode of judicial execution that the world has seen; and that Jesus endured it in full consciousness of being innocent before God and man, and yet of being despised and rejected, whether in malicious conceit or in sheer fecklessness, by persons he had loved and tried to save – this is ground common to all views, and tells us already that the love of Jesus, which took him to the cross, brought him appallingly low. But the penal substitution model adds to all this a further dimension of truly unimaginable distress, compared with which everything mentioned so far pales into insignificance.

This is the dimension indicated by Denney – 'that in that dark hour He had to realise to the full the divine reaction against sin in the race'. Owen stated this formally, abstractly and non-psychologically: Christ, he said, satisfied God's justice, 'for all the sins of all those for whom he made satisfaction, by undergoing that same punishment which, by reason of obligation that was upon them, they were bound to undergo. When I say the same I mean essentially the same in weight and pressure, though not in all accidents of duration and the like ...'[43] Jonathan Edwards expressed the thought with tender and noble empathy: 'God dealt with him as if he had been exceedingly angry with him, and as though he had been the object of his dreadful wrath. This made all the sufferings of Christ the more terrible to him, because they were from the hand of his Father, whom he infinitely loved, and whose infinite love he had had eternal experience of. Besides, it was an effect of God's wrath that he forsook Christ. This caused Christ to cry out ... "My God, my God, why hast thou forsaken me?" This was infinitely terrible to Christ. Christ's knowledge of the glory of the Father, and his love to the Father, and the sense and experience he had had of the worth of his Father's love to him, made the withholding the pleasant ideas and manifestations of his Father's love as terrible to him, as the sense and knowledge of his hatred is to the damned, that have no knowledge of God's excellency, no love to him, nor any experience of the infinite sweetness of his love.'[44] And the legendary 'Rabbi' Duncan concentrated it all into a single unforgettable sentence, in a famous outburst to one of his classes: 'D'ye know what Calvary was? what? what? what?' Then, with tears on his face – 'It was damnation; and he took it lovingly.' It is precisely this love that, in the last analysis, penal substitution is all about, and that explains its power in the lives of those who acknowledge it.[45]

What was potentially the most damaging criticism of penal substitution came not from Socinus, but from McLeod Campbell, who argued that by saying that God must punish sin but need not act in mercy at all (and in fact does not act in mercy towards all), Reformed exponents of this view reduced God's love to an arbitrary decision which does not reveal his character, but leaves him even in blessing us an enigma to us, 'the unknown God'.[46] The real target of Campbell's criticism is the Scotist model of divine personality with which, rightly or wrongly, he thought Reformed theologians worked; and a sufficient reply, from the standpoint of this lecture, would be that since the Bible says both that Christ's death was a penal substitution for God's people and also that it reveals God's love to sinful men as such, and since the Bible further declares that Christ is the Father's image, so that everything we learn of the Son's love is knowledge of the Father's love also, Campbell's complaint is unreal. But Campbell's criticism, if carried, would be fatal, for any account of the atonement that fails to highlight its character as a revelation of redeeming love stands self-condemned.

The ingredients in the evangelical model of penal substitution are now, I believe, all before us, along with the task it performs. It embodies and expresses insights about the cross which are basic to personal religion, and which I therefore state in personal terms, as follows:

(1) God, in Denney's phrase, 'condones nothing', but judges all sin as it deserves: which Scripture affirms, and my conscience confirms, to be right.

(2) My sins merit ultimate penal suffering and rejection from God's presence (conscience also confirms this), and nothing I do can blot them out.

(3) The penalty due to me for my sins, whatever it was, was paid for me by Jesus Christ, the Son of God, in his death on the cross.

(4) Because this is so, I through faith in him am made 'the righteousness of God in him', i.e. I am justified; pardon, acceptance and sonship become mine.

(5) Christ's death for me is my sole ground of hope before God. 'If he fulfilled not justice, I must; if he underwent not wrath, I must to eternity.'[47]

(6) My faith in Christ is God's own gift to me, given in virtue of Christ's death for me: i.e. the cross procured it.

(7) Christ's death for me guarantees my preservation to glory.

(8) Christ's death for me is the measure and pledge of the love of the Father and the Son to me.

(9) Christ's death for me calls and constrains me to trust, to worship, to love and to serve.

Thus we see what, according to this model, the cross achieved – and achieves.

V. Conclusion: the cross in the Bible

In drawing the threads together, two general questions about the relation of the penal substitutionary model to the biblical data as a whole may be briefly considered.

(1) Are the contents and functioning of this model inconsistent in any way with the faith and religion of the New Testament? Is it degrading to God, or morally offensive, as is sometimes alleged? Our analysis has, I hope, served to show that it is not any of these things. And to have shown that may not be time wasted, for it seems clear that treatments of biblical material on the atonement are often influenced by prejudices of this kind, which produce reluctance to recognize how strong is the evidence for the integral place of substitution in biblical thinking about the cross.[48]

(2) Is our model truly based on the Bible? On this, several quick points may be made.

First, full weight must be given to the fact that, as Luther saw, the central question to which the whole New Testament in one way or another is addressed is the question of our relationship, here and hereafter, with our holy Creator: the question, that is, how weak, perverse, estranged and guilty sinners may gain and guard knowledge of God's gracious pardon, acceptance and renewal. It is to this question that Christ is the answer, and that all New Testament interpretation of the cross relates.

Second, full weight must also be given to the fact that all who down the centuries have espoused this model of penal substitution have done so because they thought the Bible taught it, and scholars who for whatever reason take a different view repeatedly acknowledge that there are Bible passages which would most naturally be taken in a penal substitutionary sense. Such passages include Isaiah 53 (where Whale, as we saw, [n. 36] finds penal substitution mentioned twelve times); Galatians 3:13; 2 Corinthians 5:21; 1 Peter 3:18; and there are many analogous to these.

Third, it must be noted that the familiar exegetical arguments which, if accepted, erode the substitutionary view – the arguments, for instance, for a non-personal concept of God's wrath and a non-propitiatory understanding of the *hilaskomai* word-group, or for the interpreting of bloodshed in the Old Testament sacrifices as the release of life to invigorate rather than the ending of it to expiate – only amount to this: that certain passages may not mean quite what they have appeared to mean to Bible students of earlier generations. But at every point it remains distinctly arguable that the time-honoured view is the true one, after all.

Fourth, it must be noted that there is no shortage of scholars who maintain the integral place of penal substitution in the New Testament witness to the cross. The outstanding contributions of James Denney and Leon Morris have already been mentioned, and they do not stand alone. For further illustration of this point, I subjoin two quotations from Professor A. M. Hunter. I do so without comment; they speak for themselves.

The first quotation is on the teaching of Jesus in the synoptic gospels. Having referred to theories of the atonement 'which deal in "satisfaction" or substitution, or make use of "the sacrificial principle"', Hunter proceeds: 'It is with this type of theory that the sayings of Jesus seem best to agree. There can be little doubt that Jesus viewed his death as a representative sacrifice for "the many". Not only is His thought saturated in Isa. liii (which is a doctrine of representative suffering), but His words over the cup – indeed, the whole narrative of the Last Supper – almost demand to be interpreted in terms of a sacrifice in whose virtue His followers can share. The idea of substitution which is prominent in Isa. 1iii appears in the ransom saying. And it requires only a little reading between the lines to find in the "cup" saying, the story of the Agony, and the cry of dereliction, evidence that Christ's sufferings were what, for lack of a better word, we can only call "penal".[49]

The second quotation picks up comments on what, by common consent, are Paul's two *loci classici* on the method of atonement, 2 Corinthians 5:21 and Galatians 3:13. On the first, Hunter writes: 'Paul declares that the crucified Christ, on our behalf, took the whole reality of sin upon himself, like the scapegoat: "For our sake he made him to be sin who knew no sin, so that in him we might become the righteousness of God." Paul sees the Cross as an act of God's doing in which the Sinless One, for the sake of sinners, somehow experienced the horror of divine reaction against sin so that there might be condemnation no more.

'Gal. 3:13 moves in the same realm of ideas. "Christ redeemed us from the curse of the law, having become a curse for us."' (I interpose here my own comment, that Paul's aorist participle is explaining the method of redemption, answering the question 'how did Christ redeem us?', and might equally well therefore be translated 'by becoming a curse for us'.) 'The curse is the divine condemnation of sin which leads to death. To this curse we lay exposed; but Christ on his cross identified himself with the doom impending on sinners that, through his act, the curse passes away and we go free.

'Such passages show the holy love of God taking awful issue in the Cross with the sin of man. Christ, by God's appointing, dies the sinner's death, and so removes sin. Is there a simpler way of saying this than that Christ bore our sins? We are not fond nowadays of calling Christ's suffering "penal" or of styling him our "substitute"; but can we avoid using some such words as these to express Paul's view of the atonement?'[50]

Well, can we? And if not, what follows? Can we then justify ourselves in holding a view of the atonement into which penal substitution does not enter? Ought we not to reconsider whether penal substitution is not, after all, the heart of the matter? These are among the questions which our preliminary survey in this lecture has raised. It is to be hoped that they will receive the attention they deserve.

Questions for study

1. Why does Packer regard this subject as being of such great importance?
2. What biblical passages does Packer focus on in the course of his analysis?

3. Set out in your own words Packer's understanding of the various theories of the atonement.

4. What precisely is Packer's criticism of the views of John McLeod Campbell?

5. What does Packer understand by the term 'substitutionary'? Once this definition is conceded, how does this secure the remainder of his argument?

6. What does Packer mean by the following statement: 'Christ's saving work has two parts, his dealing with his Father on our behalf by offering himself in substitutionary satisfaction for our sins and his dealing with us on his Father's behalf by bestowing on us through faith the forgiveness which his death secured'? How does this statement undergird Packer's approach?

7. How does Packer deal with the argument that the transfer of sin or guilt from one individual to another is immoral?

8. Why does Packer open the lecture with an extended discussion of the nature of theological language, and in particular the importance of models?

Notes

Preamble

1. G. W. H. Lampe, 'The Atonement: Law and Love', in A. R. Vidler, *Soundings*, Cambridge: Cambridge University Press, 1962, pp. 187–191.

2. An important defence of the classic evangelical position was provided by the Australian writer Leon Morris, *The Cross in the New Testament*, London: Tyndale Press, 1955.

3. *The Nottingham Statement*, London: Falcon Press, 1977, p. 13.

Essay

1. Socinus' arguments were incorporated in the *Racovian Catechism*, published at Racow (the modern Cracow) in 1605, which set forth the Unitarianism of the 'Polish Brethren'. After several revisions of detail down to 1680 the text was finalized and in due course translated into English by Thomas Rees (London, 1818). It is a document of classical importance in Unitarian history.

2. See L. Berkhof, *Systematic Theology*, Grand Rapids: Eerdmans; London: Banner of Truth, 1949, pp. 373–383. Berhof's zeal to show that God did nothing illegal or unjust makes a strange impression on the post-Watergate reader.

3. See F. Turretin, *Institutio Theologiae Elenchticae*, Geneva (1682), II. xiv, 'De Officio Christi Mediatoris', and A. A. Hodge, *The Atonement*, London: Nelson, 1868. Turretin's position is usefully summarized in L. W. Grensted, *A Short History of the Doctrine of the Atonement*, Manchester: Manchester University Press, 1920, pp. 241–252. Cf. J. F. Heidegger's parallel account in his *Corpus Theologiae Christianae*, Zurich (1700), which R. S. Franks reviews in *The Work of Christ*, London: Nelson, 1962, pp. 426ff.

4. In his influential book *Christus Victor*, tr. A. G. Herbert, London: SPCK, 1931, which

advocated a 'dramatic', non-rational way of declaring God's conquest of evil through the cross, Gustaf Aulén describes the 'Latin' account of the atonement (i.e. that of Anselm and Protestant orthodoxy) as 'juridical in its inmost essence' (p. 106), and says: 'It concentrates its effort upon a rational attempt to explain how the Divine Love and the Divine Justice can be reconciled. The Love of God is regulated by His Justice, and is only free to act within the limits that Justice marks out. *Ratio* and *Lex*, rationality and justice, go hand in hand ... The attempt is made by the scholastics to elaborate a theology which shall provide a comprehensive explanation of the Divine government of the world, which shall answer all questions and solve all riddles ...' (pp. 173–174). What Aulén fails to note is how much of this implicitly rationalistic cast of thought was a direct reaction to Socinus' rationalistic critique. In fact, Aulén does not mention Socinus at all; nor does he refer to Calvin, who asserts penal substitution as strongly as any, but follows an exegetical and Christocentric method which is not in the least scholastic or rationalistic. Calvin shows no interest in the reconciling of God's love and justice as a theoretical problem; his only interest is in the mysterious but blessed fact that at the cross God did act in both love and justice to save us from our sins. Cf. P. van Buren, *Christ in our Place: The Substitutionary Character of Calvin's Doctrine of Reconciliation*, Edinburgh: Oliver and Boyd, 1957.

5. Ayer voiced his doubts in *Language, Truth and Logic*, London: Gollancz, 1936; 2nd edition, 1946; and Flew his in 'Theology and Falsification', *New Essays in Philosophical Theology*, ed. A. G. N. Flew and Alasdair MacIntyre, London: SCM, 1955, pp. 96–130. There are replies in, among other books, E. L. Mascall, *Words and Image*, London: Longmans, 1957; *Faith and Logic*, ed. Basil Mitchell, London: Allen and Unwin, 1957; Frederick Ferré, *Language, Logic and God*, London: Eyre and Spottiswoode, 1962; Fontana edition 1970; W. Hordern, *Speaking of God*, New York: Macmillan, 1964.

6. Of the church in the patristic period H. E. W. Turner writes: 'Its experience of Redemption through Christ was far richer than its attempted formulations of this experience.' *The Patristic Doctrine of Redemption*, London: Mowbray, 1952, p. 13; cf. chapter V, 'Christ our Victim'. On T. F. Torrance's sharp-edged thesis in *The Doctrine of Grace in the Apostolic Fathers*, Edinburgh: Oliver and Boyd, 1948, that the Apostolic Fathers lapsed from New Testament faith in the cross to a legalism of self-salvation, Robert S. Paul's comment in *The Atonement and the Sacraments*, London: Hodder and Stoughton, 1961, p. 37, note 2, is just: 'To me he has made his case almost too well, for at the end I am left asking the question, "In what sense, then, could the Church change this much and still be the Church?"' In fact, Torrance's thesis needs the qualification of Turner's statement quoted above.

7. *Inst.* II. xvii. 2. This thought is picked up in Anglican Article II: 'Christ ... truly suffered ... *to reconcile his Father to us*, and to be a sacrifice, not only for original guilt, but also for all actual sins of men.' On propitiation, cf. note 21 below.

8. For surveys of the present state of play, cf. Ferré's *Language, Logic and God*; Ian G. Barbour, *Myths, Models and Paradigms*, London: SCM, 1974; John Macquarrie, *God-Talk*, London: SCM Press, 1967.

9. The pioneer in stating this was Ian T. Ramsey: see his *Religious Language*, London: SCM Press, 1957; *Models and Mystery*, London: Oxford University Press, 1964; *Christian Discourse*, London: Oxford University Press, 1965. For further discussion of models in theology cf. John MacIntyre, *The Shape of Christology*, London: SCM Press, 1966, especially pp. 54–81; Thomas Fawcett, *The Symbolic Language of Religion*, London: SCM Press, 1970, pp. 69–94; Barbour, op. cit.

10. *The Shape of Christology*, 63.

11. The idea of analogy is formulated by the *Oxford Dictionary of the Christian Church*, *s.v.*, as follows: 'A method of predication whereby concepts derived from a familiar object are made applicable to a relatively unknown object in virtue of some similarity between the two otherwise dissimilar objects.' Aquinas' account of analogy is in *Summa Theologica* I. xiii, and can be read in *Words about God*, ed. Ian T. Ramsey, London: SCM, 1971, pp. 36ff. For

Thomists, the doctrine of analogy serves to explain how knowledge of creatures gives knowledge of their Creator (natural theology) as well as how biblical imagery gives knowledge of the God of both nature and grace (scriptural theology). For a technical Thomist discussion, concentrating on analogy in natural theology, see E. L. Mascall, *Existence and Analogy*, London: Longmans, 1949, pp. 92–121.

12. See my *'Fundamentalism' and the Word of God*, London: Inter-Varsity Fellowship, 1958, *God has Spoken*, London: Hodder and Stoughton, 1965; 'Inspiration' in the *New Bible Dictionary*, ed. J. D. Douglas et al., London: Inter-Varsity Fellowship, 1962.

13. For Ramsey's overall view of models, see the works cited in note 9. On most theological subjects his opinions, so far as he reveals them, are unexceptionably middle-of-the-road, but it is noteworthy that in his lecture on 'Atonement Theology' in *Christian Discourse* (pp. 28ff.) he hails Hastings Rashdall's Aberlardian treatise *The Idea of Atonement in Christian Theology* (1919) as 'definitive' (p. 29; no reasons given); limits the 'cosmic disclosure' evoked by the cross to a sense of 'the victorious will of God', whose plan to maintain a remnant did not fail (pp. 32, 34), and whose love this victory shows (pp. 59–60); rejects the grounding of justification on substitution or satisfaction as involving 'frontier-clashes with the language of morals' (p. 40; the old Socinian objection); and criticizes the exegeting of justification, substitution, satisfaction, reconciliation, redemption, propitiation and expiation as if these words 'were *not models at all, but* described procedural transactions ... each describing a species of atonement engineering' (p. 44). Profound confusion appears here. Certainly these words are models, but what they are models of is precisely procedural transactions for achieving atonement, transactions in which the Father and the Son dealt with each other on our behalf. The contexts of apostolic argument in which these models appear make this unambiguously plain, and to assume, as Ramsey seems to do, that as models they can only have a directly subjective reference to what Bultmann would call a new self-understanding is quite arbitrary. Indeed, Ramsey himself goes on to show that the model-category for biblical concepts does *not* require an exclusively subjective reference, for he dwells on 'love' as a model of *God's activity* (p. 59); and if love can be such a model, why not these other words? It seems evident that Ramsey brought Abelardian-Socinian assumptions to his study of the biblical words, rather than deriving his views from that study.

14. Cf. Vincent Taylor's remark, in *The Atonement in New Testament Teaching*, London: Epworth Press, 1940, pp. 301–302: 'The thought of *substitution* is one we have perhaps been more anxious to reject than to assess; yet the immeasurable sense of gratitude with which it is associated ... is too great a thing to be wanting in a worthy theory of the Atonement.'

15. Wolfhart Pannenberg, *Jesus – God and Man*, tr. Lewis L. Wilkins and Duane A. Priebe, London: SCM Press, 1968, pp. 268, 259.

16. See R. E. Davies, 'Christ in our Place – the Contribution of the Prepositions', *Tyndale Bulletin* 21 (1970), pp. 72ff.

17. F. W. Camfield, 'The Idea of Substitution in the Doctrine of the Atonement', *Scottish Journal of Theology* 1 (1948), pp. 282–283, referring to Vincent Taylor, *The Atonement in New Testament Teaching*. Taylor, while allowing that Paul 'in particular, is within a hair's breadth of substitution' (p. 288), and that 'a theologian who retires to a doctrinal fortress guarded by such ordnance as Mark x. 45, Romans vi. 10f., 2 Corinthians v. 14, 21, Galatians iii. 13, and 1 Timothy ii. 5f., is more difficult to dislodge than many New Testament students imagine' (p. 289), rejects substitution as implying a redemption 'wrought entirely outside of, and apart from, ourselves so that we have nothing to do but to accept its benefits' (p. 125). He describes Christ's death as a representative sacrifice, involving endurance of sin's penalty plus that archetypal expression of penitence for humanity's wrongdoing which was first conceived by McLeod Campbell and R. C. Moberly. We participate in this sacrifice, Taylor continues, by offering it on our own behalf, which we do by letting it teach us to repent. Taylor admits that from this standpoint there is 'a gap in Pauline teaching. With clear eyes

St Paul marks "the one act of righteousness" in the obedience of Christ (Romans v. 18f.) and the fact that He was "made to be sin on our behalf" (2 Corinthians v. 21), but he nowhere speaks of Him as voicing the sorrow and contrition of men in the presence of His Father' (p. 291).

18. See Pannenberg, op. cit., pp. 258–269; Barth, *Church Dogmatics* IV. 1, tr. G. W. Bromiley, Edinburgh: T. and T. Clark, 1956, pp. vii–viii, 230ff., 550ff.

19. 'He turned the penalty He endured into sacrifice He offered. And the sacrifice He offered was the judgment He accepted. His passive suffering became active obedience, and obedience to a holy doom.' *The Work of Christ*, London: Hodder and Stoughton, 1910, p. 163. In a 2,000–word 'Addendum' Forsyth combats the Ritschlian view, later to be espoused by C. H. Dodd, that the wrath of God is simply the 'automatic recoil of His moral order upon the transgressor … as if there were no personal reaction of a Holy God Himself upon the sin, and no infliction of His displeasure upon the sinner' (p. 239). He argues for the position that 'what Christ bore was not simply a sense of the connection between the sinner and the impersonal consequences of sin, but a sense of the sinner's relation to the personal *vis-à-vis* of an angry God. God never left him, but He did refuse Him His face. The communion was not broken, but its light was withdrawn' (p. 243).

20. Op. cit., pp. 164, 182, 223, 225–226. 'Substitution does not take account of the moral results (of the cross) on the soul' (p. 182, note).

21. 'Propitiation' (which means quenching God's wrath against sinners) is replaced by 'expiation' (which means removing sins from God's sight) in RSV and other modern versions. The idea of propitiation includes that of expiation as its means; thus the effect of this change is not to bring in a sacrificial motif that was previously absent, but to cut out a reference to quenching God's anger that was previously thought to be present. The case for 'expiation' was put forward by C. H. Dodd in 1935 and at first gained wide support, but a generation of debate has shown that 'the linguistic evidence seems to favour "propitiation"' (Matthew Black, *Romans*, New Century Bible, London: Oliphants, 1973, p. 68). See the full coverage of literature cited by Black, and also David Hill, *Greek Words and Hebrew Meanings*, Cambridge: Cambridge University Press, 1967, pp. 23–48.

22. Denney, *The Death of Christ*, 2nd edition, including *The Atonement and the Modern Mind*, London: Hodder and Stoughton, 1911, p. 73. Denney's summary of the meaning of Rom. 3:25–26 is worth quoting. 'It is Christ set forth in His blood who is a propitiation; that is, it is Christ who died. In dying, as St Paul conceived it, He made our sin His own; He took it on Himself as the reality which it is in God's sight and to God's law: He became sin, became a curse for us. It is this which gives His death a propitiatory character and power; in other words, which makes it possible for God to be at once righteous and a God who accepts as righteous those who believe in Jesus … I do not know any word which conveys the truth of this if "vicarious" or "substitutionary" does not, nor do I know any interpretation of Christ's death which enables us to regard it as a demonstration of love to sinners, if this vicarious or substitutionary character is denied' (p. 126). Denney's point in the last sentence is that Christ's death only reveals God's love if it accomplished something which we needed, which we could not do for ourselves, and which Christ could not do without dying.

23. It should be noted that in addition to the rather specialized usage that Denney has in view, whereby one's 'representative' is the one whose behaviour is taken as the model for one's own, 'representative' may (and usually does) signify simply this: that one's status is such that one involves others, for good or ill, in the consequences of what one does. In this sense, families are represented by fathers, nations by kings, presidents and government ministers, and humanity by Adam and Christ; and it was as our representative in this sense that Jesus became our substitute. Cf. pp. 120–121 below.

24. *The Death of Christ*, p. 304; cf. p. 307, 'Union with Christ' (i.e. personal, moral union, by faith) '… is not a presupposition of Christ's work, it is its fruit.'

25. Leon Morris, *The Cross in the New Testament*, Exeter: Paternoster Press, 1965, p. 401.

26. *Christus Victor*, p. 175, etc.

27. G. W. H. Lampe, 'The Atonement: Law and Love', in *Soundings*, ed. A. R. Vidler, Cambridge: Cambridge University Press, 1962, pp. 187ff.

28. Denney, op. cit., pp. 271–272; from *The Atonement and the Modern Mind*. Denney's last sentence over-states; as J. S. Whale says, 'the Christian religion has thought of Christ not only as Victor and as Victim, but also as "Criminal"', and all three models (Whale calls them metaphors) have biblical justification. *Victor and Victim*, Cambridge: Cambridge University Press, 1960, p. 70.

29. Denney, *The Christian Doctrine of Reconciliation*, London: Hodder and Stoughton, 1917, pp. 187, 214, 208, 273. On pp. 262–263 and elsewhere Denney rejects as unintelligible all notions of a quantitative equivalence between Christ's actual sufferings and those which sinners would have to endure under ultimate judgment; 'to realise to the full the divine reaction against sin in the race', whatever it meant, did not mean that.

30. Emil Brunner, *The Mediator*, tr. O. Wyon, London: Lutterworth Press, 1934, p. 443.

31. Two quotations give Luther's viewpoint here. The first is from his exposition of Psalm 21 (22): 'This is that mystery which is rich in divine grace to sinners: wherein by a *wonderful exchange* our sins are no longer ours but Christ's: and the righteousness of Christ is not Christ's but ours. He has emptied himself of his righteousness that he might clothe us with it, and fill us with it: and he has taken our evils upon himself that he might deliver us from them ... in the same manner as he grieved and suffered in our sins, and was confounded, in the same manner we rejoice and glory in his righteousness.' *Werke*, Weimar, 1883, vol. 5, p. 608. The second is from a pastoral letter to George Spenlein: 'Learn Christ and him crucified. Learn to pray to him and, despairing of yourself, say: "Thou, Lord Jesus, art my righteousness, but I am thy sin. Thou hast taken upon thyself what is mine and hast given to me what is thine. Thou hast taken upon thyself what thou wast not and hast given to me what I was not."' *Letters of Spiritual Counsel*, ed. Theodore G. Tappert (Library of Christian Classics), London: SCM Press, 1955, p. 110.

32. Article in *Journal of Theological Studies* 22 (1971), pp. 349–361.

33. Luther puts this dramatically and exuberantly, as was always his way. 'All the prophets did foresee in spirit, that Christ should become the greatest transgressor, murderer, adulterer, thief, rebel, blasphemer, etc., that ever was ... for he being made a sacrifice, for the sins of the whole world, is not now an innocent person and without sins ... our most merciful Father ... sent his only Son into the world and laid upon him the sins of all men, saying: Be thou Peter that denier; Paul that persecutor, blasphemer and cruel oppressor; David that adulterer; that sinner which did eat the apple in Paradise; that thief which hanged upon the cross; and, briefly, be thou the person which hath committed the sins of all men; see therefore that thou pay and satisfy for them. Here now cometh the law and saith: I find him a sinner ... therefore let him die upon the cross ...' *Galatians*, ed. Philip S. Watson, London: James Clarke, 1953, pp. 269–271; on Gal. 3:13. Aulén (*Christus Victor*, chapter VI) rightly stresses the dynamism of divine victory in Luther's account of the cross and resurrection, but wrongly ignores the penal substitution in terms of which Christ's victorious work is basically defined. The essence of Christ's victory, according to Luther, is that on the cross as our substitute he effectively purged our sins, so freeing us from Satan's power by overcoming God's curse; if Luther's whole treatment of Gal. 3:13 (pp. 268–282) is read, this becomes very plain. The necessary supplement, and indeed correction, of the impression Aulén leaves is provided by Pannenberg's statement (op. cit., p. 279): 'Luther was probably the first since Paul and his school to have seen with full clarity that Jesus' death in its genuine sense is to be understood as vicarious penal suffering.' Calvin makes the same point in his more precise way, commenting on Jesus' trial before Pilate. 'When he was arraigned before a judgment-seat, accused and put under pressure by testimony, and sentenced to death by the words of a judge, we know by these records that he played the part (*personam sustinuit*) of a guilty wrongdoer ... we see the role of sinner and criminal represented in

Christ, yet from his shining innocence it becomes obvious that he was burdened with the misdoing of others rather than his own ... This is our acquittal, that the guilt which exposed us to punishment was transferred to the head of God's Son ...' 'At every point he substituted himself in our place (*in vicem nostram ubique se supposuerit*) to pay the price of our redemption' (*Inst.* II. xvi. 5, 7). It is inexplicable that Pannenberg (loc. cit.) should say that Calvin retreated from Luther's insight into penal substitution.

34. For 'representative', cf. M. D. Hooker, art. cit., p. 358, and G. W. H. Lampe, *Reconciliation in Christ*, London: Longmans 1956, chapter 3; for 'first-fruits', cf. D. E. H. Whiteley, *The Theology of St Paul*, Oxford: Blackwell, 1964, pp. 132ff. The preferred usage of these authors seems to reflect both awareness of solidarity between Christ and us and also failure to recognize that what forgiveness rests on is Christ's vicarious sin-bearing, as distinct from the new obedience to which, in Dr Hooker's phrase, we are 'lifted' by Christ's action.

35. Cf. pp. 113–114 above.

36. Is. 53:6. J. S. Whale observes that this Servant-song 'makes twelve distinct and explicit statements that the Servant suffers the *penalty* of other men's sins: not only vicarious suffering but penal substitution is the plain meaning of its fourth, fifth and sixth verses. These may not be precise statements of Western forensic ideas' – and our earlier argument prompts the comment, a good job too! – 'but they are clearly connected with penalty, inflicted through various forms of punishment which the Servant endured on other men's behalf and in their stead, because the Lord so ordained. This legal or lawcourt metaphor of atonement may be stated positively or negatively: either as penalty which the Redeemer takes upon himself, or as acquittal which sets the prisoner free. But in either way of stating it the connotation is substitutionary:

> In my place condemned he stood:
> Sealed my pardon with his blood' (op. cit., pp. 69–70).

37. Cf. Anglican Article XI: 'We are accounted righteous before God, only for the merit of our Lord and Saviour Jesus Christ by Faith, and not for our own works or deservings.'

38. Cf. Rom. 1:6–7, 8:28, 30; 9:11, 24; 1 Cor. 1:9, 24, 26; Gal. 1:15; Eph. 4:4; 1 Thess. 2:12, 5:24; 2 Thess. 2:14; 2 Tim. 1:9; John 1:12–13, 3:3–15; 1 John 5:1.

39. 'Unless we believe in the final restoration of all mankind, we cannot have an unlimited atonement. On the premise that some perish eternally we are shut up to one of two alternatives – a limited efficacy or a limited extent; there is no such thing as an unlimited atonement.' John Murray, *The Atonement*, Philadelphia: Presbyterian and Reformed, 1962, p. 27.

40. Cf. W. Cunningham, *Historical Theology*, London: Banner of Truth, 1960, vol. 2, pp. 237–370; C. Hodge, *Systematic Theology*, London: Nelson, 1974, vol. 2, pp. 544–562. The classical anti-Arminian polemic on the atonement remains John Owen's *The Death of Death in the Death of Christ* (1648: *Works*, ed. W. Goold, London: Banner of Truth, 1968, vol. 10, pp. 139ff.), on the argumentation of which J. McLeod Campbell commented: 'As addressed to those who agreed with him as to the nature of the atonement, while differing with him as to the extent of its reference, this seems unanswerable' (*The Nature of the Atonement*, 4th edition, London: Macmillan, 1873, p. 51).

41. Thus, in *The Atonement* (1868), A. A. Hodge, while speaking freely, as his Reformed predecessors did, of Christ as our substitute in a strict sense under God's penal law, complained that in theology the word 'substitution' had no fixed meaning, and organized his exposition round the idea of 'satisfaction', which he claimed was more precise than 'atonement' and was the word 'habitually' used by all the Reformers in all the creeds and great classical theological writings of the seventeenth century, both Lutheran and Reformed' (pp. 31ff., 37–38). By contrast the IVF-UCCF Basis (1922) speaks of 'redemption from the guilt, penalty and power of sin *only* through the sacrificial death (as our Representative and Substitute) of Jesus Christ', not mentioning satisfaction at all, and L. Berkhof's textbook

presents Hodge's view, which it accepts entirely, as 'the penal substitutionary or satisfaction doctrine' (*Systematic Theology*, p. 373).

42. Cf. Rom. 8:28–39; Eph. 1:3–14; 5:25–27; John 6:37–45; 10:11–16, 27–29; 17:6–26.

43. *Works*, vol. 10, p. 269. To construe Owen's statement of equivalence between what threatened us and what Christ endured in 'quantitative' terms, as if some calculus of penal pain was being applied, would be a misunderstanding, though admittedly one which Owen's constant reliance on the model of payment invites, and against which he did not guard. But Denney's statement expresses what Owen means.

44. Edwards, *Works*, ed. E. Hickman, London: Banner of Truth, 1975, vol. 2, p. 575. Cf. Luther: 'Christ himself suffered the dread and horror of a distressed conscience that tasted eternal wrath'; 'it was not a game, or a joke, or play-acting when he said "Thou hast forsaken me"; for then he felt himself really forsaken in all things even as a sinner is forsaken' (*Werke*, vol. 5, pp. 602, 605); and Calvin: 'he bore in his soul the dreadful torments of a condemned and lost man' (*Inst.* II. xvi. 10). Thus Calvin explained Christ's descent into hell: hell means Godforsakenness, and the descent took place during the hours on the cross. Jesus' cry of dereliction has been variously explained as voicing (a) depressive delusion, (b) genuine perplexity, (c) an 'as-if' feeling, (d) trust in God (because Jesus quotes the first words of Psalm 22, which ends with trust triumphant), (e) a repressed thought forcing its way into the open (so that the cry was a Freudian lapse), (f) a truth which Jesus wanted men to know. Surely only the last view can be taken seriously as either exegesis or theology. For a compelling discussion, cf. Leon Morris, op. cit., pp. 42–49.

45. C. F. D. Moule is right to say that costly forgiving love which, in the interests of the offender's personhood, requires him to face and meet his responsibility evokes a 'burning desire to make reparation and to share the burdens of the one who forgave him ... The original self-concern which, in the process of repentance, is transformed into a concern for the one he has injured, makes the penitent eager to lavish on the one who forgives him all that he has and is.' It is certainly right to explicate God's forgiveness of our sins in terms of this model; though whether Moule is also right to define God's justice non-retributively and to eliminate penal satisfaction and to dismiss New Testament references to God's wrath and punishment as atavistic survivals and 'anomalies' is quite another question. 'The Theology of Forgiveness', in *From Fear to Faith: Studies of Suffering and Wholeness*, ed. Norman Autton, London: SPCK, 1971, pp. 61–72, esp. 66f., 72.

46. Op. cit., 55.

47. Owen, *Works*, vol. 10, p. 284.

48. See on this Leon Morris, op. cit., ch. 10, pp. 364–419.

49. A. M. Hunter, *The Words and Works of Jesus*, London: SCM, 1950, p. 100.

50. A. M. Hunter, *Interpreting Paul's Gospel*, London: SCM, 1954, pp. 31f.

8. 'On knowing God' (1975)

Although J. I. Packer has published many works, he is best known for the work entitled *Knowing God* (1973), which has become a landmark in modern evangelical spirituality. The work had its origins in a series of articles published over a period of five years in *The Evangelical Magazine*, an obscure publication with a limited readership. The objective which Packer set himself in writing the work was to allow his readers to encounter and experience the reality of God, rather than just refine the way in which they thought about God. God is one who is known, not merely known about. Underlying *Knowing God* can be discerned a set of theological guidelines which – like the title of the book itself – can be argued to derive from the Reformer John Calvin (1509–64), for whom Packer had considerable admiration. Packer identifies four main themes which occur in Calvin's writings.

First, 'knowledge of God' does not refer to some natural human awareness of God, but to a knowledge which arises within a relationship.

Secondly, knowledge of God is more than any particular experience of God. Faith is about trust in God, from which particular experiences of God have their origins.

Thirdly, knowledge of God is 'more than knowing about God, although knowing about God is its foundation'. Packer here draws a distinction between 'knowledge by description' and 'knowledge by acquaintance'. While it is necessary to have a correct understanding of God as the righteous, wise and merciful creator and judge, true knowledge of God must also be 'relational knowledge, knowledge that comes to us in the relation of commitment and trust, faith and reliance'.

Fourthly, to know God is also to know God's relationship to us. Calvin affirmed that all human wisdom could be summed up as 'knowledge of God and of ourselves', and stressed that these two were inseparable. To know God is to know ourselves; to know ourselves truly, we must know God. 'Knowing God' is therefore 'not knowing God in isolation; it is knowing God in his relationship to us, that relationship in which he gives himself and his gifts to us for our enrichment'. To know God, we need to know his gracious gifts to us, and our need for such gifts in the first place.

On the basis of this analysis, Packer concludes by declaring that 'knowing God' consists of three components, which must be taken together:

1. apprehension of what God is;
2. application to ourselves of what God is and what God gives;
3. adoration of God, as the one who gives these gifts.

Packer's major work *Knowing God* can be seen as a careful exposition of these three components, which are presented in a closely inter-related manner. Packer's general strategy is to begin by allowing his readers to apprehend the reality of God; then to move on to allow them to apply these insights to their lives; and finally, to respond to God in adoration.

Packer's spiritual insights are rigorously grounded in theology. The application of theology to life – a key theme in Puritan writings – can be seen at point after point in Packer's writings, especially *Knowing God*. The passage noted above is a remarkably fine application of the doctrine of providence to the personal life of the Christian believer. Notice how Packer uses a series of phrases and statements to develop and explore what is substantially the same rich theme – the providential care of God for his people. In this case, Packer focuses this theological theme on the individual; elsewhere, he applies this and other themes to different contexts, such as the life of the church. Packer does not merely state a theological premiss; he aims to apply it to the life of the believer – in short, he seeks to make it real.

The passage selected for discussion is not taken from *Knowing God* itself, but from a lecture which Packer gave in which he set out some of the major insights which he held before him in writing the book. In addition to stressing the important link between theology and spirituality, the work explores the richness of the theme of 'knowing God'.

Related works by Packer

Knowing God, London: Hodder and Stoughton; Downers Grove, IL:

InterVarsity Press, 1973.
'Knowing Notions or Knowing God?', *Pastoral Renewal* 6/9 (March 1982), pp. 65–68.
'An Introduction to Systematic Spirituality', *Crux* 26/1 (March 1990), pp. 2–8. (Essay 12 in this collection.)
'Evangelical Foundations for Spirituality', in M. Bockmuehl and K. Burkhardt (eds.), *Gott Lieben und seine Gebote halten*, Basel: Brunner Verlag, 1991, pp. 149–162. (Essay 14 in this collection.)

On knowing God

'Knowing God!' Is there any greater theme which we could study together? I hardly think so. To know God is the promise of the gospel. To know God is the supreme gift of grace. Jeremiah, looking forward to what God was going to do, spoke in these terms: 'Behold, the days come, saith the Lord, that I will make a new covenant with the house of Israel.' And the consequence will be this: 'They shall teach no more every man his neighbour, and every man his brother, saying, Know the Lord; for they shall all know me, from the least of them unto the greatest of them.' That is the glory of the new covenant.

Jesus Christ came as a preacher of eternal life. On one occasion, in prayer to his Father, he defined eternal life. 'This is life eternal,' he said, 'that they might know thee, the only true God, and Jesus Christ, whom thou hast sent' (John 17:3). The apostle John, the beloved disciple who leaned on Jesus' breast at the Last Supper and perhaps saw deeper into Jesus' heart of love than anyone, looking back at the end of his first letter sums up what Christ had brought to him and his fellow believers: 'We know that the Son of God is come, and hath given us an understanding, that we may know him that is true' (1 John 5:20). This is a glorious reality, knowing God. This is what we were made for; this is what we have been redeemed for. This is the sum of the biblical Christian's ambition and his hope. Let the apostle Paul assure us of this. Paul tells us his own hope thus: 'That I may know him' (Phil. 3:10). The hope to which he looks forward he sums up in this way: 'Now I know in part, but then shall I know even as also I am known.' His ambition and his hope are summed up in terms of the knowledge of God. It is man's highest dignity to know God; it is man's final fulfilment to know God. There is, I repeat, no more vital subject that any of us can ever study than knowing God according to the Scriptures.

In Reformed theology knowing God has always been a key concept. And the first and best of the Reformed expositors of this theme was John Calvin himself. Calvin's *Institutes*, that basic text for the whole Reformed tradition, went through five editions from 1536 to 1559. Part of what happened during its growth from the little pocket book that it was in 1536 to the big folio that it became in 1559 was that the theme of knowing God, dealt with sketchily in the first edition, dismissed in scarcely more than a sentence, came to dominate the whole structure. The opening sentence of the 1536 *Institutes* was this: 'The sum of sacred doctrine is contained in these two parts: the knowledge of God and of ourselves.' In the second edition that sentence was changed into this: 'The sum of our wisdom is contained in our knowledge of God and of ourselves.' From the second to the fourth edition that sentence was then expanded in separate chapters, one on the knowledge of God, one on the knowledge of ourselves. And those chapters were further expanded in the final edition. In the final edition the sum of Calvin's material was arranged in four distinct books. The first book was called 'Of the Knowledge of God the Creator'. The second book was called 'Of the Knowledge of Christ the Redeemer'. The theme of knowing God is expanding, you see, and coming to dominate the whole work.

I am sure you have noticed that the full title of Calvin's *Institutes* is not *Institutio Christianae Theologiae*, which would be translated as 'Basic Instruction in Christian Theology', but *Institutio Christianae Religionis*, 'Basic Instruction in the Christian Religion', which is more than theology – not less than theology, I hasten to say, but more than theology. And the knowing of God is more than theology. Knowing God is not simply cultivating true notions about God; knowing God is quite simply the practice of the Christian religion, the practice of godliness. It is in truth the basic biblical concept and the basic Reformed concept which sums up the life that the Christian gospel proclaims.

Let us focus on this concept and try to define it to ourselves. I take all my points from Calvin.

Not awareness only

First, knowledge of God is more than the natural man's awareness of God. Calvin has a different phrase for that. He calls it *notitia dei* (awareness of God) rather than *cognitio dei* which is his regular phrase for 'knowledge of God'. Calvin is very emphatic that the natural man is aware of God and, try as he might, cannot get rid of this awareness. He speaks of the sense of deity, the impression of God, the conviction about God, the seed of religion which is planted in the human heart and which the natural man, try as he might, cannot eliminate. The natural man wishes to pretend that there is no God; but pretence it remains, because deep down he knows that God is. Nonetheless, this awareness of God that he has is not to be equated with the knowledge of God that the Christian has, for to Calvin knowledge of God is knowledge within a covenanted relationship.

Knowledge of a covenant God who has given himself to you as your God is basic to Calvin's understanding and to the Bible's understanding. Knowledge of God means knowledge of God as the one who has given himself to you. 'Religion', says Luther, 'is a matter of personal pronouns, I being able to say to God, "My God," and I knowing that God says to me "My child."' It is in that relationship that knowledge of God becomes a reality.

More than experience

Knowledge of God is also more than any particular experience of God. For Calvin, like the Bible, comes from an era when people were less self-absorbed than we are and were more interested in the realities that we experience than in our experiences of them. It is rather difficult, I think, for us twentieth-century men quite to understand this distinction. We are self-absorbed. We are interested in experiences for their own sake. We are inclined to jump to the conclusion that the more intense any experience is (when I say 'experience' I mean 'feeling' or 'reaction to something'), the more of God there must be in it. But by Bible standards this is not so at all. Not even a conversion experience may be equated with the knowledge of God. 'For', says Calvin (and the Scripture before him), 'we know God by faith.' Faith is an outgoing of the heart in trust. Experiences flow from it. But faith is a relationship of trust and not in itself an experience. Without faith there would be no conversion experience. Without faith there would be no Christian experience at all. But faith is something distinct from the experience. Faith is the outgoing of heart to the God and Christ who are there giving themselves to us and saying, 'Come and put your trust in the Father and the Son.'

Knowledge by acquaintance

Third, knowledge of God is more than knowing about God, although knowing about God is its foundation. There is a difference between knowledge by description, in which you simply know about something, and knowledge by acquaintance, in which you are in direct contact with that reality. The knowledge of God is by acquaintance, which is more than knowledge by description.

When it comes to knowledge by description Calvin is very emphatic as to what must be known about God. In the very first chapter of the very first edition of the *Institutes* Calvin wrote that there are four things that must be known about God. First, God is 'infinite wisdom, righteousness, goodness, mercy, truth, power and life, so that there is no other wisdom, righteousness, goodness, mercy, truth, power and life save in him'. Second, 'All things, both in heaven and earth, were created to his glory.' Third, 'He is a righteous judge who sternly punishes those who swerve from his laws and do not wholly fulfill his will.' And fourth, 'He is mercy and gentleness, receiving kindly the rich and the poor who flee to his clemency and entrust themselves to his faithfulness.' These are the four basics that we must know about God if ever we are to come and know him. But, says Calvin, to know these things and to have these things clear in our minds is not yet to know God. For knowledge of God, *cognitio dei*, is relational knowledge, knowledge that comes to us in the relation of commitment and trust, faith and reliance.

More than knowing God

The fourth point is this. Knowing God – this is paradoxical, but you will see what I mean – is, in fact, more than knowing God. For it is not knowing God in isolation; it is knowing God in his relationship to us, that relationship in which he gives himself and his gifts to us for our enrichment. In other words, knowledge of God takes place only where there is knowledge of ourselves and our need and thankful reception of God's gifts to meet our need. Calvin is so right. The knowledge of God and of ourselves – these two things together – make the sum of our wisdom. In fact, one does not begin to know God until one knows God's gracious gift offered to one in one's weakness, sin and wretchedness; then and only then does one know God's grace.

Apprehension, application, adoration

This brings us to the point where we can speak positively of what knowing God is, and we can say this: knowing God is three things together. It is apprehension of what he is; it is application to ourselves of what he is and what he gives; and it is adoration of him, the giver.

Let Calvin say this to us in his own terms: 'The knowledge of God, as I understand it, is that by which we not only conceive, that is, form the concept of there being a God, but we also grasp what benefits us, what profits us from his giving. Nor shall we say that God is, strictly speaking, known where there is no religion or godliness.' That is the response of adoration and worship, both by lip and by heart and in life. Again Calvin says this: 'We are called to a knowledge of God which does not just flip about in the brain, content with empty speculations.' It is not just, in other words, a matter of ideas. But it is a knowledge which, if we rightly grasp it and allow it to take root in our hearts, will be solid and fruitful. Calvin, when he says 'fruitful', means life-changing'. So true knowledge of God means bringing forth the fruit of Christ-likeness. Again he says: 'The knowledge of God is not identified with cold speculation but it brings with it worship of him.'

Communication

So, this is what knowing God meant to Calvin and what it has meant to all Reformed theologians and what it means, I am persuaded, in the Scriptures. But how does this knowledge of God come about? What are the means of our knowing God?

The usual Reformed formula, indeed, the usual Christian formula, is that knowledge of God depends upon God's revelation of himself to us. Knowledge and revelation are correlative. And that is right. Calvin insisted on it and Reformed theologians insist on it as strongly as any Christians have ever insisted on it. And yet, sometimes I find myself wishing that in place of that word 'revelation' we could form the habit of substituting another word which I think in modern discussion and debate would express more. In place of 'revelation' I would like to say 'communication'. The word 'revelation', you see, suggests to modern minds little more than a general display, a general exhibition of something. I believe it is very important when we think of the revelation of God always to keep in view the fact that it is personal communication from the Creator to his creatures. That word 'communication' seems to me to carry all the right vibrations and to convey all the right thoughts.

What does communication suggest? It suggests a person who is approaching us, coming close to us, speaking to us, telling us about himself, opening his mind to us, giving us what he has, revealing what he knows, asking for our attention, asking for our response to what he is saying. This is the word we need in order to make clear how the knowledge of God comes to us. It comes to us through divine communication. God comes to us and makes himself known.

At this point there is a specific problem, God made us in order that he might communicate himself to us and thus draw us into loving fellowship with himself. But man has turned away from God; sin has come in; human nature has become twisted. Man is now anti-God in his basic attitudes. He is not interested in fellowship with God. It is no longer in his nature to love God; it is no longer in his nature to respond to God. He has his back to God. In consequence of the fall it is now human nature to do over and over what Adam and Eve are found doing in Genesis 3. We treat ourselves as though we were God. We live for ourselves; we seek to bend everything to our own interest. In doing so we fight God; that is, we fight the real God. We say No to him. We push him away from the centre of our life to its circumference.

So God's communication to man in sin has to do more than simply present truth to his mind. It has to work in him in such a way in his heart and change his nature. God's communication must do all that.

There is, says Calvin, a general communication of God – normally it is called 'general revelation', but I am using this word 'communication' – to men in nature (the created order with which we are all of us in contact every day of our lives). And in our own nature, too, there is a revelation, a communication from God. It comes through in the same way that an awareness of light comes through. It is immediate, inescapable, undeniable. But fallen man denies it nevertheless and turns the light that is in him into darkness.

Calvin is very strong on this. He says, 'God has so shown himself in the whole workmanship of this world that men cannot open their eyes without being forced to see him.' Again, 'The orderly arrangement of the world is like a mirror in which we may contemplate the otherwise invisible God.' Again, 'The world is created for the display of God's glory.' Again, 'The world is the theatre of God's glory.' Again, 'The Lord clearly displays both himself and his immortal kingdom in the mirror of his works.' And again, 'In the splendour of the heavens there is presented to our view a lively image of God.'

The awareness of the Creator comes through in all our commerce with his creatures, in all our knowledge and awareness of ourselves and our own identity and the workings of our conscience and the thoughts of our own hearts. But man denies this awareness and turns it into darkness and superstition. So the world, for all its wisdom, does not know God, though this general communication of God through nature is a reality for every man.

Three stages

What, then, is there to do? Well, what God has done is to add this general communication of himself in the natural order, a special communication of himself in grace, in which there are three stages. Stage one is redemption in history. By words and by works God makes himself known on the stage of history in saving action. The words are basic, for first God tells men what he is going to do. He makes the announcement. Then he acts, fulfilling his word and doing what he said. That is how it was at the exodus when he saved Israel out of captivity in Egypt. That is what he did when in the fullness of time he sent his own Son, born of a woman, to redeem those who were under the law, sinners like you and me, that we might receive the adoption of sons and so become children in his family.

Stage two is the recording of revelation in writing. That is the work of God inspiring the Holy Scriptures. God caused to be written interpretive records of what he had said and done, so that all men in all generations might know and through this knowledge come into the enjoyment of the redemptive revelation that he had made. The written record is our Bible.

The third stage in the communicative process is reception by individuals of the realities of redemption declared in the Scriptures, a reception which becomes a reality through the work of the Holy Spirit. The Holy Spirit opens hearts to give the word entrance and renews hearts so that we might turn around again to face God. We become new creatures in Christ. When the New Testament speaks of God revealing himself to men it is this third stage in the process of divine communication that is normally in view, as when Jesus said, 'Neither knoweth any man the Father, except the Son, and he to whomsoever the Son will reveal him' (Matt. 11:27) or, as when Jesus said again, 'Blessed art thou, Simon Bar-jona; for flesh and blood hath not revealed it unto thee, but my Father, who is in heaven' (Matt. 16:17). Paul uses the word in the same way when he says in Galatians that 'it pleased God ... to reveal his Son in me' (Gal. 1:15–16). The same thought is being expressed by Paul in other words when he says in 2 Corinthians 4:6 that 'God, who commanded the light to shine out of darkness, hath shone in our hearts, to give the light of the knowledge of the glory of God in the face of Jesus Christ'.

Scripture essential

Do you see now that stage two in the process, the inspiring of the Bible, is absolutely crucial? Calvin saw that. He regularly referred to the Bible as the 'oracles of God'. That, of course, is a scriptural phrase. It is Paul's own phrase, in Romans 3. Calvin took it and used it again and again to express the thought that what we have in Scripture is God's own witness to his work of salvation. Says Calvin, 'The Bible has a double function in relation to us sin-blinded sinners. It functions as our schoolmaster, teaching us the truth, operating as the rule of our teaching and our speaking.' Again, 'We should seek in the Scripture a sure rule, both of thinking and speaking, a rule by which we may regulate all the thoughts of our minds and all the words of our mouth. The Scripture is our schoolmaster, to teach us the truth of God.' More than that, says Calvin, 'The Bible is not only our schoolmaster, the Bible is our spectacles.'

Calvin's illustration speaks much to me because I, like some of you, am short-sighted. I take off my glasses, and I cannot see you. I can see a sort of smudge. That is all. Calvin, who himself was short-sighted, says, in effect, that the natural man, without the Scriptures, has no more than a smudgy awareness that there is a something or a someone; but he does not know who the something or the someone is. He has just this smudgy awareness. But, says Calvin, when a short-sighted man is able to put on glasses, then he sees clearly what he saw before as only a smudge. So when we begin to study the Scriptures, he says, we begin to see clearly who it is of whom before we had that unwelcome awareness. The Scriptures come to us as glasses, enabling us to focus that awareness of God that we had before and showing us precisely who and what this God is. The Scriptures are our lifeline. They alone can guide us out of the labyrinth of ignorance.

So Calvin opposed any form of theology that sought to run apart from the Scriptures. He denounced it as speculation. He said that it is ungodly. Consequently, he summons us to that humility which acknowledges need and is willing to be taught.

I need not develop this in its full contemporary relevance, but I think you can see without my developing it how much contemporary relevance it has. Much theology today is speculative in Calvin's sense, in the sense which he condemned. It sits loose to the Scriptures; it patronizes the Scriptures; it stands above the Scriptures, going beyond and away from the Scriptures. And it is trash, says Calvin. As one whose profession obliges him to spend a great deal of his time reading it, I can only endorse that opinion. Theology which flies away from the Scripture is trash, and one of the miseries of the modern church is that much of its books, preaching, and thinking is so much trash at this point.

What is called for now, as in Calvin's day, is the humility which bows before the Scriptures and accepts them as instruction from God. They are God preaching, God talking, God telling, God instructing, God setting before us the right way to think and the right way to talk concerning him. They are God showing us himself, God communicating to us who he is and what he has done so that we in the response of faith may truly know him and live our lives in fellowship with him.

Give me that book

I want to put this question to you. We are Reformed people. What that means too often, though, is that we think of the Scriptures simply as a stick with which to beat unorthodoxy. When we use the phrase 'biblical authority' this is often all that we have in mind. But I want to ask you this: Do you recognize the place the Bible has in God's communication of himself to you? Do you thank God for the Bible as one of his greatest gifts of grace to you? Do you recognize that it is as great and as glorious as the gift of his Son to you? It is. For if you did not have the Bible to lead you to the Son, you could never know the Son as your Saviour and could never come to know God as your Father. Think of the Bible first and foremost as a gift of the grace of God and prize it accordingly.

Let us learn this from one who (quite mistakenly, really) went on calling himself an Arminian, when he was only a muddled Calvinist – John Wesley. Here is how Wesley put the point in his preface to the published edition of his sermons: 'I am a creature of a day, travelling through this world for a brief moment, soon to leave it. I want to know one thing, the way to heaven. God has written it down in a book. Give me, then, that book. At any price, give me the book of God. I have it. Here is wisdom enough for me. I sit down with it. Only God is present. I lift up my heart to him, asking for light as to its meaning.' Do you identify with that? I ask you again. Do you identify with John Wesley and his attitude to his Bible as a supreme gift of God's grace? I hope we all do. This Word is what the world needs if ever it is to know God. Thank God for it and value and prize it.

At the coronation of the sovereign of England, the Moderator of the Church of Scotland, a good Presbyterian, presents a Bible to the reigning monarch and speaks of it as – I quote the words exactly – 'the most precious thing this world affords, the most precious thing that this world knows, God's living Word'. That is true. Christ and the Scriptures belong together as gifts of the grace of God. This is where Reformed theology begins, in recognition of this truth and in glad submission to the teaching of Scripture, that from it we may learn of our Saviour. God help us to begin at what is the true beginning, then. God teach us to value and prize his Holy Word.

Questions for study

1. What are the essential elements of 'knowing God', according to Packer?
2. What point does Packer make in relation to the title of Calvin's major work? Why does it matter that the work is called not *Institutio Christianae*

Theologiae, but *Institutio Christianae Religionis*?

3. What does Packer mean by the Latin phrase *notitia Dei*? Why does he contrast this with *cognitio Dei*?

4. Locate this quotation within the text: 'true knowledge of God means bringing forth the fruit of Christ-likeness'. How does Packer come to this conclusion? And why is it so important to his overall purpose in dealing with the theme of 'knowing God'?

5. Find the following quotation: 'Christ and the Scriptures belong together as gifts of the grace of God.' What does Packer mean by this? Why would anyone want to separate Christ and the Scriptures? And what response does Packer make?

9. 'Jesus Christ the Lord' (1977)

The authority of Christ is one of the most important elements of 'the authentic biblical and credal mainstream of Christian identity, the confessional and liturgical "great tradition" that the church on earth has characteristically maintained from the start'. Packer regarded the faithful defence and exposition of the uniqueness and authority of Jesus Christ as essential to the well-being and integrity of the Christian church. In his 1977 lecture 'Jesus Christ the Lord', Packer set out an authoritative presentation of the centrality of Christ for Christianity, and offered responses to difficulties which might be discerned with such an approach.

The lecture was delivered at the 1977 National Evangelical Anglican Congress, held in Nottingham, which was intended to take forward the agenda which was set by the National Evangelical Anglican Congress of 1967. It was in 1975 that John Stott convened a meeting to plan the successor to the Keele congress of 1967, which was by now recognized as a landmark, representing a decisive change in the mood of evangelicalism within the Church of England. Stott felt that it would be appropriate to hold a follow-up conference to this event, to be held ten years afterwards in 1977. It was decided to produce three books as 'study guides' for the proposed conference. These books were given the titles *The Lord Christ*, *The Changing World* and *The People of God*, each indicating the broad area which they explored. The resulting Nottingham congress, held at the Sports Hall of the University of Nottingham over the period Thursday 14 April – Monday 18 April 1977, was well attended. Some

1,000 people had attended the Keele congress of 1967; double that number came to Nottingham.

Packer's address was not, in the event, the most memorable aspect of the Nottingham congress. A new interest in hermeneutics emerged, which eclipsed many of the more traditional topics. There can be no doubt that this concern for hermeneutics was to be welcomed; sadly, however, it led to a loss of focus on some classic themes, which bound evangelicalism together. We have already noted how the congress saw some division emerge over the issue of the doctrine of the atonement. Packer set out a vision of the centrality of Christ as a unifying ground for evangelicals. Although the lecture received relatively little attention when it was given, the passage of time has confirmed its importance.

Related works by Packer

'What did the Cross Achieve? The Logic of Penal Substitution', *Tyndale Bulletin* 25 (1974), pp. 3–45. (Essay 7 in this collection.)
'The Uniqueness of Jesus Christ', *Churchman* 92 (1978), pp. 101–111.
'A Modern View of Jesus', *Faith Today*, January 1987, pp. 28–30, 32–33. (Essay 11 in this collection.)

Jesus Christ the Lord

What think ye of Christ? That's the test
To try both your state and your scheme.
You cannot be right in the rest
Unless you think rightly of him.

So, two centuries ago, wrote John Newton, 'the old converted slave-trader'. Was he right?

By biblical standards he most certainly was. 'State' means 'spiritual condition'; 'scheme' means 'theological system'; claims to hold a 'scheme' of truth and to be in a 'state' of grace become vulnerable where one's Christology – that is, one's thoughts about the person and place of Jesus of Nazareth, whom Christians since Pentecost have called Christ (cf. Acts 2:36) – is suspect. John showed this when he condemned both the 'scheme' and the 'state' of

Gnostic separatists on the grounds that 'every spirit which does not confess Jesus [sc. as Son of God come in the flesh] … is the spirit of antichrist' (1 John 4:2–3; cf. 2 John 7), and that 'any one who goes ahead and does not abide in the [sc. apostolic] doctrine of Christ does not have God' (2 John 9).

Historically, it has not been seriously doubted till modern times that belief in the incarnation – that is, the taking of full humanity by the Son of God or, putting it the other way round, the full personal deity of the man Jesus – is essential to Christianity. Two sets of reasons have been held to show that this is so.

Christology and Christian belief

Set one has to do with theology, that is, our understanding of God and his relation to everything everywhere that is distinct from himself. The Christian consensus has been that, as Scripture is the proper source from which theology should flow, so Christology is the true hub round which the wheel of theology revolves, and to which its separate spokes must each be correctly anchored if the wheel is not to get bent. That all historic Christianity's most distinctive convictions have been decisively shaped by belief in the incarnation is not hard to see. Let me illustrate.

Take God. Why do Christians hold that the one God is plural (triple, to be exact), and that he is at once intolerably severe, terrifyingly perceptive, and infinitely good? Ultimately, it is because they hold that Jesus, who prayed to his Father and promised the Spirit, and whose character was as described, was personally divine.

Or take humanity. Why do Christians hold that personal relationships matter more than anything in this world, and that the truly human way to live – in the last analysis, the only non-bestial way – is lovingly, constantly, unreservedly to give yourself away to God and to others, and that anything less offends God? Ultimately, it is because they hold that Jesus was as fully human as he was divine, and that as he taught these things so he lived them, and that at the deepest level of personhood his was the one perfect human life that the world has seen.

Or take God's Word. Why are Christians sure, despite all the difficulties, that the Bible is God's own inspired and authoritative instruction? Ultimately, it is because Jesus, the Son of God, showed constantly that the Old Testament Scriptures were to him his Father's word, teaching him his Father's way.[1]

Or take God's church. Why do Christians view their thousands of congregations as not just a chain of clubs or interest groups, but as outcrops of a single organic entity, the one 'body' of ransomed, healed, restored and forgiven sinners, brothers and sisters in one family sharing a new supernatural life through common links with Christ their 'head'? Ultimately, it is because Jesus taught his disciples to see his Father as their Father, his death as their ransom sacrifice, and himself as their way to the Father, their bread of life, and the vine in which, as branches, they must abide.

Or take human destiny. Why do Christians hold, despite the felt limitations which aging bodies impose, and despite endless speculations and superstitions about the larger life of departed spirits, that full humanness requires re-embodiment, and hence anticipate physical resurrection? Ultimately, it is because they are sure that Jesus rose physically from death, and that his rising is the model for ours.

Or, lastly, take world history. Why do Christians, facing the chaos of an overcrowded world in which technological titans are spiritual pygmies and mass starvation seems the only alternative to nuclear holocaust, cling to the hope of a cosmic triumph of divine justice and power? Ultimately, it is because they believe that God's risen Son reigns, really if hiddenly, over all things, and is pledged to return in glory to judge and renew that world which he, with the Father and the Holy Spirit, first created.

So we see that all the main distinctives of the Christian creed spring from Christian Christology. What follows? This: that if you alter the Christology, you should alter the derived beliefs as well, since there is now no good reason for maintaining them in their original form.

Thus, if we think that Jesus did not rise, but 'lives' and 'reigns' only in his followers' memories and imaginations, and is not actively and objectively 'there' in the place of power, irrespective of whether he is acknowledged or not,' we should give up hope of our own rising, and of Jesus' public return, and admit that the idea of churches and Christians being sustained by the Spirit-given energy of a living Lord was never more than a pleasing illusion.

And in that case we ought frankly to affirm that, though the New Testament is an amazing witness to the religious creativity of the human spirit, its actual message is more wrong than right, more misleading than helpful, and we must reconstruct our gospel accordingly. Only a weak, muddled or cowardly mind will hesitate to do this.[2] But then it will be a misuse of language to call our theology Christian; for, as we have seen, the forms of faith and thought to which that name has been given over the best part of two millennia all depend on belief in the incarnation.[3]

Christology and Christian experience

Set two of reasons for regarding belief in Jesus' deity as central to Christianity must now be noted. This has to do with religion – that is, our actual response to God. The relevant facts here are that it is characteristic of Christians to approach Jesus Christ in prayer and worship, and to commune with him in a relationship of faith and hope, loyalty and love, openness and dependence; and both activities implicitly assert his deity.

Take the latter first. The Christian claim from New Testament times has been that God confronts men not only in those intimations of creaturely dependence and obligation which come to all persons alive in God's world,[4] but also in the person of the risen Christ, the divine Saviour whose portrait is in the Gospels and whose place in God's purpose is the theme of the whole New Testament. Christianity (so Christians love to say) is Christ – not just theological notions plus a code of practice, but fellowship with the Father and Jesus Christ his Son (cf. 1 John 1:3). More particularly, Christianity (so it is affirmed) is a prolonging and universalizing for all disciples of that one-to-one relationship with Jesus which his first followers enjoyed in Palestine in his earthly ministry.

There are, indeed, two differences. First, we know more of who and what Jesus is than anyone knew before his passion. Secondly, once Jesus is now physically absent from us, our connection with him is not via our physical senses, but through his own inward application of biblical material to mind and heart in a way which is as familiar to believers as it is mysterious to others.[5] But the actual sense of being confronted, claimed, taught, restored, upheld and empowered by the Jesus of the Gospels has been the essence of Christian experience over nineteen centuries, just as it is demonstrably of the essence of what New Testament writers knew, promised and expected.[6] To assume, however, that Jesus is alive, universally available, and able to give full attention simultaneously to every disciple everywhere (and this is the biblical and Christian assumption) is, in effect, to declare his divinity.

Moreover, Christians have from the start addressed prayer and praise to the Son as well as to the Father.[7] It seems that Jesus taught the propriety of praying to him once he had returned to the Father,[8] and in any case if his disciples could rightly make requests of him while he was on earth it could hardly become wrong for them to do so when 'the days of his flesh' gave way to the days of his reign. In AD 112 the younger Pliny found Christians meeting before dawn to 'recite a hymn of praise to Christ, as to a god',[9] and much Christian liturgy and hymnody goes the same way. Typical is the *Te Deum*: 'Thou art the King of glory, O Christ … we therefore pray thee, help thy servants …' And also the Prayer Book Litany:

By the mystery of thy holy Incarnation … by thy Cross and Passion …

by the coming of the Holy Ghost, good Lord, deliver us … Graciously hear us, O Christ; graciously hear us, O Lord Christ.

All this, however, as Athanasius told the Arians long ago, would be the height of irreverence were Jesus not held to be divine.

What has been said so far highlights two facts about biblical and later Christianity: first, that belief in Jesus' deity is so essential to it that at no significant point could it have become what it is had this belief not operated; secondly, that Christian faith means not just acknowledging Jesus' deity, but also seeking and finding a personal relationship with him in which we receive of his fullness and respond to his love in the devotion of his discipleship. Christians have not always achieved agreement on how this relationship is mediated (some stressing sacraments as an alternative to the gospel word), but they agree that the relationship is real, and that the deepest and saddest division in the Christian world, deeper than any gulf dividing denominations, is and always was the division within congregations between those who know Jesus Christ in experience and those who do not. It is the reality of this relationship for Christian people that explains the pain they feel when confronted with what seems to them Christological misbelief which insults and diminishes their Saviour; just as it is (so they fear) ignorance of this relationship which produces the misbelief in the first place and then creates an audience for it.

A generation ago, Dietrich Bonhoeffer posed for enquiry the theme 'Who Christ really is, for us today'.[10] Since his time, Christology has become a matter of new debate, and of fresh tension too. Teilhard de Chardin, in maximizing Christ's cosmic significance, has appeared to depersonalize him. And Protestant theologians, in stressing Jesus' humanness and historicality, have appeared to dissolve away the substance of his godhead. Should such Christologies be taken as the last word, the faith-relationship with Jesus of which we spoke would not be 'on'. And merely by existing they make that relationship harder to hold on to, just as do the current 'secular' pictures of Jesus as a troubled hysteric (e.g. Dennis Potter, *Son of Man*) and as a pleasant song-and-dance man (e.g. *Godspell; Jesus Christ Superstar*). Fresh clarification is called for, urgently!

This essay seeks to show how the record may be put straight, and the way to true faith reopened. We shall start to work out an answer to the question which Bonhoeffer left us, not subjectively, in terms of what in this confused age men feel, fancy or (worse!) 'like to think', but objectively, in terms of what is there, given and abiding, according to the nineteen-hundred-year-old principle that 'Jesus Christ is the same yesterday and today and for ever' (Heb. 13:8).

We shall in fact address ourselves to a question which underlies Bonhoeffer's, namely this: what must be said of our Lord Jesus Christ today in order first to secure for him that acknowledgment in praise, worship and obedient trust which apostolic witness and theology require, and secondly to prevent the nature and scope of his saving ministry being so misunderstood as to produce mistaken – indeed, by biblical standards unbelieving – proclamation and practice?

In order to answer this question, we shall (1) sketch out the main lines of New Testament Christology, (2) bring into focus some of the claims which it entails, (3) note some characteristic methods, assumptions, theses and problems of the 'humanitarian' Christology of our time, and (4) reaffirm an 'incarnational' account of Jesus. (The point of contrasting 'humanitarian' with 'incarnational', be it said, is not that exponents of the former approach reject incarnation of set purpose, but that their way of explaining it is an abandoning of it in fact.) Thus, hopefully, our theologizing will pay true homage to Jesus Christ the Lord.

New Testament Christology

> I have come to the point [wrote Francis Schaeffer in 1968], where, when I hear the word 'Jesus' – which means so much to me because of the Person of the historic Jesus and His work – I listen carefully because I have with sorrow become more afraid of the word 'Jesus' than almost any other word in the modern world. The word is used as a contentless banner ... there is no rational scriptural content by which to test it ... Increasingly over the past few years the word 'Jesus,' separated from the content of the Scriptures, has been the enemy of the Jesus of history, the Jesus who died and rose and is coming again and who is the eternal Son of God.[11]

Dr Schaeffer's protest against allowing the name 'Jesus' to become a 'non-defined symbol', a 'connotation word' in a world of 'semantic mysticism', is timely. That the only real Jesus is the Christ of New Testament history and theology, and that by parting company with the New Testament we do not find him, but only lose him, is a truth that cannot be too often emphasized today.

But do we find the real Jesus in the New Testament? Can we trust the records and interpretations which we find there? Do not the New Testament presentations of Jesus differ so widely as to cancel each other out, and create uncertainty at every point? Scepticism abounds, we know, but we shall be forearmed against it if we will learn to weigh the following three points.

First, the current fashion of treating the varieties of vocabulary, emphasis and development of themes within the New Testament as indicating a plurality of inconsistent theological outlooks is merely a revival of an elderly mistake which has already been many times corrected. A century and a half of scientific New Testament study has seen abundant hypotheses of this kind, setting Paul against the synoptic evangelists, or the synoptists against John, or James against Paul, or the Pastorals against the rest of Paul's letters, and so forth. None of them can be said to have stood the test of sustained scholarly examination. On the contrary, investigation has again and again underlined the real unity of the New Testament witness to Christ.[12]

Secondly, the current habit of disbelieving Gospel narratives, and treating Jesus' real history as mostly unrecoverable – a last-century habit, which owes most of its recent vogue to one outstanding but idiosyncratic teacher, the late Rudolf Bultmann, who died in 1976 at the age of 91 – comes to look silly once one realizes that the bulk of the New Testament dates from the lifetime of persons who knew Jesus (all from before AD 70, claims John A. T. Robinson),[13] and moreover that the culture of Palestinian Judaism was based on memory to a far greater extent than ours is. Nobody alive in 1977 who remembers the Second World War should think it possible that key facts of Jesus' life and teaching were forgotten, or misremembered, among his disciples before the Gospels were written; particularly in view of the importance ascribed to these facts, and Luke's emphatic claim to be well informed (Luke 1:1–4), and the attestation given to John's witness in the Fourth Gospel (John 19:25; 21:24).[14]

Thirdly, the current readiness to think that the Jesus of the Gospels could have been made up is nonsensically naïve. In 1904 Bishop Handley Moule wrote of 'that supreme miracle, the Lord', declaring that 'there is no miracle more properly miraculous than the Jesus of the Evangelists, in the profound contrasts and sublime harmony of his character'.[15] 'If anything whatever is common to all believers, and even to many unbelievers,' wrote C. S. Lewis,

> it is the sense that in the Gospels they have a personality ... So strong
> is the flavour of that personality that, even while he says things which,
> on any other assumption than that of divine Incarnation in the fullest
> sense, would be appallingly arrogant, yet we – and many unbelievers
> too – accept him at his own valuation when he says 'I am meek and
> lowly of heart.'[16]

Surely it is clear that to suppose that the sayings and doings which communicate the unique flavour of Jesus' personality are products of pious imagination, while the real Jesus was in undiscoverable ways different, is embracing the incredible. To take just one point: the Jesus of the Gospels is free from any sense of sin or dissatisfaction with himself (traits that are ordinarily psychopathic, and the negation of virtue), yet he impresses us as a supreme moral realist, and a person of supreme goodness. The remembering of so mind-blowing a personality is no problem, supposing he really existed, but the idea that he might have been invented by imagination alone is as wild as the idea that pigs may some day fly. No biblical miracle takes so much believing as that!

So we approach the New Testament with confidence, which the discovery in it of a substantial unity of witness to Christ bears out. This witness, about which there is no dispute save on details,[17] may be summed up in four propositions, thus:

1. Jesus of Nazareth is God's promised Christ

'Christ' is, of course, not a surname(!) but an 'office-title', meaning literally 'anointed one' (which is what 'Messiah' also means), and designating God's promised Saviour-King. That the Galilean rabbi who rose from death is the Christ was always the basic Christian conviction,[18] and all strands of the New Testament express it. The Messiah's fulfilment of his earthly ministry in face of incomprehension and hostility, right up to his dying and rising, is the 'plot' of all four Gospels. That 'Son of Man', Jesus' own mysterious title for himself, and 'Lord', the title given him from Pentecost on, point first to the reality of his messianic rule is nowadays generally agreed.[19]

Not that Jesus' concept of messiahship corresponded to Jewish expectation. His notion reflected his view of God's eschatological kingdom, which he preached as a reality brought into being by his own ministry. He saw the kingdom as a new relationship between penitent sinners and God as their heavenly Father, a relationship achieved through commitment to himself as their sovereign Saviour; and he saw his lordship as based on his call to be God's suffering servant, the innocent one who, having died for others' sin, is then vindicated by being restored to life, according to Isaiah 53. Calvin well summarized Jesus' notion of messiahship, and the overall New Testament view of his role, when he spoke of Jesus as fulfilling a threefold office, as prophet (bringer of messages from God), priest (offerer of sacrifice to God) and king (ruler of the people of God).

2. *Jesus of Nazareth is the unique Son of God*

There are places in the first three Gospels and Acts where 'Son of God' may be an honorific title for the Messiah, modelled on Psalm 2:6ff.;[20] but it is certain that in the Epistles and in John's Gospel it signifies a unique relation of solidarity with the Father, a relation entailing both a revelatory function[21] and also a share in the Father's work of creating, sustaining, reconciling, ruling and renewing his world;[22] and whatever 'Son of God' means in the first three Gospels, their direct witness to Jesus' knowledge of his unique filial identity is very clear.[23] Personal distinctions within the unity of God constitute perhaps the hardest notion round which the human mind has ever been asked to wrap itself, and the thought was never adequately conceptualized till the fourth century. But faith that Jesus was in a true sense the Son of God made flesh, and an emphatic rejection of Docetism (the view of Jesus as a theophany, an appearance of God, not a real or complete man at all) marked Christians from the first.

3. *Jesus of Nazareth is the only way to the Father*

The New Testament views knowing your Maker as your Father, and yourself as his child and heir, as the highest privilege and richest relationship of which any human being is capable. Not to know God in this way is, by contrast, to be in a state of fallenness and guilt, cut off from God's life, exposed to his judgment, and under demonic control, whence flows only misery. But this is every man's natural condition.

Can it be changed? Jesus said: 'I am the way, and the truth, and the life; no one comes to the Father, but by me' (John 14:6). It is as if he said: Yes, a filial relationship to God is possible through relating to me and my mediatorial ministry – though not otherwise. For sonship of God, in the sense that guarantees mercy and glory, is not a fact of natural life, but a gift of supernatural grace. 'To all who received him, who believed in his name, he gave power' [or the right, the prerogative] to become children of God' (John 1:12). The doctrine of the bestowal of sonship is part of the proper exposition of 1 Peter 3:18: 'Christ ... died for sins once for all, the righteous for the unrighteous, that he might bring us to God.' The only-begotten Son, who died for us, presents us to his Father as his brothers and sisters; thus we are adopted. But to this privilege unbelievers remain strangers, to their own infinite loss.

As contractors-out gain no benefit from a pension scheme, so one who shrugs off the gospel gains nothing from the mediation of Jesus Christ. 'You refuse to come to me that you may have life,' says Jesus (John 5:40). As unadopted roads are just pebbles and puddles, lacking a surface, so the spiritually unadopted lack a God they can call Father, and their living, however hectic, is drab in consequence. However vivid their sense of God may be, and however ardent their quest to know more of him, there is only one way they can find him as Father, and that is by coming to terms with – that is, accepting terms already announced by – God's Son, Jesus Christ, the living Lord. As no other relation to God save sonship brings salvation, so apart from Jesus, who effects our adoption, 'there is no other name under heaven given among men by which we must be saved'.[24]

4. Jesus of Nazareth is the only hope for any person

Hopelessness is hell – literally. As God made us to fulfil a function and attain an end (for 'man's chief end is to glorify God, and to enjoy him for ever'), so he made us creatures for whom hope is life, and whose lives become living deaths when we have nothing good to look forward to. As the deep hopelessness of post-Christian western culture tightens its chilly grip on us, we are made to feel this increasingly, and so can better appreciate the infinite value for life today of that exuberant, unstoppable, intoxicating, energizing hope of joy with Jesus in the Father's presence for ever which is so pervasive a mark of New Testament Christianity.

Whereas those without Christ are without God and without hope, living already in a dusk of the spirit that is destined to grow darker and colder, Christians are in the sunshine, endlessly rejoicing in 'Christ Jesus our hope'.[25] The inescapable alternatives are false hope (Marxism? spiritism? happiness through having things? endless good health? – false hopes, every one), or else no hope (total pessimism, inviting suicide), or else Christian hope, the electrifying knowledge of 'Christ in you, the hope of glory'.[26] It is a pity that so little is heard these days about what has been called 'the unknown world with its well-known inhabitant' to which the New Testament teaches Christians to look forward; for, as the hymn says: 'The Lamb is all the glory of Emmanuel's land,' and declaring that glory is part of what it means to relate the New Testament witness to the person and place of Jesus Christ.

Five crucial claims

Let us now be analytical, and spell out to ourselves five particular claims which this witness involves. Each relates to both Jesus and ourselves, and each has vital importance for present-day discussion of both. Then we shall better see the significance of what has just been written.

The first claim relates to history, and the meaning of our own place in it. Concerning Jesus, the claim is that his incarnation, death, rising and present reign are events that give saving significance to present and future occurrences. A divine plan for history is in operation, and a new community – indeed a race of new persons – is being created. The power that made the world from nothing is now active to renovate it from the chaos and disorder that sin has brought. This power of new creation first transformed Jesus' humanity when he rose. Now, through the Spirit whom Jesus sends, it touches our own personal being in the great change which Jesus, John, James and Peter referred to as new birth and which Paul described as co-resurrection with Christ.[27] One day, when Jesus reappears, it will transform our physicality as completely as it transformed his, and in that transformation the whole external universe will in some unimaginable way be involved.[28] Meanwhile, Jesus Christ is in control, world history is 'his story', and we may live in the certain knowledge that the predestined reintegration of all things in him[29] is on its way.

Concerning ourselves, the claim is that as God's rational creatures and our Lord's redeemed subjects we find the true purpose and fulfilment of our lives by embracing God's announced goals and working for them – for the spread of the gospel, the good of others, the enriching of human life, and the eliminating of what is morally evil and practically harmful. The alternative would be to turn one's back on world history as an area of meaninglessness and seek to realize God, Hindu-style, in the privacies of the psyche: a drop-out philosophy which through disillusionment with the rat-race of the 'great society' has recently had a new vogue. But Christians must set their faces against it.

The second claim relates to humanity, and the meaning of our humanness. Concerning Jesus, it is claimed that he is the yardstick at the level of motivation and attitudes of what it means to be fully human. Concerning ourselves, the claim is that only as we set ourselves to imitate Christ at this level are we fulfilling and developing (as distinct from violating and diminishing) our own human nature, which is already much diminished through sin; and only in this way can we find true joy, which is always integrally bound up with a sense of fulfilment. When Jesus said: 'My food is to do the will of him who sent me, and to accomplish his work,'[30] he was testifying to the joy which he found in his Father's service – service which, in his humanity no less than before he took flesh, was the fulfilling of his nature as the Son. But it was also, and equally, the fulfilling of his nature as man.

For us, then, as for him, full realization of all that potential which is distinctively human (a realization which is both the heart of freedom and the height of joy) is found, not in self-will, but in service – service of God (which for us means service of the Son with the Father), and of others for the Lord's sake. Other paths may bring temporary pleasure, but lead neither to fulfilment, nor to freedom, nor to joy; and enlargement of one's experience will be little enough compensation for the shrinkage of one's real humanity.

The third claim relates to encounter, and the meaning of our personhood. Concerning Jesus, it is claimed that he, the risen and enthroned Lord, is, though physically withdrawn from us, none the less 'there,' indeed 'here,' by his Spirit, in terms of personal presence for personal encounter. From such encounter (so the claim runs) trust in him, and love and loyalty to him, derive. The experience of Paul on the Damascus road, and that of Zacchaeus up and down the sycamore tree,[31] classically illustrate this. Fellowship with Jesus is not a metaphor or parable or myth of something else, but is a basic ingredient of distinctively Christian experience.

Concerning ourselves, the claim is that we were made for relationships, first with God and then with created persons; that this, indeed, is part of God's image in us, inasmuch as God himself is triune, each divine person existing in constant conscious relationship to the other two; and that through the re-creative effect of God's saving relationship to us through Jesus Christ, our capacity for relationships at the deepest level with other human beings, a capacity which sin has in large measure impaired, is progressively restored to us, so that we find ourselves free in Christ for genuinely human relationships in a way that was never true before.

The fourth claim relates to dominion, and the meaning of our circumstances. Concerning Jesus, the claim is that at every point and in every space-time event the cosmos is under the authoritative control[32] of Jesus the risen Lord, who is both the Jesus of history whom we meet in the gospel story and Jesus our saviour and friend. Concerning ourselves, the claim is that whatever happens to us, however bewildering or harrowing, has positive meaning because it was planned in love for us, and willed for our good, and others' good through us, in one way or another. Not that this good meaning is always apparent (except in the sense that we see some appropriate exercise of faith, patience and continuing obedience being called for); but what a difference it makes to living to know that a meaning is there!

The fifth claim relates to destiny, and the meaning of present choices. Concerning Jesus, the claim is that at the end of the road of each man's life Jesus the judge stands inescapable, and that each man will at that time know that this final encounter with Jesus has had final significance for determining his own final state. This is the reality of the judgment-seat of Christ, which is central in biblical thinking about both death and the parousia (royal visit) of the returning Son.[33]

Concerning ourselves, the claim is that present decisions determine ultimate destiny, for they have, in von Hügel's phrase, 'abiding consequences'. Christ as judge will from one standpoint simply ratify the choice to have God, or not to have him, which we have already made in this life.

Surely it is in terms of these claims that our answer to Bonhoeffer's question: 'Who is Jesus Christ for us today?', must be given. Whatever should be added to the above analysis, this is where thinking must start.

Humanitarian Christology

The richest theological statement of the incarnation in Scripture is, beyond question, the prologue of John's Gospel (John 1:1–18), the climactic sentence of which is verse 14: 'So the Word became flesh; he came to dwell among us, and we saw his glory, such glory as befits the Father's only Son, full of grace and truth' (NEB). 'The Word' (*logos*) here is the mysterious being who was God with God at the beginning, agent of creation, source of life and light (i.e. knowledge of the Creator), rejected visitor to his world, and yet donor of sonship to God by adoption through a new divine birth (1–13). 'Flesh' signifies those qualities of weakness, vulnerability, and limitedness in space, time and knowledge in this world which are the marks of created humanity. 'Became' implies the unimaginable reality of God assuming these qualities as modes of his own life.

The verse says that witnesses ('we') discerned in the Word thus made flesh the divine glory of God's only Son. John is clearly asserting two things: first, that the personal Son who is also God's expressive and executive Word existed and was active prior to the incarnation;[34] secondly, that he is the personal subject whose human name is Jesus, and whose humanness is apparent, as his deity, in the story John goes on to tell.

Naturally, mainstream Christian thinking about Jesus has stayed within these limits, and it is right to see the terms of theological art which the Fathers used at the Council of Chalcedon (451) when they confessed one person (*hypostasis*; better, 'entity') in two natures (*physeis*) as intended not to explain, but simply to surround and safeguard this area of mystery – namely, that a man named Jesus, a real human being, was truly and fully God, God the creator, God the Son. The general Christian consensus has been that the incarnation, no less than the divine tri-unity, cannot in any ordinary sense of the word be explained at all; it is a transcendent reality that confounds our finite minds; all we can do (and all we are asked to do) is acknowledge and adore.

In modern times, however, an approach to Christology quite different from

John's has been tried. Its theme, of which there have been many variants over a century and a half, is this: Jesus of Nazareth was a prophetic man in whom God was manifest and through whom God acted, exerting an influence that produced a community with distinctive goals, experiences, views of itself and modes of God-consciousness, of all of which the New Testament is a record. The man from Galilee was not God personally, nor did he in any sense exist before conception and birth, nor (probably) did he rise bodily from death, nor (certainly) can he be expected to 'come to be our judge'. But his life was a supreme revelation of godliness, and facing it mediates the touch of God to us with unique effectiveness.

This justifies worship of him. The fact that John and other New Testament writers speak differently is dealt with by urging that their authority lies in their witness to Christian origins and experience in a general way rather than in the particular way they put it into words. That was conditioned by their culture; so that once we have taken the measure of their experience and sense of things, we are free to express it in different words and concepts if we think they fit it better. In this case, what they are telling us, and what we need to be carefully picking up from them, is the impact of Jesus; but we are not obliged to endorse their first-century notions of who he was.

Space prohibits full and fair dealing with any one exponent of this 'humanitarian' Christology, so it is best that we should name none of the current ones, notorious though some of them have become. Instead, we shall make some general comments on this approach, as it has been developed from Friedrich Schleiermacher, the 'father of liberalism', who died in 1834, up to the present day.

First, what has given rise to it? Three factors operating together. The first is a habit of not treating the teaching of biblical writers as divinely revealed truth. Secondly, an interest in feelings and experiences which is a spin-off from the Romantic movement in European culture, and which has prompted folk to try to imagine what it felt like to be Jesus. This is a psychological question, reflecting concerns which New Testament writers do not manifest or help us much to pursue, and one wonders how far they are worth pursuing; but certainly, for many today one test of the adequacy of an account of Jesus is that it makes him psychologically comprehensible. This obviously favours 'humanitarian' Christology; to envisage a godly man's state of mind is practicable in a way that mapping the consciousness of God incarnate could hardly be.

The third factor, following from the second, is a recoil from Chalcedonian Christology; not just because it uses elusive philosophical terms ('nature', 'substance', 'entity'), but chiefly because (so it is argued) it cannot properly recognize Jesus' humanness, and so is in effect Docetic. Now it is true that some Fathers who went about the Chalcedonian way talked with maximum awkwardness about Jesus 'suffering impassibly', and divided out his experiences between his divine and human natures in a way that is quite impossible (hereby deferring to Greek rather than to biblical ideas of God). It is also true that some latter-day Chalcedonians, deprecating the smell of Docetism, have felt it needful to adopt the 'kenosis' theory, which speculates – that is, guesses – that for the Son to experience human limitations properly he had to abandon some divine powers when becoming man.

But the conviction now being discussed goes further: its burden is, quite simply, that only human persons have human experiences, and the idea of God having them is impossible. (Which begs the whole question of the incarnation! – although to many professed Christians it has none the less seemed a self-evident truth.)

Other modern dogmas have favoured humanitarian Christology: the anti-supernatural 'scientific worldview', for which incarnation was inadmissible; the evolutionary outlook, for which incarnation was an intrusion; and the scepticism of biblical historians who severed the Christ of apostolic faith from the Jesus of history and then reconstructed the latter by eliminating the miraculous from the gospel story.

But insuperable difficulties dog this Christology in all its forms. Not only does it involve in general terms a painfully low view of biblical authority, apostolic intelligence and two millennia of Christian devotion; it also invites particular objection along at least the following lines.

First, in relation to Jesus himself, humanitarian Christology calls in question not only his godhead but also his goodness. We must insist, in face of the common inability of 'humanitarians' to see it, that no view of Jesus as a uniquely God-filled, God-possessed man can ever amount to faith in his deity, nor can it function as an explanation of that faith. It is not an explanation of it, but an alternative to it. And we must also insist, in face once again of the inability of 'humanitarians' to see it, that the old dilemma, either he was God or he was not good (*aut Deus aut non bonus*), still applies. All the records (and it takes prodigies of special pleading to doubt them all) show Jesus conscious of divine sonship, claiming divine prerogatives as men's saviour and judge, and matter-of-factly demanding, expecting and accepting the unqualified trust and loyalty which by common consent are God's due alone. If he was not divine, we cannot avoid saying that he was deluded and (unwittingly, we assume) deluded others. This is compatible, no doubt, with perfect sincerity, but hardly with perfect goodness.

Secondly, in relation to the doctrine of God, the failure of the humanitarian view to distinguish the incarnation of the Son from the Spirit's indwelling a saint, and its reduction of the former to the latter, makes trinitarian faith impossible. The humanitarian view can be understood in either unitarian or binitarian terms, according to whether the Spirit's distinct personality is affirmed or denied, but it cannot be understood in trinitarian terms because, though it affirms that God was in Christ, it denies that Christ was personally divine. So the whole biblical picture of God in three persons fulfilling a saving purpose in which the incarnate Son has the key role as mediator – God for humanity and human for God, bringing God and humanity out of estrangement into fellowship – will have to be redrawn. The loss is surely as intolerable as it is inescapable.

Thirdly, in relation to the doctrine of grace, non-acknowledgment of Jesus as God incarnate requires a redefining of the gospel. The best we can now say is that by his example of faith and faithfulness, his moral and spiritual trail-blazing, and the impact of his teaching and character, Jesus (the figure in the Gospels) moves us to imitate him. (Which, as it stands, is moralism, luring us back into the world of justification by works.) What we can never now say is that Jesus' death is God propitiating his own wrath against our sins, and that Jesus' resurrection is God arising to bring us pardon and peace, and to raise us from spiritual death to new life in fellowship with himself.

So salvation is not of the Lord, nor is Jesus the object of faith, in the sense that we once thought; and prayer to Jesus as distinct from the Father seems improper, while talk of Jesus as our present help and hope must be hyperbolical. But that is a terrible impoverishing of the gospel, indeed a destruction of it, for there is no gospel left. Here again, the loss which is inescapable is also intolerable.

Fourthly, in relation to Christian experience, and also to the God-given Scriptures which shape that experience, the witness of the Holy Spirit leads away from humanitarian Christology to something higher. G. W. H. Lampe asks 'what Christians mean when they claim to "encounter Jesus Christ",' and puts alternatives. Would they say

that they encounter, here and now, or are encountered by God, the Spirit who was in Jesus, meeting them with the identical judgement, mercy, forgiveness and love which were at work in Jesus, inspiring and recreating them according to the pattern of Jesus; and that they worship God, the Spirit who was in Jesus ...? Or would they, rather, assert that in their experience Jesus of Nazareth, the man fully possessed by the Spirit and thus united with God, meets them from the other side of death? Or must Spirit Christology after all give way at this point to the concept of the incarnation of the pre-existent divine being, the Logos/Son?[35]

Surely the Christian consensus, today as yesterday, is that the first analysis is incomplete, because it is Jesus personally, the Jesus of the Gospels, whom we meet; that the second analysis is uncouth, because it is precisely of Jesus as divine saviour, calling for our faith and worship, that we are made aware; and that nothing less than acknowledging Jesus as God's pre-existent Son will express the sense of reality in the Spirit-taught heart. But when the speculations of theologians contradict the Spirit's witness to worshippers, it is time to call a halt.

Christ unchanging

It is not the case that by contrast with humanitarian Christology the incarnationalism of the New Testament and of Chalcedon is problem-free; though whereas humanitarianism ran into trouble through its deep disharmony with Scripture, the problems of incarnationalism concern only the 'how' of the biblically declared reality.

Here are three sample problems: how does the Son uphold the universe (Heb. 1:3; Col. 1:17) while living within the limits of his humanity? – for that humanity, though glorified, remains human and therefore limited still. Again, how could temptation and moral conflict have been real for Jesus when the Son, being God, cannot sin? And how could Jesus truly not have known the time of his return (Mark 13:32), when as divine Son he was omniscient? Our life of faith does not necessitate our knowing the answer to these or any similar questions, and the full answers are likely to exceed our mind's reach anyway. None the less, the questions are real and not improper, and a quick comment on each may be ventured.

On the first: are we entitled (God being God) to assume that because the fullness of a divine-human personal life appears in Jesus, therefore the Son now does all his work through his humanity? Surely not. We simply do not know. And if it worries us that we cannot imagine how the Son has upheld the universe since the incarnation, we should remind ourselves that we cannot imagine how he did it before the incarnation either. The whole matter is too high for us.

On the second: is it not a matter of experience that often the person least likely to yield to temptation is most sensitive to it, and has what feels like the hardest and most sustained battle with it?

On the third: kenoticists (those who, as we saw, understand the Son's self-emptying at the incarnation as involving loss of powers as well as of glory) suggest that omniscience was given up at the time of the incarnation; but surely omniscience should be defined as power to know all that one wills to know, and the Son's ignorance be explained in terms of the fact that he never willed to know by supernatural means more than he knew that his Father willed him to know. If he knew that his Father did not wish him to have in his mind the date of his return, that settled it; the knowledge was not there. The Son, being Son, knows, just as he acts, in dependence on the Father, never on his independent initiative.[36]

To say these things, however, is to point up a further question. If the personal subject whom we know as Jesus is in his true identity Son of God, co-creator and upholder of all things, is it possible, in the nature of the case, for him to be a man in the full sense? The Chalcedonian tradition proclaims him as one person, and that must mean one personality, and that must mean one centre of consciousness, one subject-self, one psychological ego.

So Chalcedonian incarnationalism must imply that Jesus' knowledge of himself as 'I', a distinct personal subject, involved knowing himself as divine. But is it not essential to true humanness to know that one is not God, however vividly aware of God one may be? How then can Jesus be genuinely human?

In reply, note first that this is not a new question. Older exponents of Chalcedon have faced it. Their line was to define the Son's humanity as precisely a set of qualities and capabilities for experience, both passive and active, the acquiring of which conditioned his entire personal life. The Son's humanity, once acquired, never was and never will be 'switched off', or laid aside in the way kenoticists think divine powers were laid aside when the Son took flesh; yet this humanity was and is, so to speak, adjectival to the person whose it is, and who lives for ever in the consciousness of his identity as God's Son.

The thought is that the self-awareness – that is, the being-present-to-oneself that comes with awareness of other realities – which began to crystallize in the mind of Jesus as baby and toddler, and which developed, as it does in us through adolescence into adulthood, had in it from the start awareness of a unique relationship, not just potential but actual, between himself and the ultimate Person, a relation of dependence within co-eternity, of subordination within co-equality, and of filial obedience within total mutual love.

No doubt Jesus stood in need of that knowledge of objective facts which comes through temporal and bodily existence in the world with other selves and things, and grew and developed in that knowledge, as indeed Luke 2:52 affirms. No doubt he gained his mature understanding of the kingdom and service of God, and of his own mission as Son of Man and servant-Messiah from commerce with the Scriptures (everything in the records suggests that), and so may rightly be said to have lived by faith (rather than vision, or immediate revelation, as older thinkers tended to say) so far as his vocation was concerned. (Is it wrong to see Jesus' going to a foreseen death in Jerusalem as an act of faith that the Father would then raise him, by willing him to raise himself, from the dead? Surely not.) No doubt too, although supernatural modes of knowledge at a distance, knowledge of men's secret thoughts, and knowledge of the future and of the past, were available to him,[37] no more came into his mind by these means at any time, as we said earlier, than his Father wished him to be aware of, so that while on earth he never knew all that he could have known, had the Father so willed, and was sometimes ignorant of matters of a kind which at other times he knew supernaturally.[38] But for all that, the sense of being God's Son related to his Father in an abiding fellowship of love in which each glorifies the other[39] was always in his mind, as it was expressed in all that he did.

Therefore Chalcedonians have usually said that Jesus, the Word-made-flesh, was man generically and qualitatively, but not 'a man' in the sense of an individual human being with a creaturely identity, and they have wed the technical terms 'hypostatic union' and 'enhypostasia' to express the thought that Jesus' manhood exists only as the manhood – that is, the sum of human characteristics – of the divine person who is God's eternal Son. And in voicing this thought they certainly have the backing of the apostle John! Any alternative position would be open to the criticism of not taking the Fourth Gospel seriously enough. (That some distrust John's Gospel these days is true, but not in our view good, for their scepticism is not adequately justified nor, we think, adequately justifiable, by argument.)

Of course, if in calling Jesus 'a man' we mean only to say that no constituent human quality was lacking to him, without raising the question whether his demonstrable dependence on and submission to the Father reflected a consciousness of creaturehood or not, there is no reason why we should not do it; the usage described in the previous paragraph was developed to make a different point.

Does this line of thought really impair the full humanity of our divine Lord? Not if we understand personhood and personality in the modern and, surely, correct way – that is, in terms of relatedness to other realities. If Jesus was related to the Father in terms of co-eternity, co-equality and co-creatorship, then he was a divine person. If his experience of relatedness to things and people – experience, that is, of thinking, feeling, choosing, giving, receiving; of being hungry, hurt, excited, tired, disappointed; of being aware of the opposite sex, and so on – corresponded in a fundamental and comprehensive way, not indeed to ours as it is, under sin's taint, but to what ours and Adam's would have been had the fall not happened, then he was a human person. Both things are true so we speak of him as a divine-human person. Is there really a problem here? I think not.

Bonhoeffer's question 'Who is Christ for us today?' could be taken as a plea for Christological novelty, as if only a novel account of Jesus Christ could catch men's ears today. Certainly, in our time much Christological novelty has been provided – in the reduced Jesus of humanitarianism, the revolutionary 'political Christ' drawn by some, and the concept of Christ as a principle of evolution which we find in Teilhard de Chardin, to look no further. But this essay has sought to commend the conviction that the Christ of whom the modern West, with its vast problems and growing alienation from its Christian roots, most needs to hear is precisely the Christ of the New Testament and of historic Christian teaching – the incarnate Son of God who lives, reigns, judges and saves; the Christ who prompts the confession, 'My Lord and my God' (cf. John 20:28).

For what, after all, are the world's deepest problems? They are what they always have been, the individual's problems – the meaning of life and death, the mastery of self, the quest for value and worth-whileness and freedom within, the transcending of loneliness, the longing for love and a sense of significance, and for peace.

Society's problems are deep, but the individual's problems go deeper; Solzhenitsyn, Dostoevsky or Shakespeare will show us that, if we hesitate to take it from the Bible. And Jesus Christ the God-man, who is the same yesterday, today and for ever, still ministers to these problems in the only way that finally resolves them. 'Him we proclaim,' says Paul long ago, 'warning every man and teaching every man in all wisdom, that we may present every man mature in Christ.'[40] It is for us, his late-twentieth-century servants, to proclaim him still, for the same end.

'The old converted slave-trader' opened this essay for us with words of theological warning. Now let him close it, leading us this time into doxology and devotion.

> Jesus! my Shepherd, Husband, Friend,
> My Prophet, Priest, and King;
> My Lord, my Life, my Way, my End,
> Accept the praise I bring.

Weak is the effort of my heart
And cold my warmest thought;
But when I see thee as thou art,
I'll praise thee as I ought.

Till then I would thy love proclaim
With every fleeting breath;
And may the music of thy name
Refresh my soul in death.

Questions for study

1. What are Packer's reasons for arguing for the centrality of Christ to the Christian faith?
2. Packer notes a concern expressed by Francis Schaeffer concerning the word 'Jesus'. Write down, in your own words, the basic anxiety which Schaeffer identifies. How does Packer evaluate this concern? And what response does he offer?
3. According to Packer, Jesus Christ 'is the yardstick at the level of motivation and attitudes of what it means to be fully human'. Locate this quotation, and study it in context. What does Packer mean by this? And what justification does he offer for it?
4. The address is framed by a hymn written by John Newton. What point does Packer make by enclosing his lecture in this manner?
5. What do you think that Packer would want his audience to do as a result of hearing this lecture?

Notes

1. Scholars vary in their understanding of Jesus' attitude to the Old Testament, but Rudolf Bultmann's statement seems to hit the nail on the head: 'Its authority stands just as fast for him (Jesus) as for the Scribes, and he feels himself in opposition to them only in the ways he understands and applies the Old Testament.' *Theology of the New Testament*, London: SCM Press, 1952, vol. 1, p. 16. For extended discussion, see John W. Wenham, *Christ and the Bible*, London: Tyndale Press, 1972.
2. In this connection it is worth recalling C. S. Lewis' trenchant words to theological students in *Fern-seed and Elephants*, London: Fontana, 1975, pp. 105–106.
3. Maurice Wiles urges that 'any theology that emerges out of a serious attention to the Christian tradition has a *prima facie* claim to being considered a Christian theology' (*Working Papers in Doctrine*, London: SCM Press, 1976, p. 192). But to be Christian, a

theology must do more than engage with Christian themes; it must make recognizably Christian affirmations.

4. Cf. Rom. 1:18–21, 28, 32; 2:12–15.

5. 'The watershed of the Resurrection led to the discovery by the Church of the continuing impact of the risen Lord, different in idiom but identical in impact with his fellowship with the disciples during his earthly life' (H. E. W. Turner, *Jesus the Christ*, London: A. R. Mowbray, 1976, p. 109).

6. Cf. 2 Tim. 4:17–18; 2:7, etc.

7. Cf. Acts 7:59–60; 22:7–21; 2 Cor. 12:8–9; Heb. 4:14–16.

8. John 14:13–14.

9. *Epistolae* X.xcvi.

10. Dietrich Bonhoeffer, *Letters and Papers from Prison*, enlarged edition, ed. Eberhard Bethge, London: SCM Press, 1971, p. 279.

11. Francis Schaeffer, *Escape from Reason*, London: IVP, 1968, pp. 78–79.

12. Current interest in the development of traditions within the Bible, and the pluriformity of Scripture as we have it, tends to obscure the solid achievement of the 'biblical theology' movement in exhibiting the inner unity of the scriptural message. Among books embodying this achievement are E. C. Hoskyns and F. N. Davey, *The Riddle of the New Testament*, London: Faber, 1931; A. M. Hunter, *The Unity of the New Testament*, London: SCM Press, 1943; H. H. Rowley, *The Rediscovery of the Bible*, London: James Clarke, 1945; *The Unity of the Bible*, London: Carey Kingsgate, 1953; A. G. Hebert, *The Bible from Within*, Oxford: Oxford University Press, 1950; Oscar Cullmann, *Christ and Time*, London: SCM Press, 1950; Alan Richardson, *Introduction to the Theology of the New Testament*, London: SCM Press, 1958.

13. John A. T. Robinson, *Redating the New Testament*, London: SCM Press, 1976.

14. On John, the following extract from C. S. Lewis is worth pondering: 'Turn to *John*. Read the dialogues: that with the Samaritan woman at the well, or that which follows the healing of the man born blind ... I have been reading poems, romances, vision-literature, legends, myths, all my life. I know what they are like. Of this text there are only two possible views. Either this is reportage ... pretty close up to the facts ... Or else, some unknown writer in the second century, without known predecessors or successors, suddenly anticipated the whole technique of modern, novelistic, realistic narrative. If it is untrue, it must be narrative of that kind. The reader who doesn't see this has simply not learned to read.' *Fern-seed and Elephants*, p. 108.

15. Cited from J. B. Harford and F. C. Macdonald, *Handley Carr Glyn Moule*, London: Hodder and Stoughton, n.d. [1922?], p. 294.

16. C. S. Lewis, *Fern-seed and Elephants*, pp. 110–111.

17. Among the best surveys of the material are B. B. Warfield, *The Lord of Glory*, Grand Rapids: Baker, 1974 [1907]; A. E. J. Rawlinson, *The New Testament Doctrine of the Christ*, London: Longmans, 1926; Vincent Taylor, *The Person of Christ in New Testament Teaching*, London: Macmillan, 1958; Oscar Cullman, *The Christology of the New Testament*, London: SCM Press, 1959; Leon Morris, *The Lord from Heaven*, London: IVF, 1958.

18. Cf. Acts 2:36; 9:22; Matt. 16:13–17.

19. G. W. H. Lampe writes of 'the two-way assertion implied by the credal confession, "Jesus Christ is LORD": that Jesus is the Messiah and the Messiah is none other than the man Jesus ... the same Jesus who was known before his death ... the title "LORD" signified the exaltation of Jesus to God's throne (Ps. 110:1). Against the background of its application to the patron and saviour deities of Hellenistic personal religion, on the one hand, and its reference in the Hebraic tradition to the Lord God, on the other, "LORD" expresses the conviction that Jesus uniquely mediated God's authority, that he transcended the category of ordinary humanity, and that he stood, as it were, on the side of God over against all other men, as one who exercised God's sovereignty over them.' *Christ, Faith and History*, ed. S. W.

Sykes and J. P. Clayton, Cambridge: Cambridge University Press, 1972, pp. 111–112.

20. Cf. Matt. 26:63; Acts 9:20–22.
21. Cf. John 1:18; 14:9; Heb. 1:1 – 2:4.
22. Cf. John 1:1–18; Eph. 1:9–10; Col. 1:15–20; Heb. 1:2–3.
23. Cf. Mark 1:9ff.; 9:7; 12:6; 13:32; Matt. 11:27; Luke 2:49.
24. Acts 4:12. So John A. T. Robinson writes that the Christian 'judges that empirically it is true that no one comes – or has come – to the *Father*, that is, to God conceived in the intimacy of "abba," but by Jesus Christ. Jeremias is justified in calling this one of the distinctive marks of Christianity. Certainly it is not true of Moses or Mohammed, Buddha or Vishnu, Confucius or Lao Tzu.' *The Human Face of God*, Cambridge: Cambridge University Press, 1973, p. 222.
25. 1 Tim. 1:1; cf. Eph. 2:11–13.
26. Col. 1:27.
27. For 'new birth' see John 3:3–8; Jas. 1:18; 1 Pet. 1:3, 23, and for 'co-resurrection with Christ' Eph. 2:4–6; Col. 2:11–13; 3:1; cf. Rom. 6:5–13.
28. Rom. 8:18–23.
29. Cf. Eph. 1:9–10.
30. John 4:34.
31. Act 9:1–22; Luke 19:1–10.
32. *Exousia*: Matt. 28:18.
33. See John 5:26–29; Acts 17:31; Rom. 2:5–16; 2 Cor. 5:6–10 and Heb. 9:27.
34. Cf. Col. 1:15–17; Heb. 1:2, 6.
35. Lampe in *Christ, Faith and History*, pp. 129–130.
36. Cf. John 5:19.
37. Cf. for knowledge at a distance, Matt. 17:24–27; Mark 11:2; 14:13f.; John 1:48–49; for knowledge of men's secret thoughts, Mark 2:6–8; Luke 9:46–47; John 2:24; for knowledge of the past, John 4:17–18; for knowledge of the future, Mark 13:6–83; John 13:19; 14:29; 21:18–19.
38. Cf. Mark 5:30 with John 1:47–48.
39. Cf. John 17:1, 4–5.
40. Col. 1:28.

10. 'Is Christianity credible?' (1981)

What reasons may be given for asserting that Christianity makes sense? This question is of fundamental importance to Christian apologetics, which may be thought of as that aspect of Christian theology which seeks to set out and demonstrate the credibility and plausibility of the Christian faith.[1] C. S. Lewis was, of course, an acknowledged master of this type of writing; Packer's high regard for Lewis is a matter of record, and will be considered further in the sixteenth and final essay in this volume. Yet Packer himself did not regard apologetics as a matter which demanded his full attention. The 1981 essay 'Is Christianity Credible?' is therefore of especial importance and interest, as it indicates Packer's general approach to this matter.

The value of Packer's essay can be seen as lying in two distinct, yet related, matters. First, Packer sets out clearly some – by no means all! – of the reasons Christianity makes sense. He notes in particular four tests: 'historical objectivity', 'rational coherence', 'explanatory power', and 'individual experience'. Each of these merits careful study, as does Packer's argument that it is the cumulative force of all four, rather than as individual items, which is of decisive importance. Second, however, Packer notes limitations in the scope of apologetics. Who, he asks, has the right to decide what is 'credible' and what is not? Is not apologetics ultimately – like revival – the work of the Holy Spirit, rather than of human ingenuity?

173

Is Christianity credible?

I

In the same way that beauty is in the eye of the beholder, so questions sound different in different ears, according to what each hearer brings to them. When the Editor asked me for a contribution to the 'Is Christianity Credible?' series, he almost apologized that the question sounded defeatist and reductionist. But to me it did not sound like that at all; it came, rather, as a welcome opportunity to say two things which in these days I find myself wanting to shout from the housetops. The first thing is that the intellectual credentials of thorough-going Christianity are very strong, much stronger than is often allowed, and it is only when Christians cease to be thorough-going that their faith ever sounds or looks forlorn. When it feels forlorn and dubious (and I suppose all Christians know such feelings on occasion), it is because, for whatever reason, relevant facts are not making their proper impact.

The second thing is that if thorough-going Christianity be thought incredible, it is a case of pots calling the kettle black, for the rival convictional systems which present themselves are less credible still. Scepticism, solipsism and nihilism, being philosophies of ultimate negation, cannot be refuted in the ordinary way, but can yet be shown to be paradoxical and unnecessary, while affirmations of alternative absolutes, Marxist, humanist, Freudian or whatever, prove on inspection to be inadequate to fit all the facts. What I mean by 'thorough-going' I will try to say in a moment, but let me first state my conviction that the difficulties which much contemporary Protestantism finds in commending Christianity as a believable option for folk today spring directly from the way in which, following in the methodological footsteps of Schleiermacher, we habitually scale Christianity down so as to represent it to its cultured despisers as the fulfilment of their own best thoughts, instincts and longings. Scaled-down Christianities are both the fruit and the root of uncertainty, and the supposition that the less we commit ourselves to maintain the easier it will be to maintain it never proves true. To be sure, Schleiermacher did not see himself as reducing Christianity, but rather as interpreting and indeed rejuvenating it in the cultural milieu of his time; reduce it, however, he did by the anti-transcendent, anti-revolutionary, anti-trinitarian thrust of his phenomenalist method of theologizing, and the problem with both him and his spiritual descendants is that their reduced creeds (for each has his own) seem arbitrary to a degree. In every case the question presses: why, if this man believes so much, does he not believe more? but if he believes so little, why does he not believe less? Thinkers in this tradition who, like Schleiermacher himself, have not been muddle-headed (and there have been many such, whose mental rigour merits deepest respect – Ritschl, Harnack, Troeltsch, Wiles for starters) might well seek to parry the pincers effect of this double question by saying that what determined their conclusions was strict application of their method. But since each person's method is their personal mix of phenomenalism (learning what Christianity is by inspecting it as a human phenomenon) and positivism (sieving the witness to Christian origins through the meshes of a uniformitarian worldview), the problem of arbitrariness comes up again at a deeper level, where it is not so easily banished; for why embrace such methods in any form, when the revelation-claim that is integral to biblical religion points a different way? Stimulating notions and insights have certainly sprung from surveying Christianity by the light of Schleiermacherian methods, but the inescapable plurality of them has spawned so wide a range of diverse beliefs about Christian essentials (God, Jesus Christ, salvation) as to make anyone who wants to communicate Christianity to the wider world feel completely stymied. Looked at from this standpoint, the Schleiermacherian tradition of theological subjectivity has much to answer for.

It was, perhaps, no wonder that Karl Barth, in his zeal to speak the word of God and the reactionary passion of his love-hate relationship with Schleiermacher, not only refused to scale down what he took to be the biblical faith but rejected the whole apologetic enterprise of showing faith reasonable and unbelief unreasonable as a misguided exercise which leads only to truncated Christianities pandering to unbelievers' intellectual conceit and unable to follow Paul in diagnosing the world's wisdom as folly (1 Cor. 1 – 2). Barth's emphasis was timely and invigorating in the academic theological world of the twenties and thirties, where Kant's ghost still walked and the unholy league between idealist philosophy ('the rational is the real') and liberal theology ('what is real in Christianity is rational') still stood in older men's minds; had Barth not taken this line, the recovery of confidence in the biblical message which he sought to midwife might never have come to birth. But in the long term to have no apologetic – that is, no 'natural' or, as John Macquarrie urges us to say, 'philosophical' theology that roots the God-referring language and the God-affirming content of Christian faith in the world of everyday reality – makes against credibility no less than does the solvent effect of Schleiermacherian subjectivism. Paul van Buren's switch from

Barthianism, allegedly revelation-based but epistemologically uncertain, to the linguistic relativism, indeed scepticism, of *The Secular Meaning of the Gospel* is a cautionary tale showing what sort of recoil methodological contempt for philosophical theology may prompt.[1] Such contempt cannot establish credibility; rather the reverse.

II

What, then, will confirm credibility? By what tests can a faith like Christianity, a total world-and-life view, be shown to be believable? Four tests, at least, are relevant.

First comes the test of historical objectivity. Christianity in all its forms claims to be a faith based on historical events. It will not, therefore, be credible unless its factual historical assertions are based on cogent evidence, and not significantly undermined by contrary evidence. For two centuries now much western Protestant thinking about Christian origins has been shaped by the uniformitarian *a priori* wished on it in the name of Newton, plus the Romantic stress on the decisiveness of personal factors when men reconstruct and interpret the past, and it has become almost a shibboleth to say that everything important concerning Christian origins is shrouded in deep uncertainty. If that is just a way of saying that there is always some scholar around who will challenge his colleagues' claims, let the statement stand, for it is true; but if what is meant is that, this being so, nobody is entitled to be certain about Christian origins, I for one must demur. By 'cogent' evidence I mean evidence of the flow of events which prompts the conclusion (of the Sinai covenant-making, or Elijah's triumph at Carmel, or Jesus' bodily resurrection, or Paul's conversion, to take a selection of key items), 'however strange and mysterious, it must have happened, for what followed is inexplicable without it'. Without denying for a moment the findings of modern historiographical analysis about the complexity of historical judgments and the variety of cultural and presuppositional factors that enter into them, I wish to record my conviction that cogent evidence of this kind is in fact available to us, and supremely so in connection with the life, death and resurrection of Jesus Christ.

Second comes the test of rational coherence. Christianity in all its forms says that God the Creator transcends man's understanding, but insists in the same breath that what we know about him through revelation makes good sense. For credibility, substance must be given to this claim. So the various assertions made, historical, convictional and interpretative, of present realities under God must demonstrably hang together as a meaningful, workable and wise philosophy of life. Also, the logic of, and rules for, our speech about the incomprehensible Creator must be clearly explicable, as must our speech about human decisions and actions, which Christianity sees as both free and controlled, self-determined and overruled at the same time. These are the two areas where Christianity's logical coherence is, and in fact has always been, most suspect. Down the centuries, however, Christian spokespersons have set themselves to make evident the coherence that is claimed, and I judge that where Christianity is consistently formulated the job can still be done.

Third comes the test of explanatory power. As the higher can explain the lower, and the more complex the simple, but not *vice versa*, so one test for any position claiming, as all forms of Christianity do, to embody final truth about life is its power to account for actual human behaviour and states of mind, including denial or disregard of its own claims, and preference for other options. Also, it must give good answers to humankind's inescapable questions about life's meaning, purpose and value, including the question of what death means, both others' death and our own, and whether the certainty of death does not render life senseless – the question with which Woody Allen, surely the shrewdest and most serious comedian of our time, as well as perhaps the funniest, is confessedly preoccupied. I would maintain that consistent Christianity, with its radical doctrines of this life as a preparation for the next, and of sin as touching the mind no less than the heart, and of the working of God's wrath and grace side by side in our fallen world, does not lack credibility here either.

Fourth comes the test of individual experience in relation to the expectations which Christian claims raise – perhaps the most sensitive area of evaluation today. All versions of Christianity claim that personal knowledge of God through Jesus Christ is life-transforming: for people in Christ are new creatures, and response to the gospel fulfils human nature in such a sense as to transmute realistic acceptance of what comes (to which the only alternatives are fantasy and suicide) from stoical endurance into a life of love and happiness. On this basis, Christianity claims to be the truest humanism, by comparison with which godless prescriptions for living do not merit that name at all. Such claims invite and indeed require inspection of Christianity's track record over two millennia, and their credibility will depend in measure on the credibility of Christians past and present. But the biblical call to witness, and the old truth that the proof of the pudding is in the eating, make the inspection appropriate from every standpoint. When someone like Don Cupitt concludes that incarnational faith must be queried because its moral effects have been so largely bad, we may disagree with his judgment on the facts, but on the relevance of his appeal to them there can be no argument. Nor, surely, has a faith adorned by men like Origen, Augustine, Francis of Assisi, John of the Cross, Luther, Baxter, Wesley, John Newton, Hudson Taylor, George Müller, Sundar Singh, Charles de Foucauld and C. S. Lewis, plus countless lesser lights whose lives Christ has made new for all to see, anything to fear from this appeal. Nor (to anticipate an objection) are bad Christians a significant counterweight in this assessment; that people can profess Christianity without being transformed by it is not disputed; the question is, whether faith in Jesus Christ when taken seriously has a moral and spiritual transforming effect which is characteristic of it and is not naturally explicable in naturalistic terms. The devoted love of God and humanity, expressed in what might seem extravagances of prayer and service, in such lives as those cited seems to show quite decisively that it does, however many may profess faith while their lives and characters remain unchanged.

It should be added that the full force of Christianity's capacity to pass each of these tests will be felt only when related to its capacity to pass the other three also. The significance of these criteria of credibility is cumulative. If Christianity showed up badly in relation to any one of them, its credibility would remain uncertain, no matter how adequately it met the other three. But if, as I believe, it passes all four tests impressively, its overall credibility is established beyond doubt.

III

Now the question I begged when speaking of 'consistent' and 'thorough-going' Christianity must be faced. That I have in mind a particular understanding of essential Christianity which in my view passes the credibility test better than its rivals must by now be obvious; that I hold to it because of its supposedly superior apologetic strength (in other words, on grounds less rational than rationalistic) is a suspicion to which I may have laid myself open. So I turn to ask what procedures and criteria should decide for us what is an adequate account of authentic Christianity, where various accounts are canvassed and doctors disagree? At the risk of sounding old-fashioned and cavalier, I urge that the method which is in principle decisive is that which the 'biblical theology' movement of the past half-century has aimed to follow, the method sometimes described as reading the Bible from within. In its twentieth-century form it is a reaction against imposing on Scripture alien presuppositions, but in essence it is the method of much Patristic and all Reformation theology, updated for our times.

This method takes seriously the claims of biblical authors to be witnesses to and messengers from the living God of whom they speak. Intellectually, imaginatively and existentially it seeks to identify with their faith and to see reality through their eyes, not only because their meaning and thrust are otherwise likely to be missed, but also and basically because the truths about God which they voice and apply come from God himself and are the normative word through which he speaks to us here and now. Thus the method views the teachings of each biblical author as all Christians view the recorded sayings of Jesus Christ, and seeks to comprehend, relate and apply them in their character as divine instruction.

For various reasons this method is today under a cloud. It has been thought to be tied to Barth's biblical positivism and Christological hermeneutic (which, however, it would if followed consistently have amended). Some of its practitioners, by ignoring philosophical theology, have made it seem that the method confines us to articulating biblical thoughts in biblical language of uncertain logical status. In stressing that God speaks in and through Scripture, they have appeared to minimize the cultural gap between the Bible world(s) and ours, leaving the impression that the method itself is intrinsically insensitive and naïve at this point. We may query Dennis Nineham's belief that conceptual communication across a two- or three-millennia gap is not possible, but recent hermeneutical study has shown that getting into the mind of an Old Testament prophet or a first-century apostle is a very tricky business, and it is not clear that exponents of 'biblical theology' to date have sufficiently noted its complexity. As once James Barr convicted some of them of semantic naïvety, so now they are suspected of cultural naïvety, and also of theological naïvety, for not having done justice to the conceptual pluralism (not, I think, pluralism of substance, though some today argue otherwise) of the biblical material. But these shortcomings can all be corrected – as rigour in applying the method requires that they should be without any doubt being cast on the method itself.

Two of the conclusions to which this method leads may be stated here. The first is that acknowledgment of God as the self-revealed Triune Creator and Redeemer, and of Jesus Christ as our divine human mediator and sin-bearer, risen, reigning and in due course returning, and of salvation as a new reconciled relationship with God in which the believer has been made a new creature in Christ by the Spirit, are basic and indispensable elements in any adequate account of Christianity; for these things – not as Bultmannian myths, but as revealed truths – are the core of New Testament Christian belief. The second conclusion is that the criterion whereby to test our own theological theories must be this: would the New Testament writers, were they here today, recognize these constructions as being in line with what they themselves said? This is just a way of articulating the old truth that we must test all things by the written word. Thus the contents and boundaries of thorough-going Christianity may be discerned.

IV

One last word in this all-too-brief farrago. The question, 'Is Christianity credible?' prompts the retort, 'credible to whom?' If we are thinking of the person who does not yet believe, we should remind ourselves that in New Testament evangelism and exposition the Christian gospel is always presented as God's solution to our problem – the problem, that is, of our lostness, our separation from our maker through our sins – and the good news of the solution is preceded by the bad news of divine rejection set forth in the law under which we all naturally stand. In post-biblical Christian evangelism, whether by the apologetics of Athanasius (*Contra Gentiles* and *De Incarnatione*) or Savonarola or Luther or Baxter or Whitefield or Wesley or Spurgeon or John Sung or Billy Graham, this pattern of exposition has regularly been followed, for it is observable that the dawning of a sense of personal spiritual need makes a vast difference to one's capacity to find the gospel believable. When at Corinth Paul resolved to stick to plain unvarnished proclamation of Christ crucified, 'not in plausible words of wisdom, but in demonstration of the Spirit and power, that your faith might not rest in the wisdom of men but in the power of God' (1 Cor. 2:4–5), it looks as if this was precisely his strategy; he looked to the Spirit to make folk realize that the needs of which he spoke were real for them, and the crucified Messiah whom he proclaimed was God's merciful provision for them. We should not forget that through the Spirit there is self-evidencing, convincing force in the gospel, over and above the force of any arguments to confirm its credibility; and that the New Testament approach to the problem of human incredulity is not that the gospel needs to be changed from one generation to another so as to make it more believable, but that human beings in every generation need to be changed by the Holy Spirit so that they may be able to believe it as undoubtedly God's truth. So in seeking to commend Christianity as credible to unbelievers we should not stop short at going over the kind of thing covered in this essay; we should speak to them also, and very fully, of the spiritual predicament of humankind and the abiding problem of unforgiven, unmastered sin, and we should look to the Holy Spirit as we do so to work once more as he worked in Corinth long ago.

Questions for study

1. What limitations does Packer identify in relation to apologetics?
2. Packer identifies four areas in which Christianity has credibility. Set out, in your own words, what he means by each. Which do you regard as being the most persuasive?
3. Locate this citation within the text: 'it is observable that the dawning of a sense of personal spiritual need makes a vast difference to one's capacity to find the gospel believable'. What does Packer mean by this? And what are the implications of this observation for Christian apologetics, according to Packer?
4. Find this quotation, and study it within its context: 'We should not forget that through the Spirit there is self-evidencing, convincing force in the gospel, over and above the force of any arguments to confirm its credibility.' What does Packer mean here? How important do you think this insight is in relation to apologetics?

Notes

Preamble

1. For an introduction to this aspect of theology, see Alister McGrath, *Intellectuals Don't Need God and Other Modern Myths: Building Bridges to Faith through Apologetics,* Grand Rapids, MI: Zondervan, 1993; United Kingdom edition published as *Bridge-Building: Effective Christian Apologetics,* Leicester: Inter-Varsity Press, 1992.

Essay

1. Paul van Buren, *The Secular Meaning of the Gospel,* London: SCM Press, 1963.

11. 'A modern view of Jesus' (1987)

In view of the centrality of Christ for the Christian faith, J. I. Packer has always taken the view that a loss of confidence in the orthodox understanding of the identity and importance of Christ is potentially disastrous for evangelism and Christian integrity. Picking up on a theme from the English writer W. H. Griffith Thomas (a former Principal of Wycliffe Hall, Oxford, and one of the founders of Dallas Theological Seminary), Packer argues that 'Christianity is Christ'. Having noted the centrality of Christ, Packer then proceeds to offer an analysis of some disturbing trends in modern western (and especially North American) Christianity which lead to an erosion of 'the deity, dominion and sole saviourhood of Jesus Christ', before offering a remedy to this situation.

Packer sets out a series of reasons for the observed erosion in the status of Jesus within modern western Christianity, including a misplaced confidence in the human ability to determine that status independent of the biblical witness. Common sense seems to rule. 'What seems to be assumed by all is that to say anything more about Jesus than that he was a fine man is to enter the realm of speculation, where no norms for thought exist, and no-one has any right to impose his or her views on anyone else.' This confusion and minimalism are typical of what Packer terms 'a modern view of Jesus'. It is important to note that Packer is critiquing a general trend in western Christianity, which has led to a 'massive drift into a lowered view of Jesus', rather than one specific modern view of Jesus – for example, that associated with a major writer.

Packer identifies four major factors within global Protestantism which have contributed to this trend. This is typical of Packer's approach to important theological issues: to sort things out, we need to know how we came to be where we are. In this article, as in so many of his writings, penetrating historical analysis precedes positive and concrete proposals for rectification. What is particularly interesting is Packer's identification of the widespread abandonment of the practice of learning catechisms as a significant contributing cause to doctrinal confusion. For example, consider Martin Luther's Shorter Catechism (1529), which includes the following question-and-answer sequence:

I believe in God the Almighty Father, Creator of Heaven and Earth.

Question: What does this mean?

Answer: I believe that God created me, along with all creatures. He gave to me: body and soul, eyes, ears and all the other parts of my body, my mind and all my senses and preserves them as well. He gives me clothing and shoes, food and drink, house and land, wife and children, fields, animals and all I own. Every day He abundantly provides everything I need to nourish this body and life. He protects me against all danger, shields and defends me from all evil. He does all this because of His pure, fatherly and divine goodness and His mercy, not because I have earned it or deserved it. For all of this, I must thank Him, praise Him, serve Him and obey Him. Yes, this is true!

Packer's point is that the theological education of children too often consists of little more than the recitation of Bible stories, without any firm grasp of the theological truths which underlie them.

Having noted these difficulties, Packer then proceeds to set out four ways in which belief in Christ may be rebuilt. It is important to note that each of these involves grasping the theological foundations which undergird the fully Christian understanding of his significance. Yet it must be appreciated that Packer does not believe that right belief is adequate; Christianity is about 'knowing Christ, which is more than just knowing about him'. Right belief about Christ must be complemented with personal fellowship with Christ. As Packer puts it: 'credence without this communion is only half-way to Christianity'.

Related works by Packer

'Jesus Christ the Lord', in J. R. W. Stott (ed.), *Obeying Christ in a Changing World*, London: Collins, 1977, pp. 32–60. (Essay 9 in this collection.)
'The Uniqueness of Jesus Christ', *Churchman* 92 (1978), pp. 101–111.

A modern view of Jesus

The late W. H. Griffith Thomas entitled one of his books *Christianity is Christ*. He was right; so it is. To describe Christianity as a creed plus a code would be more usual, but would not go so deep. That Christianity involves both a creed and a code is a truth that none should query. Where basic beliefs about Jesus are denied and Christian behaviour is not practised, Christianity does not exist, whatever may be claimed to the contrary.

But Thomas's point was that you can know the creed and embrace the code and still be a stranger to Christianity. Martin Luther, George Whitefield and John Wesley, to name but three, had to learn that through humbling experiences; so did I; and so have many more. For the essence of Christianity is neither beliefs nor behaviour patterns; it is the communion here and now with Christianity's living founder, the Mediator, Jesus Christ.

Stages of decline

Christianity proclaims that Jesus of Nazareth, the Galilean preacher, was a divine person, the incarnate Son of God. Christianity calls him 'Christ' because that is his official title: it identifies him as the long-awaited, God-appointed Saviour-King of mankind.

Christianity interprets the criminal's death that he suffered as fulfilling a divine purpose, the salvation of sinners. And Christianity affirms that after his death Jesus came alive again, in human flesh, mysteriously transformed, and has from that time been exercising full supremacy over the entire cosmic order.

Invisibly present to uphold us as we trust, love, honour and obey him, he supernaturalizes our natural existence, remaking our characters on the model of his own, constantly energizing us to serve and succour others for his sake.

When life ends, whether through the coming of our own heartstop day or through his public reappearance to end history with judgment, he will take us to be with him. Then we shall see his face, share his life, do his will, and praise his name, with a joy that will exceed any ecstasy of which we are now capable and that will go on literally for ever.

That is the gospel. It is indeed good news.

Being a Christian, therefore, is a matter of constantly reaching out to the invisibly present Saviour by words and actions that express three things: faith in him as the one who secured, and now bestows, forgiveness of our sins, so setting us right with the God who is his Father by essence and becomes ours by adoption; love for him as the one who loved us enough to endure an unimaginably dreadful death in order to save us; and hope in him as the sovereign Lord through whose grace our life here, with all its pains, is experienced as infinitely rich and our life hereafter will be experienced as infinitely richer.

It thus appears that Christianity is Christ relationally. Being a Christian is knowing Christ, which is more than just knowing about him. Real faith involves real fellowship. 'Our fellowship', explained the apostle John, 'is with the Father and with his Son, Jesus Christ' (1 John 1:3). Credence without this communion is only half-way to Christianity. Personal homage, trust and obedience Christ-ward are what finally count.

The Christian centuries have seen a vast company of believers who have shown that they understood this well, even when their official teachers were not stating it well. This knowledge of Christ sustained Christians in the catacombs and in the arena during 250 years of persecution before Constantine. This same knowledge upheld Protestant martyrs in Britain and Western Europe in the sixteenth century and the persecuted Puritans, Covenanters and Huguenots of the seventeenth. This knowledge has supported missionaries, who have been laying down their lives for Christ since the days of the Jesuit pioneers, and countless thousands who have suffered for Christ in our time in Africa and behind the Iron Curtain.

What should we make, and what should we ask the world to make, of these heroic believers who remained so peaceful, patient and sweet through all they endured? Their secret was an open one; it's really no secret at all. They embraced Paul's certainty that nothing can separate us from the love of God that is in Christ Jesus our Lord (Rom. 8:38–39).

They took to themselves Christ's words to the church at Smyrna: 'Be faithful, even to the point of death, and I will give you the crown of life' (Rev. 2:10). By these assurances they died, as they had lived, in joy and triumph. Their faith in, and love for, their divine Saviour and their readiness to exchange the present life for a better one at his call are the authentic marks of Bible Christianity. This is the real thing.

Christ changing lives

Against the background of this supernatural, faithful heroism which demonstrates so fully the credibility of Christianity as stated, if you were told that many in the churches have come to minimize and even deny the deity, dominion and sole saviourhood of Jesus Christ, you would conclude that they were in a state of spiritual delirium of some kind.

But such is true; sleeping sickness of the spirit, with talking in the sleep, is in fact my own diagnosis of this state of affairs. Let me describe more exactly what I see.

For a century now, not just among outsiders but within Protestant bodies too, there has been a massive drift into a lowered view of Jesus as a good and godly man who is simply an inspiring example rather than an almighty Saviour. This trend has produced great confusion and weakness. Folk nowadays don't know what the truth is about Jesus. And if they were in a church (which most of them are not), they do not know what they would be expected to believe about him; for they see the clergy as confused on the subject, and many church people holding views about Jesus that are quite different from what their church professes.

What seems to be assumed by all is that to say anything more about Jesus than that he was a fine man is to enter the realm of speculation, where no norms for thought exist and no-one has any right to impose his or her views on anyone else.

A sad scene? Yes, very. How did it come to be? By stages thus.

Three centuries ago, Protestant intellectual culture – philosophical, scientific, literary and aesthetic – tugged loose from its historic moorings in Christian faith. Brilliant men shrank the thought of God smaller and smaller, distorting it in the process, and distorting belief about Jesus with it. That is why today's man-in-the-street has only out-of-shape notions about the Father and the Son, seen, as it were, through the wrong end of a telescope.

Specifically, the Reformers had proclaimed the sovereign Lord of scriptural faith, the God who says what the Bible says and who saves sinners through Christ by grace. But seventeenth-century Deists ruled out miracles and set a fashion of denying that God is Lord over his world, and in the eighteenth century the philosopher Kant set a fashion of denying verbal revelation, and nineteenth-century thinkers domesticated God as the power behind the universal evolutionary processes that they posited, and our own twentieth century has settled for a finite, kind-hearted, ineffective, suffering God, a kind of heavenly uncle whose good will makes no real difference to anything, a being who it is nice to think exists but who, ultimately, is not worth bothering about.

You have met this rather pathetic figure: he is the God in whom the average North American today believes.

Thoughts about Jesus shrank similarly. Seventeenth-century scepticism about miracles made the incarnation an embarrassment, and eighteenth-century scepticism about revelation reduced the words of Jesus from divine disclosures to something far less. Since the nineteenth century, Jesus has been viewed as a supreme instance of human religious development, who probably did not rise from the dead and certainly does not rule the world at present, but whose memory still has influence, as does that of Socrates or Winston Churchill. This, however, does not affirm Jesus' continuing personal ministry, but denies it. It says he was not God incarnate but was a man whom God indwelt, and that he is important to us as a sample of sainthood rather than as a supernatural Saviour from the guilt and power of sin.

This was bad enough, but four further factors in world Protestantism have made it worse.

First, the theological colleges and seminaries and, in Germany particularly, the theological faculties of universities, which prepare each generation of clergy for their life's work, have largely surrendered to this scepticism about Christ. They teach it to their students, who naturally swallow it neat and spread it in the churches where they serve.

Second, the so-called 'higher' biblical criticism (which is no more than the necessary attempt to find out when, where, how, by whom and why each book was written) has for more than a century been controlled by the anti-miraculous assumptions about God of which we spoke above. As a result, it has come to be thought, quite wrongly, that scientific scholarship has shown the untrustworthiness of much of the Bible and its Christ must hence be judged unscholarly.

Third, the practice of making children memorize catechisms stating Christian doctrine has fallen out of use. Modern Sunday schools mostly limit themselves to teaching Bible stories. Children thus grow up in the church without being drilled in its creed. They learn of Jesus as friend and helper without ever hearing that he is the second person of the Trinity, and so become adults to whom this fact is altogether strange.

Fourth, as the West's sense of human sinfulness has diminished and its awareness of other religions has intensified, the idea has taken root that Christianity is a mind-set and behaviour pattern that is seen in all good men, whatever faith or lack of faith they may profess; and that it is acquired by instinct and osmosis rather than instruction.

Since no-one knows about Jesus without instruction, this view would seem to imply that Jesus himself is not essential to Christianity. That, I suspect, is what many believe deep down, though few are bold enough to say it aloud.

With all these factors as part of the scene, it's small wonder that great companies of churchgoers today should think of God in a unitarian rather than trinitarian way, of Christ in terms of God-indwelt humanity rather than of incarnate deity, and of salvation in terms of being accepted through God's forbearance for trying to do right rather than of being forgiven through Christ's atonement for actually doing wrong. But it is tragic that we who inherit so rich a legacy of true faith, past and present, should have gone so far astray on matters so fundamental. It shows of course, that, as has often been said, God has no grandchildren; grace and wisdom do not run in the blood. No doubt the devil laughs at our lapses, but I hope that no-one else does. They are too serious for that.

Rebuilding belief in Christ

What this all amounts to is that in today's church historic Christian belief in Jesus Christ is like Humpty Dumpty: it has had a great fall, and now lies before us broken in pieces. Everyone picks up some of these, but few have them all or know what to do with those they have.

There is much genuine perplexity. Persons of good will who want to be Christians look to clergy and theologians for help, find them in disarray regarding the person and place of Jesus, and with some impatience and disgust, turn away from them to settle for their own private thoughts about the man from Galilee. Yet they know that these are no more than amateurish fancies and guesses, and they would be very glad if they could be given something surer and more definite.

So for their sake as well as that of others, we ask with some urgency: can Christian certainty about Jesus Christ be reconstructed? Can Humpty Dumpty be put together again? I think the answer is yes, and I move on now to offer guidelines for doing this.

1. Link the person of Jesus with his work

All accounts of Jesus Christ really answer two questions together: not just the question about his person (who he was, and is), but also that which concerns his work (what he did, and does). The first question is ontological, the second functional, and they are distinct; none the less, one's answer to the second is likely to affect one's answer to the first.

If, under the influence of scepticism about the Bible, one should limit Jesus' work to instruction (teaching God's will) and demonstration (of God's love and of godliness) and play down as unreal all thoughts of his present heavenly reign and future return to judge mankind, and reduce communion with him to being moved by his example, then one will lose nothing by reducing him to the status of a uniquely enlightened human being, a man who reflected God in a specially clear way. Such a non-supernatural view of Jesus will seem simple, sufficient and appealing.

But for sober Christians who heed the apostles' understanding of Jesus, and his own recorded understanding of himself, as sole mediator between God and men, our substitutionary sin-bearer on the cross, our risen Redeemer here and now and the one in whom and through whom we have eternal life it is a very different story. Such Christians give full weight to the New Testament depiction of Christ's salvation as a matter of literal union and communion with him here and hereafter; that the New Testament sees prayer and praise to Jesus as no less proper than praise and prayer to the Father; that the New Testament actually hails him as the living Lord who, alongside the Father, is personally

A Scripture record of Jesus

Sole mediator between God and men	John 14:6; 1 Tim. 2:5
Substitutionary sin-bearer	Mark 10:45; Matt. 26:28; Gal. 2:20; 3:13; Col. 2:13–14
Risen Redeemer	John 15:1–7; Eph. 1:19 – 2:10
Literal union and communion with him	John 14:1–6; Rom. 6:3–11; 2 Cor. 5:6–9; Phil. 1:20–23; Rev. 7:14–17
Prayer and praise to Jesus	Acts 7:59; Rom. 10:8–17; 2 Cor. 12:7–10; Rev. 5:12–12
Living Lord	John 1:1–14; 20:28–30; Rom. 9:5 KJV, NASB, NIV; Heb. 1:8
Personal fellowship with the risen Lord	Acts 9:4–6, 10–17; 2 Cor. 12:9; 2 Tim. 4:17; 1 John 1:3; cf. John 14:21–23; Rev. 1:17–18; 22:16

divine; and that in the New Testament, as in the Christian community since, personal fellowship with the risen Lord is a reality of experience.

Their conclusion is that to categorize Jesus as a God-indwelt man, now dead, is to fall grievously short, for such a Christ could not bring us the salvation that the New Testament proclaims.

Where the dimensions of salvation are diminished or obscured, there the New Testament account of Jesus' role as redeemer is likely to be scaled down to match. What else would you expect? This is the explanation for most of the poor Christology that the world has seen in our time.

2. Understand Jesus' identity in trinitarian terms

The one God is a complex unity, to whose personal life oneness and threeness are equally basic. For this unique and unparalleled fact the New Testament has no technical terminology, and it took Christians 300 years of debate before they learned to express and safeguard it by confessing one God in three persons, the Son and Spirit being one in essence with the Father.

But trinitarian thinking about God is found constantly throughout the New Testament, most strikingly so when Jesus explains that after his going to the Father 'another counsellor', the Holy Spirit, will come to replace him, and that through the Spirit's coming he himself will come to the disciples in personal presence. They will then know that they live in him (John 14:12–23; 16:5–28).

The New Testament writers see salvation as the joint work of Father, Son and Holy Spirit, the Father arranging it, the Son accomplishing and administering it, and the Holy Spirit applying it. Therefore if one denies the Trinity, the truth about salvation will inevitably be lost also. It is basic to Christianity, as distinct from all other world religions, always to think about God in trinitarian terms.

So rather than loosely referring to Jesus as 'God incarnate', as if unitarianism is true and 'Jesus' is a second role that the eternal Father has played, we should always describe him as 'Son of God incarnate'. For it was only the second person of the eternal three who took humanity to himself.

Among New Testament scholars today it is fashionable to maintain that passages like John 1:1–14; Philippians 2:5–7; Colossians 1:15–17 and Hebrews 1 – 2 affirm that the Son pre-existed before the incarnation only as a thought in the Father's mind, not as an eternal person distinct from the Father. Whether they see that this view denies the Trinity I do not know, but it does. It is so unnatural and forced as an interpretation, however, that we need not spend time discussing it here.

3. Do not soft-pedal Jesus' humanness

John's statement that the Word became flesh (John 1:14) means more than that he encased himself in a physical body. It means that he took to himself, and entered right into, everything that contributes to a fully human experience. From the moment he became a fetus in Mary's womb up to the present, human experience has been one dimension of the life of the Son of God, and will continue so for ever.

By virtue of what he experienced as a healthy first-century Jewish male before his death at thirty-three, he can now enter sympathetically into all human experiences, those of girls and women, sick folk, the aged, and addicts (for instance) no less than those of young males like himself (see Heb. 2:18; 4:15–16). Thus he is able to give to all the help towards right living that we all need.

The church has always known this. That is why such ideas as that Jesus really was not human (though he appeared to be), or that the incarnate Son had no human mind or will, have always been condemned as heresy. And that's why Christians have been constantly asking Jesus to help them in their struggles ever since the days of the apostles and constantly testifying that he does.

For more than a hundred years it has been argued that those who believe that Jesus' humanness is adjectival, so to speak, to his deity cannot take his humanness seriously. Such people believe that the deepest secret of his identity is that he is 'God plus', a divine person ontologically and experientially enlarged by his manhood rather than being 'man plus', a human person uniquely indwelt and enriched by God.

It is certainly true that believers in the incarnation have often trailed their coat at this point by talking as if there were some experience – the suffering of Calvary, for one – that Jesus went through 'in his humanity' but not 'in his deity'. But that idea should be replaced by the thought that the Jesus of the New Testament experienced everything in the unity of his divine-human person.

The true Christian claim at this point is that incarnation made direct entry into human frustration and pain possible for the Son of God, who then out of love actually entered in person into the agony of crucifixion and the greater agony of God-forsakenness (see Mark 15:34) in order to bear our sins and so redeem us. Never let this claim be played down.

4. Do not diminish Jesus' divinity

An unhappy speculation that has mesmerized many during the past century is the so-called 'kenosis theory' which suggests that in order to enter into a fully human experience of limitation, the Son of God at his incarnation forfeited his natural powers of omnipotence and omniscience; as a result, there were things that he wanted to do that he could not do, and mistakes due to ignorance could enter into his teaching. Four comments seem to be called for by way of reaction.

First, there is no hint of any such forfeiture in the Scripture.

Second, the suggestion seems to undermine Jesus' authority as a teacher and thus dishonour him.

Third, it raises a problem about Jesus' present heavenly life. If Jesus' exercise of the two abilities mentioned (the Son's natural power to do and know whatever he willed to do and know) is incompatible with a fully human experience, it would seem to follow that either – having in heaven resumed these powers – his experience is not now fully human, or, since his heavenly experience remains fully human, he has not regained these powers, and never will. I leave it to the proponents of the kenosis theory to struggle with this dilemma; it is not my problem, nor I hope yours.

Fourth, the natural explanation of the one bit of evidence from the Gospels cited in support of the theory – Jesus' acknowledged ignorance of the time of his return (Mark 13:32) – is that since the Son's nature is not to take initiatives (see John 5:19) but to follow his Father's prompting, his reason for not doing certain things, or bringing to conscious knowledge certain facts, was simply that he knew that his Father did not wish this done.

In other words, Jesus' human limitations should be explained in terms, not of the special conditions of the incarnation, but of the eternal life of the Trinity.

To follow these paths of thought is, I believe, to avoid the pitfalls that in our day threaten incarnational thinking. Then we will be led back out of confusion to regain a truly biblical faith in Jesus Christ. How we in our churches today need to do this! Surely there will be no renewal of life and power from God among us until we learn again to see the glory of Jesus Christ, our incarnate Lord! May God teach us all this lesson – soon!

Questions for study

1. 'Christianity is Christ relationally.' Locate this quotation in the text, and establish the context in which it is set. What does Packer mean by this?

And do you think that it allows him to distinguish between a notional faith and a fully relational faith?

2. How does Packer describe 'the God in whom the average North American today believes'? And what relevance does this have to the question of the identity of Jesus Christ?

3. Packer identifies four factors which he believes have led to a dilution of the traditional Christian understanding of the person of Jesus Christ. Set these out, in your own words. Which does Packer seem to regard as most important? Which do you think is the most significant?

4. In response to this weakening of the traditional view of Christ, Packer sets out four elements of a programme of recovery of confidence. Summarize each of these in your own words.

12. 'An introduction to systematic spirituality' (1990)

The relation between theology and spirituality has become one of the most hotly debated topics in theological education since about 1980, not least because of the experience of many seminary students who found theological education destructive of their personal faith.[1] On 9 March 1987, J. I. Packer delivered the commencement address at the Tokyo Christian Institute.[2] In this address, he noted a problem which he had encountered extensively in his educational ministry – that theology and Christian living all too often seem to go their separate ways, as if they have nothing to offer or learn from each other. Packer noted the tendency of many seminary students to declare that God was less real to them after their theological studies than he had been prior to them. So what had gone wrong? For Packer, one of the most significant failings of seminaries was that they failed to make any real connection between Christian theology and Christian living. College courses were too often one-sided, dealing with academic issues rather than questions of Christian living. The books of the New Testament were written to make disciples, not simply to convey Christian concepts.

The whole issue of the relation between theology and spirituality was one to which Packer had given considerable thought throughout his career as a theological educator. Although Packer was prepared to use the term 'spirituality', it is clear that he did not regard it as quite the *mot juste*. In his lectures at Trinity College, Bristol, during the 1970s, Packer had used the term 'spiritual theology' to refer to the general Christian discipline of 'conceiving and living the life of communion with God'. Although he glossed this with the term 'spirituality', Packer's fundamental position was that it was quite improper to treat 'spirituality' as something distinct from theology. 'Spiritual theology' concerned the proper application of systematic theology, and was not an independent discipline in its own right.

Perhaps Packer's finest statement of his views on spiritual theology are to be found in his inaugural lecture as the first Sangwoo Youtong Chee Professor of Theology at Regent College. The lecture, delivered in the college chapel on 11 December 1989, and published the following year, was entitled 'An Introduction to Systematic Spirituality'. The title itself is of significance, in that it immediately suggests a close connection between 'systematic theology' and 'spirituality' – a connection which the lecture proceeded to explore and explain.

Packer offered his audience a definition of spirituality as 'enquiry into the whole Christian enterprise of pursuing, achieving, and cultivating communion with God, which includes both public worship and private devotion, and the results of these in actual Christian life'. The definition included an emphasis on the application of truth to life, which Packer had long regarded as of vital importance. 'I have always conceived theology, ethics and apologetics as truth for people, and have never felt free to leave unapplied any truth that I taught ... To speak of the application of truth to life is to look at life as itself a relationship to God; and when one does that, one is talking spirituality.'

For Packer, spirituality was an integral part of theological education, especially for those who were called to pastor. 'We cannot function well as counsellors, spiritual directors and guides to birth, growth and maturity in Christ, unless we are clear as to what constitutes spiritual well-being as opposed to spiritual lassitude and exhaustion, and to stunted and deformed spiritual development.' But where do these norms come from? For Packer, the answer was clear – from systematic theology. But immediately, Packer qualified what he understood by that term, and specifically criticized as inadequate two influential understandings of the nature of that discipline, as practised in North America. For Packer, 'the proper subject-matter of systematic theology is God actively relating in and through all created things to human beings'. This leads to theology being seen as 'a devotional discipline, a verifying in experience of Aquinas' beautiful remark that theology is taught by God, teaches God, and takes us to God'.

The two models which Packer criticizes lack this distinguishing mark. In the first place, there is the view that the proper subject-matter of systematic theology is 'Christian feelings and ideas about God'. The New Testament is thus treated as the earliest example of Christians and feelings. Packer here delineates the general trajectory of liberal theology, from F. D. E. Schleiermacher through to Rudolf Bultmann and process thought. God's revelation has no cognitive content. For Packer, this was quite false and unacceptable. As it would almost certainly have been regarded as such by his audience, Packer felt no pressing need to continue his analysis of its weaknesses, and passed on to deal with the second approach.

According to this second view, the proper subject-matter of systematic theology is 'revealed truth about the works, ways and will of God'. This view places considerable emphasis on the authority of Scripture, which is seen as God's own didactic witness to himself. Packer had no difficulties with this view up to this point. His anxieties concerned the next stage in this process of doing theology – the argument that 'all the data about God that exegesis has established must be brought together in a single coherent scheme'. This was the common task of medieval writers prior to the Reformation, Protestant scholastic writers of the seventeenth century, and most of the theological writers of the evangelical theological renaissance since the Second World War. Packer's difficulties with this view did not relate to the need to ensure that the didactic content of Scripture should be brought together into a coherent whole, lacking contradiction. His anxiety had more to do with the possible consequences of such an approach.

> I question the adequacy of conceptualizing the subject-matter of systematic theology as simply revealed truths about God, and I challenge the assumption that has usually accompanied this form of statement, that the material, like other scientific data, is best studied in cool and clinical detachment. Detachment from what, you ask? Why, from the relational activity of trusting, loving, worshipping, obeying, serving and glorifying God: the activity that results from realizing that one is actually in God's presence, actually being addressed by him, every time one opens the Bible or reflects on any divine truth whatsoever. This ... proceeds as if doctrinal study would only be muddled by introducing devotional concerns; it drives a wedge between ... knowing true notions about God and knowing the true God himself.

There was therefore a need to bring systematic theology and spirituality together. 'I want to see spirituality studied within an evaluative theological frame ... I want to arrange a marriage, with explicit exchange of vows and mutual commitments, between spirituality and theology.'

That marriage can be seen in Packer's *Knowing God* and other writings. It can be argued to be a distinctive aspect of the Puritan tradition, so that Packer is urging a recovery of older insights at this point. But this is not the issue. Packer's concern is to ensure that 'knowing true notions about God' and 'knowing the true God himself' go hand in hand, with the one reinforcing the other. Theological students should not find that knowing more about theology impoverishes their spiritual development, or that deepening their love for God and personal relationship with him allows them to dispense with the need for critical theological reflection. The two could and should go together, as inseparable companions and friends.

In view of the immense importance of Packer's inaugural lecture of 1989, it is here reprinted for detailed study.

Related works by Packer

Knowing God, London: Hodder and Stoughton; Downers Grove, IL: InterVarsity Press, 1973.
'On Knowing God', *Tenth: An Evangelical Quarterly* (July 1975), pp. 11–25. (Essay 8 in this collection.)
'Knowing Notions or Knowing God?', *Pastoral Renewal* 6/9 (March 1982), pp. 65–68.
'Evangelical Foundations for Spirituality', in M. Bockmuehl and K. Burkhardt (eds.), *Gott Lieben und seine Gebote halten*, Basel: Brunner Verlag, 1991, pp. 149–162. (Essay 14 in this collection.)

An introduction to systematic spirituality

Speaking from a newly founded Chair, I find myself freed from one embarrassment only to fall into another. I have no great predecessors to overshadow me; on the other hand, I must try (as the theatrical people say) to 'create the part'. The responsibility is heavy. If I miscarry, the University may come to regret not only my election – an error which, at worst, can be left to the great healer – but even, what matters very much more, the foundation of the Chair itself.[1]

Thus C. S. Lewis began his inaugural lecture in Cambridge, in 1954, as the

University's first Professor of Medieval and Renaissance Literature; and I would make his words my own, merely substituting 'Regent College' for 'the University', as I launch out on this, my own inaugural discourse as your first Sangwoo Youtong Chee Professor of Theology. I, too, have a part to create. Lewis' next sentence was: 'That is why I have thought it best to take the bull by the horns and devote this lecture to explaining as clearly as I can the way in which I approach my work.' With that also I identify; I propose in what follows to sketch out my own approach to my future work in the Chee Professorship; and I hope you will not take it amiss if I start anecdotally, for I think I can get furthest fastest by doing that.

I

Molière was the Alan Ayckbourn of his day, and in one of his comedies a character discovers that he has been talking prose all his life, and never knew it. When he makes the discovery he is as pleased as Punch. Some years ago I made a similar discovery. A man said to me: 'These books of yours, they're all spirituality, aren't they?' Up to that moment I had never thought so; all my books had been commissioned for didactic, apologetic, evangelistic, or controversial purposes, as their titles show. ('*Fundamentalism' and the Word of God, Evangelism and the Sovereignty of God, God has Spoken, God's Words*, do not sound like the titles of devotional books, do they?) But when he said it I realized that he was right, and rejoiced accordingly. I should have known all along that I was writing spirituality, for the Puritan passion for application got into my blood quite early; I have always conceived theology, ethics, and apologetics as truth for people, and have never felt free to leave unapplied any truth that I taught, whether orally or on paper; and to speak of the application of truth to life is to look at life as itself a relationship with God; and when one does that, one is talking spirituality. So the man spoke the truth, and I remain grateful to him for helping me to appreciate what I was actually up to.

A definition of spirituality will help us at this point. I am using the word in its twentieth-century Christian sense, according to which it means, in the words of Henry Rack, 'enquiry into the whole Christian enterprise of pursuing, achieving, and cultivating communion with God, which includes both public worship and private devotion, and the results of these in actual Christian life'.[2] By spirituality, therefore, I mean the study of what Henry Scougal, in the title of his book which so helped George Whitefield, called 'The Life of God in the Soul of Man'; or, putting it another way, the study of godliness in its root and in its fruit. Prior to this century, spirituality went under a number of names: Roman Catholics called it ascetic theology, from the Greek *askēsis*, which means to practise some discipline or routine; the Puritans called it 'practical divinity', and also 'casuistical divinity', because so much of it had to do with 'cases', that is, specific problems and anxieties of conscience; mainstream Anglicans, from the seventeenth century onward, called it 'moral' or 'devotional' theology; the Orthodox have called it 'spiritual theology' or 'mystical theology' or, quite simply, 'spiritual life'.[3] Today, it is a field of specialist academic interest, with its own journals, books, editions of key texts, and professional conferences. It is also a focus of ecumenical, pastoral and devotional interest at lay level, hence the retreats, retreat centres, schools of prayer, and writings on the inner life that abound at the present time. All branches of the church are involved, and a great deal of wisdom is currently breaking surface. These may be lean days for some other of the church's endeavours, but they are good days for spirituality.

Back, now, to anecdote. When I came to join the Regent faculty in 1979 I was delighted to discover that my old friend Dr Houston, who when he approached me about the job in 1976 had been Professor of Interdisciplinary and Environmental Studies, had shifted his field of interest, was in process of becoming Professor of Spiritual Theology, as he is now, and had started teaching the courses on spirituality and prayer that he teaches today. I had come prepared to offer Regent my own foundation course on the theology of the Christian life that I had been teaching in a British theological college since 1970, but now there was no need. It is a pleasure to contemplate, and celebrate, Dr Houston's achievements in this field – his series of Classics of Faith and Devotion;[4] his recent book, *The Transforming Friendship*;[5] and the enormous influence that his classes and counselling have had on successive generations of Regent students. Regent has, in fact, set an example to other theological teaching institutions by its emphasis on spirituality, and its unwillingness that theology should ever be taught and learned in a way that, however much it enriches the head, impoverishes the heart. When people ask me, as they sometimes do, why I feel I belong at Regent, this emphasis on spirituality always bulks large in my answer.

What gives spirituality its special importance in the educational organism offered by Regent College? Regent is committed to two principles that mesh together – first, every-member ministry in the body of Christ; second, the priority of person over function (in other words, that what you are matters more than what you do and does in fact determine and delimit what you can do in ministry). Therefore, Regent people need wisdom and insight in the realm of spirituality for the following reasons at least:

First, as ministering servants of Jesus Christ we are required to be promoters and guardians of health and humanness among God's people, and we need spirituality for that. Let me explain.

When I say 'health', I am thinking of spiritual health, and when I describe us as its promoters and guardians I am remembering the Puritan pastors, who saw their calling precisely as that of 'physicians of the soul'. Now, a would-be physician is set at an early stage to study physiology, so that she will understand the healthy functioning of the marvellously complex unit that we call the human body, and so become fit to move on to pathology, where she learns of the many ways in which a body that is diseased, debilitated, or wounded can malfunction, and how to diagnose and treat these malfunctionings. A moment's thought makes it obvious that it has to be this way round. She cannot become competent in treating bad health till she knows what constitutes good health, and can plot a route for recovery of good health from the sick state in which she found her patient. In the same way, we cannot function well as counsellors, spiritual directors, and guides to birth, growth, and maturity in Christ unless we are clear as to what constitutes spiritual well-being as opposed to spiritual lassitude and exhaustion, and to stunted and deformed spiritual development. It thus appears that the study of spirituality is just as necessary for us who hope to minister in the gospel as is the study of physiology for the medical trainee; it is something that we cannot really manage without.

What has to be said about the need for spirituality in order that we may fulfil our calling as promoters and guardians of humanness is similar.[6] North American culture effectively lost God two generations ago; now, by inevitable consequence, it is in the process of losing man. What does it mean to be truly and fully human? The post-Christian world around us no longer knows, and is being sucked down into deep cultural decadence for lack of this knowledge. Biblical Christianity, however, still has the answer, if anyone is still willing to listen. The Bible proclaims that humanness is more than just having a mind and a body; it is essentially a personal and relational ideal, the ideal of living in the image of God, which means being like Jesus Christ in creative love and service to our Father in heaven and our fellow men on earth. When Scripture speaks of humans as made in God's image and thus as being God's image-bearer, what it means is that each human individual is set apart from the animal creation by being equipped with the personal make-up, the conscious selfhood, feelings, brains, and capacity for love-relationships, without which Christ-like holiness would be impossible; as it is impossible, for instance, for cats and dogs. But Scripture also speaks of the new creation of believing sinners, and defines this as the motivational and dispositional renewing of us in Christ by the Holy Spirit, and assures us that it is only through new creation that Christ-like holiness ever becomes actual.

We may state the matter this way: structurally, God's image in us is a natural given fact, consisting of the rational powers of the human self, as such; substantively, however, God's image in us is an ongoing moral process, the fruit and expression of a supernatural character change from self-centredness to God-centredness and from acquisitive pride to outgoing love – a change that only Christians undergo. So the conclusion of the matter is that the true and full image of God is precisely godliness – communion with God, and creativity under God, in the relational rationality and righteousness that spring from faith, gratitude to one's Saviour, and the desire to please and honour God and to be a means of helping others; and the true goal of life is to know and receive and co-operate with God's grace in Christ, through which our potential for Christ-likeness may be realized.

But who nowadays know this? Secular humanism, which pretty much controls the chief opinion-making institutions in our culture – the media, the press, the educational establishment, the arbiters of taste and fashion, all in fact except the church itself – does not know it; secular humanism may tolerate religion as a quaint private hobby for those who still want it, but deep down it rejects religion in any form as dehumanizing, a debilitating crutch that ideally no-one would need because we would all be able to stand on our own feet without it. The challenge to Christians, and particularly perhaps to Regent people, with our announced concern for integration of all life under God, is to show that Christianity – yes, old-fashioned, self-denying, God-fearing, sin-hating, Christ-honouring, Bible-believing, altruistic, monogamous, frugal Christianity – is the true humanism, making for the authentic fulfilment and contentment of human individuals.[7] But the making of this case is precisely a venture in spirituality, and without some study of spirituality we are not likely to do our job very well.

And then, secondly, in addition to needing some understanding of spirituality – that is, of how God draws people into deeper fellowship with himself in order that we can fulfil our purpose of witness and ministry, we need it also for our own spiritual well-being. Not since ancient Sparta have any people in any era shown such an obsessive concern for physical well-being as I observe on the West Coast of North America today. Have you, I wonder, been circularized as yet with a request to subscribe to *The Wellness Letter*, put out from California's Berkeley campus? Don't worry, friends, you will be, I am sure, before very long; I have been thrice, already. *The Wellness Letter*, which is all about physical and mental health, is a typical product of our times. Now, should not we who are Christians be as concerned about the quality of our relationship with God as the world is about the quality of its digestion and muscle tone? Surely the question answers itself: of course we should! But the resources we need for pursuing that concern are those provided by the study of spirituality.

It appears, then, that all Regent College's characteristic interests do in fact converge here; and for myself, as I have already indicated, I greatly value Regent's pioneer role in setting spirituality at the centre of the Christian curriculum, where it belongs.

II

'But wait a minute,' says someone; 'your praise of spirituality is all very well, and it's nice to hear, but are you not a theologian?' (Well, yes, that is what I am supposed to be.) 'And have you not been employed at Regent these past ten years as a teacher of historical and systematic theology?' (Yes, I have.) 'And is it not in your capacity as a theologian that you have been appointed to the Chee Chair, which has attached to it a trust deed requiring you to (this is a quotation) "specialize within the area of systematic, philosophical, historical or ethical theology"? and is not this your inaugural lecture in that Chair?' (Yes, yes, it's all true.) 'Well then,' says my questioner, 'haven't you rather wandered off the point?'

Have I? Let me tell you a story. Cricket, as you know, is England's national game, and the phrase, 'the Wars of the Roses', is kept alive in England to describe the intense rivalry that marks the annual games between the counties of Lancashire and Yorkshire. At one of these encounters an enthusiast from the South of England was watching Lancashire bat well before a Yorkshire crowd. He applauded several scoring shots, with cries of 'Well played,' 'Good stroke,' and so forth, oblivious of the stony silence around him. Then he felt a tap on his shoulder, and the shoulder-tapper said, 'Art tha Lancashire?' 'No,' said he. 'Art tha Yorkshire?' 'No, I'm from London.' 'Then, lad, this is nowt to do wi' thee: shut up.' Have I, like the man from London, strayed into a world of concern where I have no business to be, and where my expressions of enthusiasm do not belong? Should I, as a theologian, keep clear of spirituality? Frankly, I do not think so, and the next stage in my argument requires me to tell you why. In order to make my point, however, I need now to don my professional theologian's hat in an explicit way, and back up a bit.

What is the subject-matter of systematic theology, and what is the proper method for studying it? My argument requires that I now block in my position on this pair of questions with some exactness; and the best way, I think, for me to do that is to review with you at the level of principle the two views on the subject that are most commonly met in North American Protestantism.

The first view, stated in terms of principle, is this: the proper subject-matter of systematic theology is Christian feelings and ideas about God, and the proper way of studying this material is threefold. It is partly exegetical, treating the New Testament in particular as the earliest example of Christian feelings and ideas; it is partly historical, tracing the forms that Christian feelings and ideas have taken down the centuries; and it is partly critical, letting present-day beliefs and belief-systems call in question thoughts and attitudes that belong to the Christian tradition and to suggest alternatives. This has been the generic view of Protestant subjectivists for two centuries, from the historical mysticism of Schleiermacher to the individualistic existentialism of Bultmann and the process theologians' mythology of God the poor struggler. Its basis is the belief that God's revelation, whatever else may be true of it, has no cognitive content. Bible teaching may trigger off some awareness of God, understood in more or less impersonal terms and the immanence of the transcendent and the transcendence of the immanent, and also some veneration for the more or less misty figure of Jesus; but no part of the Bible is in any sense the uttered Word of our Creator telling us things about himself and us. All theologies are therefore necessarily relative, depending for their thrust and content on the private mind-set and selective preferences of the theologians who put them together, and we may expect as many different systematic theologies to emerge in the church as there are theologians to think them up. Theological pluralism, on this view, argues theological health.

As you can see, this view trivializes theology, reducing it to a learned exercise of the religious imagination which no-one is the worse for not bothering with. However, my reason for rejecting it is not that it is trivial, but that it is false. With Karl Barth, I affirm against it the reality of the God who speaks to us in and through Jesus Christ, using the words of Holy Scripture as his instrument. I go beyond Barth in affirming that the Bible is the Word of God intrinsically as well as instrumentally, and I insist that the authority of Bible teaching – the authority, that is, of the Holy Spirit speaking in Scripture, as the Westminster Confession puts it – is the authority of God himself, and specifically of Jesus Christ the Lord in person. And, though I do not join Barth in his denial of general revelation through the created order, I further affirm, as he also did, the total inability of the fallen human mind to think correctly about God, and gain true knowledge about him, apart from the instruction of Holy Scripture mediated by the illumination of the Holy Spirit. The first fact to be reckoned with, so I maintain, is the reality of the self-revealed, self-revealing God who in and through the Scriptures has spoken and still speaks to make himself known, and all accounts of the content and method of systematic theology that fail to do justice to this fact are to be rejected. Discard, therefore, view number one.

View number two is that the proper subject matter of systematic theology is revealed truth about the works, ways, and will of God, and that the proper method of studying it is twofold. The first task is exegetical. Treating the biblical material as God's own didactic witness to himself, given in the form of the didactic witness to him of the Bible writers, we are to draw from the canonical text everything we can find relating to the Creator, and receive it as pure truth from God's own mouth. This view and use of Scripture, the historic mainstream view of the Christian church,[8] comes to us directly from Christ and his apostles, who, as has often been shown, both modelled and taught it,[9] and its claims on our assent, as Christ's disciples, are just the same, and just as strong, as are the claims of any other teaching that was demonstrably given by the Master. Let me say, up to this point I am in comfortable agreement with this second view, and I hope you are too.

The second task for students, on this view, is synthetic. All the data about God that exegesis has established must be brought together in a single coherent scheme, just as a historian schematizes all his facts into a single flowing narrative, or scientists observing the love-life of frogs (or, shall I say, Masters and Johnson studying human sexual behaviour in the manner of scientists observing the love-life of frogs)[10] schematize their findings into a single analytical report. This, essentially, was what medieval theologians were doing with their data before the Reformation; this, essentially, is what the Protestant scholastics of the seventeenth century did, and it is what most of the theology teachers of the evangelical theological renaissance of the past half-century have done. The massive theological systems inherited from the Protestant past bear impressive witness to the thoroughness of these endeavours, and similar productions, written for textbook purposes, are still emerging.[11]

'Well,' says someone, 'you are called an evangelical theologian; do you not go along with this passion for system-building?' To a large degree, I do, though I think that the older descriptions of the method of doing it were over-simplified; but I demur at one rather basic point. When Protestant scholastics of the older type insist that the didactic content of Scripture must be brought into a unity and seen as a whole, and when they refuse to allow contradictions, paradoxes, dialectical thought-forms, or any other mode of rational incoherence into their systematic syntheses, I am with them one hundred percent; I think this is the only reverent, wise, and docile way to go. But I question the adequacy of conceptualizing the subject-matter of systematic theology as simply revealed truths about God, and I challenge the assumption that has usually accompanied this form of statement, that the material, like other scientific data, is best studied in cool and clinical detachment. Detachment from what, you ask? Why, from the relational activity of trusting, loving, worshipping, obeying, serving, and glorifying God: the activity that results from realizing that one is actually in God's presence, actually being addressed by him, every time one opens the Bible or reflects on any divine truth whatsoever. This second stage in theological method, as commonly practised, separates the questions of truth from those of discipleship; it proceeds as if doctrinal study would only be muddied by introducing devotional concerns; it drives a wedge between theology and doxology, between orthodoxy and orthopraxy, between knowing true notions about God and knowing the true God himself, between one's thinking and one's worshipping. Done this way, theology induces spiritual pride and produces spiritual sleep (physical sleep, too, sometimes). Thus the noblest study in the world gets cheapened. I cannot applaud this.

So now for my own view, which is a re-angling, small perhaps but (I think) significant, of the second position that we have reviewed. I put it to you that the proper subject-matter of systematic theology is God actively relating in and through all created things to human beings; God, about whom those biblically revealed truths teach us, and to whom they point us; God, who lives, loves, rules, speaks, and saves sinners; God, who calls us who study him to relate to him through penitence and faith and worship as we study, so that our thinking about him becomes an exercise of homage of him. From this basis (if one accepts it) it follows that the proper state of mind for us as we come to synthesize the exegeted teaching of Scripture will be one not of detachment but of commitment, whereby we bring to our theologizing the attitude not of a critic but of a disciple; not of one who merely observes God, but of one who actively worships him. Then we shall be in less danger of speculative extrapolations that go beyond Scripture, which it is almost impossible to keep out of theologies that the detached intellect, often (be it said) aided by Aristotle, puts together. We shall be in less danger of forgetting the transcendent mystery of God's being and action, and of putting him in a box constructed out of our own concepts, which the detached intellect, longing to master that which it studies, is very prone to do. We shall be in less danger of the irreverence of treating God as if he were an impersonal object below us, frozen fast by us for the purposes of our study, and of failing to remember that he is the great personal Subject, far above us, apart from whose ongoing life we should not exist at all. And we shall be shielded from the further irreverence of allowing ourselves to grade God's work in connection with the sovereign mysteries of predestination and evil, and to conclude that if we ourselves were God we could do a better job. 'Your thoughts of God are too human,' said Luther to Erasmus.[12] He might have said, your theology has too little worship in it; whichever he had said, the point would have been the same. In short, we are called to make our study of theology a devotional discipline, a verifying in experience of Aquinas' beautiful remark that theology is taught by God, teaches God, and takes us to God.[13] So may it be, for all of us.

III

Now do you see what I have been driving at all this time? I want to arrange a marriage. I want our systematic theology to be practised as an element in our spirituality, and I want our spirituality to be viewed as an implicate and expression of our systematic theology, just as ethics is already viewed, at least by the discerning. The current framework in ecumenical spirituality studies seems to me to need more biblical and theological control; too often the perspective remains egocentric, and the inward journey, with its rhythms of time and place and its alternations of desert and oasis, feast and fast, solitude and fellowship is expounded from the experience of saints, in whatever pattern of significance impresses the expositor, without any theological assessments being directly made. Spirituality books are written that contain no application of Scripture, just as theological tomes are written that contain no application of truth to life. As I want to see theological study done as an aspect and means of our relating to God, so I want to see spirituality studied within an evaluative theological frame; that is why I want to arrange a marriage, with explicit exchange of vows and mutual commitments, between spirituality and theology, or (if you would rather hear it put this way) between systematic and spiritual theology. That is what my lecture title was pointed to. Given the marriage, both our theologizing and our devotional explorations will become systematic spirituality, exercises in (allow me to say it) knowing God; and we shall all be the richer as a result.

Maybe you have already had enough theology for one lecture; but I thought I ought to illustrate my concern by giving an example of how the spirituality of some would benefit from more solid, Bible-based theological controls. Here then is my example. Sound spirituality needs to be thoroughly trinitarian. In our fellowship with God we must learn to do full justice to all three persons and the part that each plays in the team job (please allow me that bold phrase) of saving us from sin, restoring our ruined humanness, and bringing us finally to glory. Neglect the Son, lose your focus on his mediation and blood atonement and heavenly intercession, and you slip back into the legalism that is fallen man's natural religion, the treadmill religion of works. Few evangelicals, perhaps, need to be reminded of this, but some do. Again, neglect the Spirit, lose your focus on the fellowship with Christ that he creates, the renewing of nature that he effects, the assurance and joy that he evokes, and the enabling for service that he bestows, and you slip back into orthodoxism and formalism, the religion of aspiration and perspiration without either inspiration or transformation, the religion of low expectations, deep ruts, and grooves that become graves. More evangelicals, I think, need reminders here. Finally, neglect the Father, lose your focus on the tasks he prescribes and the discipline he inflicts, and you become a mushy, soft-centred, self-indulgent, unsteady, lazy spoiled child in the divine family, making very heavy weather of any troubles and setbacks that come. This loss of focus is surely a widespread weakness in these days, and very many of us need to be admonished about it.[14]

That is my example; and now I will bring this discourse to an end. From all of what I have said you can, I trust, form some idea of what to expect from the first occupant of the Chee Chair (which, I take it, is what you wanted to know, for why else would you be reading this?). Strengthening every way I can the links between spirituality and systematic theology will certainly be high on my agenda. I do not think I shall cramp Dr Houston's style; what I do will be more in the nature of digging out foundations and putting in drains, leaving the air clear for him to fly in, as at present. So now you know!

At the close of the inaugural lecture from which I quoted when I began, C. S. Lewis described himself as a cultural dinosaur, and begged his hearers, even if they disagreed with his old-fashioned approach to literature, to value him as a specimen of a vanished breed. 'Use your specimens while you can,' he said. 'There are not going to be many more dinosaurs.'[15] My theology, I know, is old-fashioned enough to be described as dinosauric in some quarters, and sociologists like Jeffrey Hunter are sure that such theology cannot survive; but I wonder. Does God change with the passing years? If the Bible is his Word for the world, will it ever go out of date? Will its meaning change with the culture? Will the human heart change with technological advance? Will the gospel change as the world's religions talk to each other? And are the inward exercises of godliness essentially any different from what they were one, two, five, ten, fifteen centuries ago? Some things do not change; and it is out of the conviction that God and godliness are among them, and are in fact to be classed among what Carlyle called the 'eternities and immensities', that I do my work in the way I do. The day will declare it; meantime, let us all labour to do what, as we see it, needs to be done.

Questions for study

1. What does Packer understand by the phrase 'systematic spirituality'? Why do you think he chose this as the title of the lecture?

2. In this lecture, Packer outlines two approaches to theology which he regards as unsatisfactory. Summarize them in your own words. Do you agree with Packer's assessment of their weaknesses?

3. Locate the following quotation, and study it in context: 'The proper subject-matter of systematic theology is God actively relating in and through all created things to human beings.' What is the significance of this statement? Where does it lead Packer as he explores the relation between theology and spirituality?

4. Packer argues that the Bible has a very specific understanding of what it means to be human. Locate his discussion of this point in the passage. What, according to Packer, is that understanding? And how does it bear on spirituality?

Notes

Preamble

1. For an introduction to the debate, see Alister E. McGrath, *Christian Spirituality: An Introduction*, Oxford: Blackwell, 1999, pp. 27–34; Walter L. Liefield and Linda M. Cannell, 'Spiritual Formation and Theological Education', in J. I. Packer and L. Wilkinson (eds.), *Alive to God: Studies in Spirituality*, Downers Grove, IL: InterVarsity Press, 1992, pp. 239–252.
2. J. I. Packer, 'To Make our Theology Serve our Godliness', *Leadership* (Tokyo Christian Institute), Spring–Summer 1987, pp. 1–2.

Essay

1. C. S. Lewis, 'De Descriptione Temporale', in *They Asked for a Paper*, London: Geoffrey Bles, 1962, p. 9.
2. Henry Rack, *Twentieth Century Spirituality*, London: Epworth Press, 1969, p. 2.
3. For some historical background, see T. Wood, *English Casuistical Divinity during the Seventeenth Century*, London: SPCK, 1952; H. R. McAdoo, *The Structure of Caroline Moral Theology*, London: Longmans, 1949; V. Lossky, *The Mystical Theology of the Eastern Church*, London: James Clarke, 1957; and Gordon S. Wakefield (ed.), *The Westminster Dictionary of Christian Spirituality*, Philadelphia: Westminster Press, 1983, *passim*.
4. Portland: Multnomah Press, 1981.
5. Oxford and Batavia: Lion Publishing, 1989.
6. I tried to make this point in *Knowing Man*, Westchester: Cornerstone, 1979, and more fully with Thomas Howard in *Christianity: The True Humanism*, Waco: Word Books, 1985.
7. This is the thesis which *Christianity: The True Humanism*, seeks to demonstrate.
8. This description is sometimes disputed, on the grounds that pre-Reformation and post-Reformation exegesis were two significantly different things. In approaching Scripture as the didactic utterance of the God and Father of our Lord Jesus Christ, who is our Father in him, there was however not the least difference or divergence in the Christian church until the days of the Enlightenment. For an overview, see R. P. Preus, 'The View of the Bible Held by the Church: the Early Church through Luther', in Norman Geisler (ed.), *Inerrancy*, Grand Rapids: Zondervan, 1979, pp. 357–392; John D. Hannah (ed.), *Inerrancy and the Church*, Chicago: Moody Press, 1984.
9. See, for instance, J. W. Wenham, 'Christ's View of Scripture', *Inerrancy*, pp. 3–36; B. B. Warfield, *The Inspiration and Authority of the Bible*, Philadelphia: Presbyterian and Reformed, 1952, pp. 51–226; Wayne A. Grudem, 'Scripture's Self-Attestation and the Problem of Formulating a

Doctrine of Scripture', in D. A. Carson and J. D. Woodbridge (eds.), *Scripture and Truth*, Grand Rapids: Zondervan, 1983.

10. I do not mean to imply that the love-life of frogs is not an intrinsically interesting topic.
11. Millard J. Erickson, *Christian Theology*, Grand Rapids: Baker Book House, 1983–85; Gordon R. Lewis and Bruce A. Demarest, *Integrative Theology*, vol. 1, Grand Rapids: Zondervan, 1987; Paul Enns, *The Moody Handbook of Theology*, Chicago: Moody Press, 1989; Alan F. Johnson and Robert E. Webber, *What Christians Believe: A Biblical and Historical Summary*, Grand Rapids: Zondervan, 1989; etc.
12. Martin Luther, *On the Bondage of the Will*, tr. O. R. Johnston and J. I. Packer, London: James Clarke; Old Tappan, NJ: Revell, 1957, p. 87.
13. *Theologia a Deo docta, Deum docet, ad Deum ducit.*
14. On this latter point, see Thomas Smail, *The Forgotten Father*, London: Hodder and Stoughton, 1979.
15. Lewis, op. cit., p. 25.

13. 'The problem of eternal punishment' (1990)

Packer has consistently shown himself to be a staunch defender of traditional evangelical teachings, even when these are the subject of considerable discussion within the evangelical constituency. A case in point is Packer's vigorous defence of the concept of eternal punishment – a notion which has come under considerable revisionary scrutiny on the part of evangelicals since about 1980, with growing interest in the idea of 'conditional immortality'.[1] Those who affirm 'conditional immortality' – who are often referred to as 'conditionalists' – deny that the human soul is created inherently immortal. Conditionalists argue that immortality is not a natural attribute of humankind but is a specific additional gift to humanity, and is conditional upon faith and repentance. Immortality is thus 'conditional' in the sense that certain conditions must be met before the sinner can receive everlasting personal existence. Conditionalists contrast their position with what they perceive to be the traditional teaching, namely, that the soul is by nature absolutely impervious to destruction. At present, it seems that most evangelicals continue to hold that the doctrine of conditional immortality is unbiblical. However, a related debate has also developed, in which some of the arguments associated with universalism appear to have found at least a degree of acceptance in some evangelical circles. How, universalists demanded, could a God of love consign anyone to eternal torment? Was not the traditional doctrine of hell inconsistent with the idea of a loving God?

For some evangelicals, this question had merit. The idea that no-one will suffer eternal torment has gradually emerged as a significant viewpoint within evangelicalism since 1988, when two leading evangelical writers committed themselves in print to the idea of 'conditional immortality'. This idea can be defined as the belief that God created humanity with the potential to be immortal. Immortality is a gift conveyed by grace through faith when the believer receives eternal life and becomes a partaker of the divine nature. The distinctive feature of the teaching is that it sees no continuing place for human beings to exist in continuous torment, unreconciled to God.[2] The traditional view held that humanity was immortal, and was therefore subject to eternal life or eternal punishment. The 'conditionalist' approach argued that immortality was bestowed only on those who were to be saved, so that none would endure the torment of eternal punishment in hell.

In 1988, two leading conservative evangelicals published their doubts concerning the traditional understanding of the nature of hell and eternal punishment, and tentatively advocated annihilationism as a serious option for evangelicals. Philip E. Hughes, a former Librarian of Latimer House (see p. 13), and subsequently a member of the faculty of Westminster Theological Seminary, published his views in *The True Image*; John R. W. Stott contributed to a dialogue with David L. Edwards, in which he affirmed (although very tentatively) his inclination to believe in the final annihilation of the wicked, rather than their eternal punishment. Stott stressed that he stated this view with some hesitation, partly on account of his 'great respect for longstanding tradition which claims to be a true interpretation of Scripture' and partly because of his high regard and concern for 'the unity of the worldwide evangelical constituency'.[3] Additional support for such views also came from John Wenham, the veteran English conservative evangelical, who indicated that he had come round to this way of thinking as early as 1934, partly through the influence of Basil Atkinson, widely regarded as a bastion of orthodoxy in evangelical student circles.[4]

All of these writers were colleagues of Packer, with whom he had worked closely in the past, especially in connection with Latimer House. It was not an easy situation for Packer, in that his personal regard for the people concerned had to be set against his fundamental belief that their ideas were misguided and misleading. Another noted proponent of conditional immortality was Clark Pinnock, whom Packer had succeeded as Professor of Systematic and Historical Theology at Regent College.[5]

Packer responded to these developments in the annual Leon Morris Lecture, delivered to the Evangelical Alliance in the Australian city of Melbourne on Friday 31 August 1990. The lecture commemorated the considerable achievements of Leon Morris, one of Australia's leading evangelicals, who served with great distinction as Principal of Ridley College, Melbourne. Packer chose as his topic 'The Problem of Eternal Punishment', and indicated that he wished his lecture to be seen as 'a dissuasive from universalism and conditionalism, and particularly from conditionalism'. Packer argued that the doctrine of eternal punishment was an integral aspect of 'the Christianity taught by the Lord Jesus Christ and his apostles', pointing out that it was also found in the writings of Christian theologians as diverse as Tertullian, Thomas Aquinas and Jonathan Edwards. The teaching is also found in the Westminster Confession, which affirmed that 'the souls of the wicked are cast into Hell, where they remain in torments and utter darkness'. Packer appealed to W. G. T. Shedd's famous work *The Doctrine of Endless Punishment*, first published in 1885, and reprinted by the Banner of Truth Trust in 1986. Shedd pointed to the teaching of Christ himself as the strongest warrant for the doctrine of endless punishment. Packer concurred, and pointed particularly to the parable of the sheep and the goats, in which Christ speaks explicitly of the goats being sent away to 'eternal fire' and 'eternal punishment' (Matt. 25:41, 46). Eternal punishment is thus, according to Jesus, departure into eternal fire.

The debate is complex, and involves a number of issues. The interpretation of a substantial number of biblical passages is clearly of importance, although other questions also emerge as significant. Perhaps the most important of these is the question whether God creates human souls in a state of immortality (the traditional view) or with the potential for immortality (the conditionalist view). Packer was quite clear that conditionalism missed out on 'the awesome dignity of our having been made to last for eternity'. However, it is clear that one of Packer's major concerns was the impact of conditionalist teaching on evangelism. Conditionalism seriously detracted from the motivation for evangelism, in that if there is no everlasting punishment from which a sinner is to be delivered, there is correspondingly little reason to preach a gospel of deliverance. There can be no doubt that one of Packer's major concerns here – shared by others defending this position – is that missionary activity is seriously endangered by the belief, which removes a fundamental motivation for preaching the gospel.

Related works by Packer

'The Way of Salvation: I. What is Salvation. II. What is Faith? III. The Problem of Universalism. IV: Are Non-Christian Faiths Ways of Salvation?' *Bibliotheca Sacra* 129 (1972), pp. 105–125; 291–306; 130 (1973), pp.3–10; 110–116.

'Good Pagans and God's Kingdom', *Christianity Today*, 17 January 1986, pp. 27–31.

'Evangelicals and the Way of Salvation: New Challenges to the Gospel', in C. F. H. Henry and K. Kantzer (eds.), *Evangelical Affirmations*, Grand Rapids, MI: Zondervan, 1990, pp. 107–136.

The problem of eternal punishment

I count it a great privilege, and feel it as a great pleasure, to be delivering this Leon Morris Lecture today: for Dr Morris, an old friend and one still happily with us, is a man whom I, with many more, am delighted to honour. A versatile and productive scholar, a fluent speaker, and above all a man of God, he has made an outstanding contribution to biblical and theological study, and to ongoing evangelical life, in Australia, Britain, North America, and in a more diffused sense worldwide. I would honour him both as an academic of highest ability who has never compromised his intellectual integrity and also as an evangelical for whom the cross of Christ, as an achievement of redemptive penal substitution, has always been the main theme, and the person of Christ, as the proper object of faith, hope, and love, has always been the central focus. So it seems to me most appropriate that I should offer you in this lecture a subsidiary to Dr Morris' own work, and that was one factor determining the subject that I have chosen. The article, 'Eternal Punishment', in the *Evangelical Dictionary of Theology*, published in 1984, was written by Dr Morris, and, following a dismissal of universalism and conditional immortality, it ends thus: 'If we are to be true to the whole teaching of Scripture, we must come to the conclusion that the ultimate fate of the wicked is eternal punishment, though we must add that we have no way of knowing in exactly what that punishment consists.' That statement is the springboard off which I dive in what follows.

I

At Regent College, from time to time, we have fun. (We are not, of course, alone in that; what serious community does not need an occasional giggle to speed it on its way?) One bit of Regent fun was the appearance in faculty mail boxes on

April 1st this year of a spoof course programme. Our New Testament pundit, who writes on hermeneutics, was down to lecture on 'How to Prove Anything from the Bible'. The Principal of the Baptist college with which we work was to give instruction in 'What the Bible Teaches about Infant Baptism', and his colleague, whose speciality is family ministries, was slated for one course on 'How to Conquer Self-Doubt through Pretence and Ostentation', and for another on 'Motivating your Children by Guilt and Fear'. My assignment was 'Guilt without Sex: an Introduction to Puritan Theology', and our new Professor of Theology was given the theme, 'Overcoming Peace of Mind: the Doctrine of Eternal Punishment'.

Overcoming peace of mind ... Many a true word is spoken in jest, and it certainly is true that to any normal person the thought that people one knows and cares for, not to mention oneself, might face a destiny that could be described as eternal punishment, will be profoundly disturbing. It rudely disrupts the sort of peace of mind that we in the western world cultivate today – the peace of mind, that is, that is gained by constantly telling oneself that there is nothing to worry about, and everything will work out all right in the end. But since this complacency is part of our culture, and is sniffed like glue in the air we breathe, and does in fact operate as a deadening drug on the mind, it is a kind of knee-jerk reaction with us to resent having it disturbed, and hence to dismiss the doctrine of eternal punishment in all its forms as debased Christianity. We scoff at hell fire as a bad dream, the murky stamping-ground of redneck fundamentalists, backwoods preachers, and old-fashioned Roman Catholics. For ourselves, we write off the idea as a hangover from primitive ages now long past, and when we meet someone who still believes in eternal punishment we regard him as at least quaint, and perhaps weird; we certainly do not take him seriously. We know, of course, that belief in eternal punishment has been part of the mainstream of Christian conviction from the first. Maybe we know that Tertullian in the third century, and Thomas Aquinas in the thirteenth, taught that the sufferings of those in hell would be a joyful spectacle to those in heaven – a notion affirmed also by Jonathan Edwards, whose famous or infamous sermon, 'Sinners in the Hands of an Angry God', was, of course (so we were all taught at school), the product of a sick mind. We know, too, that belief in eternal punishment bulked large in all forms of Victorian Christianity; but, just as we would not dream of aping the Victorians in other matters, so we acquit ourselves of any responsibility to go along with them in this. Hell is dead, we say; so back to peace of mind!

How should we respond to this? I hold no special brief for Victorian Christianity, or for Edwards, or Aquinas, or Tertullian; but I do hold a brief for that to which they all appealed, namely the Christianity taught by the Lord

Jesus Christ and his apostles, and my first task now must be to point out as forcefully as I can that Jesus and the apostles do not let us off the hook with regard to eternal punishment as we so blithely let ourselves off it. Rather, they impale us on that hook and make us face this issue directly. The doctrine of eternal punishment stems directly from Jesus, and the apostolic teaching on the subject simply echoes what the founder of Christianity first said. And no Greek myth-maker or Jewish apocalyptic fantasist ever spoke of eternal punishment with such weight and gravity as Jesus did. As W. G. T. Shedd affirmed in a landmark statement a century ago: 'The strongest support of the doctrine of Endless Punishment is the teaching of Christ, the Redeemer of men ... Christ could not have warned men so frequently and earnestly as He did against "the fire that shall never be quenched," and "the worm that dieth not," had he known that there is no future peril to fully correspond to them ... Jesus Christ is the Person who is responsible for the doctrine of Eternal Perdition. He is the Being with whom all opponents of this theological tenet are in conflict.' This is a strong statement, but the evidence warrants it, as we shall now see.

'Eternal punishment' is Jesus' own phrase. It comes from the passage that pictures the day of judgment in terms of the Son of Man, now returned as King, separating sheep from goats (that is, two classes of human beings from each other). To the goats his word is: '"Depart from me, you who are cursed, into the eternal fire prepared for the devil and his angels" ... Then they will go away to eternal punishment, but the righteous to eternal life' (Matt. 25:41, 46). 'Eternal' in these phrases is *aiōnios*, meaning, as has often been pointed out, not 'endless', but pertaining to the 'age to come', as distinct from the order of things that now is. However, the age to come, as Jesus and the Jews conceived it, was to be unending; therefore *aiōnios* implies the unending continuance of that to which it refers, unless something is said to show the contrary. In verse 46, Jesus' statement about the eternal life into which the sheep enter and the eternal punishment into which the goats go is clearly a conscious parallelism on his part; so if eternal life is taken to be unending, as surely it must be, the only natural supposition is that eternal punishment is unending also.

Eternal punishment, then, as Jesus declares it, is departure into eternal fire. Of this fire Jesus had spoken often, using for it the word *gehenna*, the Greek form of Ge Hinnom, 'Valley of Hinnom'. This was an area outside the wall of Jerusalem where children had once been offered as burnt sacrifices to Molech (2 Chr. 28:3; 33:6), and which had become the city's incinerator area where the city's garbage and the discarded corpses of the familyless were daily burned. In the Sermon on the Mount we find Jesus saying to his own professed disciples that anyone calling his brother a fool (an index of malicious contempt in one's heart) 'will be in danger of the fire of hell' (literally, 'the Gehenna of fire') (Matt. 5:22). In Matthew 18:9 he refers again to 'the Gehenna of fire', as an equivalent of 'eternal fire' (literally, 'the fire that is *aiōnios*') in the verse before. The passage runs: 'If your hand or your foot causes you to sin, cut it off and throw it away. It is better for you to enter life maimed or crippled than to have two hands or two feet and be thrown into eternal fire. And if your eye causes you to sin, gouge it out and throw it away. It is better for you to enter life with one eye than to have two eyes and be thrown into the fire of hell.'

Another version of this same bit of teaching in Mark's Gospel speaks of a person with two hands going into 'Gehenna, where the fire never goes out' and of a person with two eyes being 'thrown into Gehenna, where their worm does not die, and the fire is not quenched' (Mark 9:43, 48, echoing imagery from Is. 66:24, which speaks of the worm and the fire destroying corpses, but applying the imagery to the fate of living souls).

With all this should be linked Jesus' picture of tares and bad fish being finally taken out of the kingdom and thrown into 'the fiery furnace' (literally, 'the furnace of the fire'), where there will be 'weeping and gnashing of teeth' (Matt. 13:42, 50), and also the grim form of Jesus' call for courage as he sends out the twelve on mission: 'Do not be afraid of those who kill the body but cannot kill the soul. Rather, be afraid of the One who can destroy both soul and body in hell' (Matt. 10:28). 'Destroy' in that verse is *apollymi*, the regular Greek word for wrecking and ruining something, so making it useless for its intended purpose, and 'hell' is Gehenna; and the One to be feared is not the devil, but the One whom Jesus called Father.

What does all this add up to? We may summarize as follows: Jesus speaks of a destiny of being in the fire for all people everywhere (in Matt. 25:32 the sheep and the goats are between them 'all the nations') whom he does not accept as his own. He calls the fire Gehenna, and describes it as *aiōnios*, part of the abiding future order of things, and as never going out. To enter or be thrown into it (Jesus uses both verbs) brings unqualified distress ('weeping and gnashing of teeth': a condition that Jesus elsewhere ascribes, we should note, to those banished at judgment day to 'the darkness outside', Matt. 8:12; 22:13; 25:30). Clearly, we are in the world of imagery here, for the fire and the darkness are both picturing the same condition, one of painful and hopeless desolation; and equally clearly, what is being pictured is a condition that is unimaginably dreadful, one that it is worth any labour and any cost to avoid. And the speaker is the incarnate Son of God, our divine instructor, who if anyone should know what he is talking about and should therefore be heard as having authority when he deals with these things.

The apostolic writers use their own vocabulary, but for substance they do no more, just as they do no less, than follow in their Master's footsteps. Here are some sample passages.

Paul warns each impenitent person thus: 'you are storing up wrath against yourself for the day of God's wrath, when his righteous judgment will be revealed. God "will give to each person according to what he has done" ' (a quote from Ps. 62:12). 'For those who are self-seeking and who reject the truth and follow evil, there will be wrath and anger. There will be trouble and distress for every human being who does evil ... God does not show favouritism. All who sin apart from the law will also perish apart from the law, and all who sin under the law will be judged by the law ... This will take place on the day when God will judge men's secrets through Jesus Christ, as my gospel declares' (Rom. 2:5–6, 8–9, 11, 16). Thus Paul states the principle, and affirms the certainty, of final judgment and final ruin.

More dramatically, Paul also declares: 'When the Lord Jesus is revealed from heaven in blazing fire ... he will punish those who do not know God and do not obey the gospel of our Lord Jesus. They will be punished with everlasting destruction and shut out from the presence of the Lord ...' (2 Thess. 1:7–9). 'Everlasting' is *aiōnios*, reasonably so translated, as we have seen; 'destruction' is *olethros*, a noun from *apollymi*, signifying a reduction to ruin, which Paul also used in 1 Thessalonians 5:3 and 1 Timothy 6:9.

Jude's brief letter includes both Jesus' images for the state of final loss. Verse 7 reads: 'Sodom and Gomorrah and the surrounding towns gave themselves up to sexual immorality ... They serve as an example of those who suffer the punishment of eternal fire.' Verse 13 speaks of certain immoral folk in the church as 'wandering stars, for whom blackest darkness' (literally, as in KJV, 'the blackness of darkness') 'has been reserved for ever'. It has sometimes been suggested that the eternal fire is an image of immediate annihilation, but Jude's phrase, 'darkness ... reserved for ever', surely indicates that he did not mean his words about the fire to be taken that way.

In the book of Revelation, the long visionary appendix to the Lord's letters (chs. 4 – 22) intensifies the Lord's picture of eternal fire in a deliberately excruciating way, doing canonically what 'Sinners in the Hands of an Angry God' attempted later, and for the same pastoral reason: to lead people to embrace and hold fast life in Christ, and not to risk the alternative. Revelation 14:9–11 warns that anyone who worships the beast 'will be tormented with burning sulphur in the presence of the holy angels and of the Lamb. And the smoke of their torment rises for ever and ever.' Revelation 20:10 pictures a lake of burning sulphur into which at the last judgment the devil, the beast, and the false prophet are thrown, to be 'tormented day and night for ever and ever'; then in verse 14 death and Hades are thrown into it, and it is identified with 'the second death', which verse 6 had told us would have no power over God's saints; and then, climactically, verse 15 declares: 'If anyone's name was not found written in the book of life' (of which we heard in 3:5, and will hear again in 21:17) 'he was thrown into the lake of fire.' In the context of this build-up, and in the light of the explicit statement of 14:11, it is excessively unnatural to suppose, as some do, that being thrown into the lake of fire means anything less than pain and grief without end.

It is true that in the inter-testamental literature of Judaism (such books as 2 and 4 Maccabees, the Wisdom of Solomon, Judith, Ecclesiasticus, Jubilees, 2 Baruch, and the Assumption of Moses) the imagery of Gehenna and predictions of unending future torment for the ungodly are already present. Jesus and the apostles were therefore drawing on a stock of ideas and beliefs that already existed. This does not, however, in any way lessen the divine authority of these notions when the New Testament teachers endorse them. Moreover, 'endorse' is hardly the right word; for in using these ideas Jesus and the apostles purged them of the overtones of gloating that they had often carried before and imparted to them a nuance, or temper, or feeling-tone of what I can only call traumatic awe: a passionate gladness that justice will be done for God's glory, linked with an equally passionate sadness that fellow human beings, no matter how perverse, will thereby be ruined. This traumatic awe is reflected in Jesus' tearful words of Jerusalem (Luke 19:41–44), and in his compassionate admonition to the woman walking with him to Calvary ('Daughters of Jerusalem, do not weep for me; weep for yourselves and for your children ...', Luke 23:28–31). Similar submissive sadness comes out in Paul's heart-cry about the Jews whose rejection by God he announces – 'I have great sorrow and unceasing anguish in my heart. For I could wish that I myself were cursed and cut off from Christ for the sake of my brothers ...'; 'my heart's desire and prayer to God for the Israelites is that they may be saved' (Rom. 9:2–3; 10:1).

The same traumatic awe, or awe-filled trauma, will strike the soul of every thoughtful Christian with unconverted relatives and friends who takes seriously the promise that Jesus the Saviour will one day return to judge the living and the dead. And surely we may boldly say that, though it is not in the least comfortable, yet it is healthy for us to feel this trauma, and to be unable, like Paul before us, to find relief from the pain save in whole-hearted commitment to the ministry of spreading the gospel, in which we become all things to all men that by all means we may save some (1 Cor. 9:22), and so fulfil Jude's blunt summons: 'Snatch others from the fire and save them' (Jude 23). The only spiritual method of alleviating distress at the prospect of souls being lost is to take action to win them; and the theological way of stating that is to say that God enables us to live with the prospect of people we know, or know of, possibly being lost by moving us to pray and work so that they may not be lost, and indeed using that prospect in our consciences to stir us to this mode of action.

But the eternal punishment of all the ungodly none the less remains a distressing truth to discuss; which makes it vital to have at command for the purpose a form of words that is conceptually clear but not emotionally loaded. I have made a policy decision about this, which I shall try to hold to for the rest of this lecture, and I would like to share it now. It has both a negative and a positive side.

Negatively: though the language of punishment, in the sense of God's judicial infliction, is abundantly scriptural, as we have seen, I am now going to drop it, for it conjures up unhelpful suspicions. The dictum of Goethe, 'we should always distrust anyone who has a desire to punish', would nowadays be reinforced by the followers of Freud; modern thought is sceptical as to whether punishment that does not serve the purpose of reforming the offender and safeguarding others can ever be justified; and talk about God's punitive role on the last day, when neither of these further goals can enter into the reckoning, is bound to feed the suspicion that God is in truth arbitrary and vindictive in a way that is not quite admirable, because it is not quite moral. Indeed, the widespread revolt against the idea of eternal punishment during the past century has sprung from this suspicion, and from a desire for doctrine that does not thus impugn God's character, rather than from any other source. So I think it best not to use vocabulary of punishment at all.

By the same token, I do not propose at any point to use the word 'torment', scriptural though it is (see the story of Dives and Lazarus: Luke 16:23, 28) for describing the state of the ungodly beyond this world. Its vibrations, too, are bad: to the modern mind, it suggests sadism and cruelty and torture, and what we are talking about is none of these things, but the adorable justice of a holy Creator who deals righteously with people according to their works.

In what terms, then, do I propose to carry on this discussion? I propose, positively, to speak henceforth of the divinely executed retributive process that operates in the world to come. This rule of speech has three advantages.

First, though admittedly clumsy, the phraseology is not emotionally loaded, and it should not cloud discussion by evoking prejudicial attitudes, for in our culture retribution retains its status as a moral rather than an immoral idea.

Second, individual retribution, as one aspect of the larger reality of divine judgment whereby evil is stopped in its tracks and righteousness restored, is precisely what we are talking about: the word fits. Punishment can be arbitrary and not proportionate to the wrongdoing, but retribution means that one's past becomes the decisive factor in determining one's present, for one gets what one deserves.

And then, third, the language of retribution permits, in a way that punishment language does not, the blending in our minds of two thoughts that are blended in the Bible – namely, that the condemnation justly imposed by God as the Judge, vindicating righteousness, is also, and in a sense primarily, self-inflicted through our own perversity in choosing death rather than life. This biblical blending is clearest in John 3:18–20, where, having stated that 'whoever does not believe stands condemned already, because he has not believed in the name of God's one and only Son', John continues: 'This is the process.' (So Dr Morris himself renders *krisis*, the Greek word used here. NIV has 'verdict', but that does not seem to be right; nor does NEB's 'test'. The thought being expressed is that this is how the process of judgment works in the present case.) 'Light has come into the world, but men loved darkness instead of light because their deeds were evil. Everyone who does evil hates the light, and will not come into the light for fear that his deeds will be exposed …' In other words, we choose to retreat from God rather than repent before God, and God's judicial sentence is a ratifying for eternity of the sentence of separation from God that we by our own choice have already passed on ourselves. Teachers like C. S. Lewis stress the thought that no-one is in hell who has not chosen to be there, in the sense of choosing to be self-absorbed and to keep God out of his or her life, and that is evidently one aspect of the grim truth. It is an aspect that the idea of retribution readily covers.

II

It may be that someone is still wondering why I chose to lecture on this sombre theme rather than on any other subject. This is the moment for me to explain why. In today's Christianity, what I am now calling the divinely executed retributive process that operates in the world to come is becoming more and more a problem area for belief. Uncertainty is growing, and growing in a way that has a very weakening effect on Christian witness. Let me describe to you the uncertainties that I see.

(1) Christians in general are increasingly uncertain about the finality of God's condemnation of sinners at the judgment.

As we have noted already, belief in the everlasting conscious distress of those that Jesus pictured as the goats whom he banished from his presence belonged to the Christian consensus from the first. Fathers, medievals, and moderns up to the time of the Enlightenment were unanimous about it; Protestants,

Catholics, and Orthodox were divided on many things, but not on this. The consensus existed not because the doctrine was congenial – Charles Hodge called it 'a doctrine which the natural heart revolts from and struggles against, and to which it submits only under stress of authority' – but because Bible-believers of all schools of thought and all church allegiances found it inescapable. But when the European Enlightenment, with the Romantic movement riding on its shoulders, invaded the Protestant churches in the eighteenth and nineteenth centuries, it elbowed biblical authority aside, reconceived God's moral character in terms of benevolence without judgment, exalted man against the Bible as the real measure of all things – and, with increasing emphasis, rejected any thought of endless existence for anyone in hell. Universalism, which had hardly been heard of since its condemnation at the fifth general council in 543, re-emerged and gathered strength, and today it is a widespread and potent view among both Protestant and Roman Catholics. It is worth our while to pause for a moment and take a look at it.

Universalism, the doctrine that every human being, no matter how sinful, perverse, and guilty at this moment, will ultimately be brought to eternal life, has occasionally been formulated as an optimism of nature – 'no-one is really bad enough for God to condemn' – but it is generally stated as an optimism of grace. Its exponents do not question that all human beings deserve hell; but, they say, God's love is such that he will not finally damn any of us, or lose any of us, and Christ's cross is the guarantee of everyone's final salvation. Nothing less than a doctrine of universal salvation, so they claim, can do justice to the reality of God's love, and the magnitude of Christ's victory, and the wisdom of God in making a world into which sin could enter. Wishful thinking gives universalism a strong appeal: who would not like it to be true? Who can take pleasure in the thought of people being eternally lost? If you want to see folk damned, there is something wrong with you! Universalism is a comfortable doctrine in a way that the alternatives to it are not. But is universalism true? Only Scripture can tell us that; and when universalists move from general theological notions to the specific study of texts, insuperable difficulties arise to explode their hopeful and generous guesswork.

The universalist's problem is to circumvent the seemingly solid New Testament witness to the fate of unbelievers, whom Paul declares to be under sin, law, wrath, and death (so says Romans: 3:9, 19; 1:18; 5:17), alienated from God and without hope (so says Ephesians 2:12), and facing exclusion from God's presence for non-subjection to what they knew of his truth (Rom. 1:18 – 2:16), and for whom Jesus himself, as we have seen, predicts only fire and darkness. The problem is tackled in different ways by different universalists.

Thus, some Protestants simply jettison the dominical and apostolic teaching about future retribution as a bad dream, effectively contradicted by a set of texts taken to affirm that universal salvation will one day be a fact. This solution depends on setting Scripture against Scripture.

Other Protestants affirm that those who leave this world in unbelief do indeed go to hell, but eventually come out of it, having been brought to their senses, and to a positive response to Christ who has met them there. Hell, on this view, does for unbelievers what Roman Catholics claim that purgatory does to believers – that is, it prepares them for heaven. What is being affirmed is salvation out of what the New Testament calls 'eternal destruction', 'eternal punishment', and 'perdition', through post-mortem encounter with Christ (a 'second chance' for some, a 'first chance' for others). This solution depends on relativizing an apparent biblical absolute, namely the fixed character of one's destiny after this life ends.

Roman Catholic universalists go another way: they refuse to believe that any human beings fail to receive grace that moves them to seek God inwardly here and now, or that any form of religion in this world fails to bring its faithful adherents into God's salvation. In the famous phraseology of Karl Rahner, the claim is that every human being is an 'anonymous Christian', so that the biblical threat of retribution for unbelievers does not touch any real people. This solution depends on positing grace in the heart where no sign of it appears in the life.

Older evangelicalism equated universalist teaching with the world's first lie, the devil's assurance to Eve in Eden, 'You will not surely die' (Gen. 3:4). In this the older evangelicalism, in my view, was right. But universalist speculations, hazardous and unconvincing as they are, continue to gain ground, especially among Protestants of liberal and ecumenical outlooks, and they undermine evangelistic concern wherever they take root. This is the increasing uncertainty that I see regarding the finality of condemnation of judgment day, and I confess that it troubles me greatly. So does the second uncertainty that I see around me, to which I now turn. Here it is.

(2) Evangelicals in particular are increasingly uncertain about the ongoing existence of those who leave this world in unbelief.
That one aspect of the hellishness of hell will be its endlessness has been a traditional evangelical conviction, often proclaimed in evangelistic and pastoral sermons, and never queried with any seriousness until the twentieth century. Evangelicals regretted the appearance in the last century of sects (Seventh-Day Adventists, Christadelphians, Jehovah's Witnesses, to which must now be added Herbert W. Armstrong's World-wide Church of God) which, along with some otherwise orthodox Christian teachers, affirmed the

extinction of unbelievers either at death or at the moment of final judgment or after a period in hell; all forms of this extinction idea were at first rated heretical. Recently, however, persons who may fairly be called accredited evangelicals of the main stream have written in favour of extinction, which they call either annihilationism or conditional immortality. These writers include John Wenham, veteran of the Tyndale Fellowship, the theological research unit of Britain's UCCF (IVF under its new name), in *The Goodness of God*, 1974 (retitled in the USA *The Enigma of Evil*); Edward Fudge, member of America's Evangelical Theological Society, in *The Fire that Consumes*, 1982; the late Philip Edgcumbe Hughes, senior Anglican Reformed theologian, in *The True Image*, 1988; and John Stott, one of the best-known and most admired evangelical leaders anywhere in the world, in *Essentials*, 1988.

In 1986 Peter Toon wrote, with reference mainly to Britain and North America: 'In conservative circles there is a seeming reluctance to espouse publicly a doctrine of hell, and where it is held there is a seeming tendency towards a doctrine of hell as annihilation.' He went on to refer to 'conditional immortality, which appears to be gaining acceptance in evangelical orthodox circles'. His words, I guess, are truer in 1990 than when they first appeared. John Stott wrote: 'The ultimate annihilation of the wicked should be accepted as a legitimate biblically founded alternative to their eternal conscious torment.' But we need to ask: are the biblical foundations of conditionalism solid? Its advocates appear to back into it in horrified recoil from the thought of billions in endless distress, rather than move into it because the obvious meaning of Scripture beckons them. Let us look at the biblical arguments that are used. They reduce to four.

First, it is said that the New Testament terms for the fate of the lost – destruction and death, perdition and punishment, the worm and the fire – could mean annihilation; and various exegetical expedients are developed to show this. I will not say that these expedients are impossible, though none of them convinces me; but I will say, as emphatically as I can, that none of them is natural. In all the contexts, the natural meaning of the death-destruction-punishment-fire language is entry upon ruin and distress, not non-existence; and in all Bible study it is surely the natural meaning that should be embraced. Conditionalists' attempts to evade the natural meaning of some dozens of relevant passages impress me as a prime case of avalanche-dodging.

Second, it is said that everlasting retribution would be needless cruelty, since God's justice does not appear to require it. Reverence, I think, will leave it to God to know that his justice requires a means to his own fullest glory; but I would point out that this argument, if it proves anything, proves too much. For if it is needlessly cruel for God to keep the lost in being after judgment, no reason can be given why it is not needlessly cruel for him to keep the lost in the conscious misery of the interim state (which Jesus' story of Dives shows that he does, Luke 16:23ff.), and then to raise them bodily in what Jesus calls 'the resurrection of judgment' (John 5:28). What God ought to do, on conditionalist principles, is annihilate unbelievers at death – but, as biblical conditionalists confess, he does not do this. So the conditionalist argument, which sought to clear God of the suspicion of needless cruelty, actually puts him under it. And in fact, the only way to dispel this suspicion is to affirm that every moment of the unbeliever's continuance after death, in the experience of reaping what he has sown and learning the bitterness of the choice he made, furthers the glory of God's holy justice: which is what I, for one, do affirm. But if that is so, then no reason can be given why the unbeliever's continuance should ever be thought to cease – particularly when, as I said when dealing with the first point, the natural implication of the New Testament language is that it does not cease.

Third, it is said that the harmony of the new heaven and earth will be marred if somewhere the lost continue to exist in impenitence and distress. But how can the conditionalists possibly know this? Their argument is pure speculation.

Fourth, it is said that the joy of heaven will be marred by knowledge that some continue under merited retribution. But this cannot be said of God, as if the expressing of his holiness in retribution hurts him more than it hurts the offenders; and since in heaven Christians will be like God in character, loving what he loves and taking joy in all his self-manifestation, including his justice, there is no reason to think that their joy will be impaired in this way.

In *The True Image*, Philip Hughes sets these considerations within the frame of the thesis that God's one and only purpose in creating human beings was to perfect us in the image of his Son, who was later incarnate as Jesus Christ to be our Saviour from sin. God's re-creation of his sin-spoiled world now involves him in eliminating all traces of sin, and it is as part of that activity that he annihilates the lost. This is a kind of universalism in reverse, ensuring not that all who exist will be saved, but that only those who are saved will exist. But clearly, the logic of Hughes' view of God's sovereign purpose requires full universalism, and makes it inexplicable that God should not save everyone! There is real incoherence in Hughes' argument at this point.

Are the biblical foundations of conditionalism secure? I think not. Does it matter whether an evangelical is a conditionalist or not? I think it does: for a conditionalist's idea of God will miss out on the glory of divine justice, and his idea of worship will miss out on praise for God's judgments, and his idea of heaven will miss out on the thought that praise for God's judgments goes on (cf. Rev. 16:5–7; 19:1–5), and his idea of man will miss out on the awesome dignity of our having been made to last for eternity, and in his preaching of the gospel he will miss out on telling the unconverted that their prospects without Christ are as bad as they possibly could be – for on the conditionalist view they aren't! These, surely, are sad losses. Conditionalism, logically thought through, cannot but impoverish a Christian man, and limit his usefulness to the Lord. That is why I am concerned about the current trend towards conditionalism. I hope it may soon be reversed.

If you think of this lecture as a dissuasive from universalism and conditionalism, and particularly from conditionalism, since that is the more tempting by-path for evangelicals at this moment, you will be correct.

III

One final admonition. Do not speculate about the retributive process. Do not try to imagine what it is like to be in hell. The horrific imaginings of the past were hardly helpful, and often in fact proved a stumbling-block, as people equated the reality of hell with the lurid word-pictures drawn by Dante, or Edwards, or C. H. Spurgeon. Not that these men were wrong to draw their pictures, any more than Jesus was wrong to dwell on the fire and the worm; the mistake is to take such pictures as physical descriptions, when in fact they are imagery symbolizing realities of possible experience of which we can only say they are far, far worse than the symbols themselves. The words used by theologians, on the basis of Scripture, to describe hell – loss of all good, all pleasure, all rest, and all hope; exclusion from God's favour and exposure to his anger; remorse, frustration, fury, despair; self-hate as a form of self-absorption; introversion to the point of idiocy – are formal category-words only; what they might mean in actual experience for anyone is more than we can imagine, and we shall not be wise to try. Our wisdom is rather to spend our lives finding ways of showing gratitude for the saving grace of Christ which ensures that we shall not in fact ever go to the hell that each of us so richly deserves, and to school our minds to dwell on heaven rather than on the other place, except when we are seeking, in Jude's phrase, to snatch others from the fire. Let us labour to be wise.

Questions for study

1. What general considerations does Packer consider to underlie the erosion of belief in eternal punishment within evangelical circles in the late

twentieth century? You will find it helpful to state these factors in your own words.

2. What is meant by 'conditional immortality'? And how is this related to the theme of 'annihilation'?
3. List the authors whom Packer identifies as supporters of conditional immortality. Do they have anything in common?
4. What arguments does Philip Hughes set forward in support of conditional immortality in his book *The True Image*, according to Packer? And what are Packer's responses to those arguments?
5. What is Packer's most fundamental response to the suggestion that the notion of eternal punishment may be abandoned?
6. How important is evangelism to Packer's reflections on this topic? What does Packer believe the impact of abandoning this doctrine would be on the motivation for preaching the gospel?

Notes

1. For an early and brief analysis, see Millard J. Erickson, 'Is Universalistic Thinking Now Appearing Among Evangelicals?', *United Evangelical Action* 48/5 (September-October, 1989), pp. 4–6. A useful survey can be found in Tony Gray, 'Destroyed for Ever: An Examination of the Debates Concerning Annihilation and Conditional Immortality', *Themelios* 21 (1996), pp. 14–18.
2. I take this definition from a lecture by John Wenham, 'The Case for Conditional Immortality', delivered at Rutherford House, Edinburgh, Scotland, on 29 August 1991.
3. David L. Edwards with John R. W. Stott, *Essentials* (London: Hodder and Stoughton, 1988), pp. 312–339; quote at p. 319. Stott has subsequently indicated that, although he is inclined towards annihilationism, he ultimately remains agnostic on the issue.
4. Wenham, 'Case for Conditional Immortality', p. 2.
5. See Clark H. Pinnock, *A Wideness in God's Mercy* (Grand Rapids: Zondervan, 1992), and especially his earlier article 'The Destruction of the Finally Impenitent', *Criswell Theological Review* 4 (1990), pp. 243–259.

14. 'Evangelical foundations for spirituality' (1991)

The question of the theological foundations of Christian spirituality is now recognized to be of major importance. For J. I. Packer, who is firmly committed to the 'primacy of theology', it is clear that good spirituality rests upon good theology. Packer's early experience with the Keswick holiness movement in the late 1940s had led him to distrust forms of Christian spirituality which rested on weak or erroneous theological foundations. In the case of the then highly influential Keswick teaching, Packer believed that it was grounded on Pelagian ideas, especially the idea of the human ability to make the critical decisions necessary to sanctification. For Packer, this was an uninformed Pelagianism, which took a hopelessly optimistic view of fallen human nature. The Keswick teaching was Pelagian, in that it diminished the role of God and falsely elevated the role of human will and freedom.[1]

Most important of all was Packer's suggestion that a theologically naïve pietism inevitably lapsed into precisely such a Pelagianism. 'After all, Pelagianism is the natural heresy of zealous Christians who are not interested in theology.' It was therefore clear to Packer that theological clarity and precision were essential prerequisites for a sound spirituality.

Yet many writers in the field of spirituality argue that there is actually a serious tension between the disciplines of 'theology' and 'spirituality'. There can be no doubt that this is the case if theology is defined in highly abstract terms – such as 'the study of Christian concepts or doctrines'. Yet it needs to be realized that, partly in response to pressures within western academic culture in general,

227

the western understanding of 'theology' has undergone a shift in the last two centuries which inevitably leads to precisely this tension emerging. It is therefore important to appreciate that the tension is not primarily between theology and spirituality, but between modern western concepts of theology and spirituality.

In his important study *Theologia: The Fragmentation and Unity of Theological Education* (1983), the noted American writer Edward Farley (1929–) points to a series of developments in theological education which have led to the loss of a defining theological vision characterized by the coinherence of piety and intellect.[2] Farley argues that the term *theologia* has lost its original meaning, which he defines as 'sapiential and personal knowledge of divine self-disclosure' leading to 'wisdom or discerning judgement indispensable for human living'. Theology used to be – and, in Farley's view, still should be – 'not just objective science, but a personal knowledge of God and the things of God'.

This is an important point, as it indicates that the term 'theology' has suffered a serious and detrimental shift in meaning in the twentieth century. Properly understood, theology embraces, informs and sustains spirituality. It is easy to argue for a gulf having opened up between theology and spirituality in the last hundred years or so – but this must be seen in the light of cultural assumptions, especially within the western academy, which have forced theology to see itself as an academically neutral subject, not involving commitment on the part of its teachers or students, which is primarily concerned with information about abstract ideas. This is not how theology was understood in earlier generations. It is perfectly proper to point out that Christian theology cannot remain faithful to its subject matter if it regards itself as purely propositional or cognitive in nature. The Christian encounter with God is transformative. As Packer, following John Calvin (1509–64), pointed out, to know God is to be changed by God; true knowledge of God leads to worship, as the believer is caught up in a transforming and renewing encounter with the living God.

In his 1991 essay 'Evangelical Foundations for Spirituality', Packer undertook to lay the necessary theological foundations for spirituality. Some of those foundations were hinted at in his 1990 article 'An Introduction to Systematic Spirituality'. In the present article, which took the form of a contribution to a volume honouring Packer's Regent College colleague Klaus Bockmuehl, Packer developed those ideas further. The essay deals with two major issues, each of which merits close consideration.

The first major issue concerns what a distinctively evangelical spirituality might look like. How does the distinctive ethos of evangelicalism find its expression in matters of spirituality? Notice, incidentally, that Packer now uses the term 'spirituality' to designate this critically important area of Christian thought, where he earlier would have preferred 'spiritual theology' or some related phrase.

The second issue relates to the theological foundations of evangelical spirituality. What are the theological foundations and distinctives of such a spirituality? Packer suggests that there are three such theological perspectives which govern and inform evangelical spirituality: thoroughgoing theocentricity; thoroughgoing trinitarianism; and thoroughgoing two-worldliness. Yet Packer argues that these theological perspectives are to be supplemented by three basic biblical themes, each of which illuminates the quest for an authentically evangelical spirituality.

It is instructive to read this essay after having engaged with the 1990 essay 'An Introduction to Systematic Spirituality', and to note how the two interact.

Related works by Packer

Knowing God, London: Hodder and Stoughton; Downers Grove, IL: InterVarsity Press, 1973.

'On Knowing God', *Tenth: An Evangelical Quarterly* (July 1975), pp. 11–25. (Essay 8 in this collection.)

'Knowing Notions or Knowing God?', *Pastoral Renewal* 6/9 (March 1982), pp. 65–68.

'An Introduction to Systematic Spirituality', *Crux* 26/1 (March 1990), pp. 2–8. (Essay 12 in this collection.)

Evangelical foundations for spirituality

I

For Christians in the historic main stream, theology means thinking and talking about God and his creatures in the light of God's own self-disclosure in history and Scripture; ethics means determining what types of action and qualities of character please God; and spirituality (which has also been called spiritual, moral, ascetic, devotional, and casuistical theology in its time) means

enquiry into the whole Christian enterprise of pursuing, achieving, and cultivating communion with God, which includes both public worship and private devotion, and the results of these in actual Christian life[1]

– or, more briefly, mapping what Henry Scougal labelled 'the life of God in the soul of man'.[2] One could fairly characterize spirituality as the study of godliness in its root and its fruit.

These definitions show that, on the one hand, ethics and spirituality should be viewed as departments of theology and be controlled by the truths of theology and, on the other hand, theology should always have an eye to the ethical and devotional implications of its theses, since God's truth is given to be practised.

But it does not always work out this way. Because theology is commonly anchored in universities and similar academic settings, where the advancement of learning rather than the direction of life is the goal, some theologians never see ethics and spirituality as their business, and limit their interest to abstract and formal truth in a way that ultimately trivializes theology itself; while some exponents of spiritual life, not seeing themselves as theologians or theology as basic to their task, let their wisdom appear as comments from experience for those who care rather than as elucidation of the summons to commune with God that the gospel issues to every believer.

Since the age of the great Puritan and pietist theologians ended, this disjunction between theology, ethics, and spirituality at the conceptual level, and the consequent distribution of their study between three different groups of specialists, have brought great weakness into the churches. This distribution is now, however, firmly institutionalized in the course structures and syllabi and in the make-up of teaching faculties in most centres of Christian learning, and hence cannot easily be changed. In practice, it is only when individual instructors labour of set purpose to bring the three fields of concern together in their own teaching that the disjunction is ever nowadays overcome.

Perhaps the most memorable feature of Klaus Bockmuehl's career as a professional theologian was that he set himself to do precisely that. He saw ethics and spiritual life as branches of theology, just as Augustine and Luther and Calvin and Wesley and Edwards had done before him. He kept the three together in the classroom, and in two small books, the latter finished only weeks before his death, he highlighted some of the deepest roots of discipleship.[3] He saw his teaching role as requiring him to be transparently a believer, letting his own evangelical spirituality appear, and the renewing of a literate, honest, childlike evangelical spirituality in others was a matter of constant concern to him. In this respect he was a shining example of a theologian, so to speak, in the round.

As a former colleague, I would now pay tribute to his memory and his purpose by offering a sketch of what seem to be key perspectives for the realizing of authentic evangelical spirituality in our time.

II

By addressing two preliminary questions I can clarify my standpoint and thrust.

First: is evangelical spirituality distinctive? If so, how?

For me, as for Klaus Bockmuehl, 'evangelical' means, not Lutheran, Reformational, pietistic or Baptistic as distinct from Catholic, Orthodox, or post-Enlightenment, but relating and witnessing biblically to Jesus Christ. An evangelical is one who honours and proclaims the Christ of the Scriptures, who is Jesus of Nazareth, God incarnate, humankind's crucified and risen Saviour and reigning Lord, Son of the Father and way to the Father, focus of Christian faith, hope, love, worship and service. Christ, for the evangelical, is not just the potent memory, kept alive in the church, of a good man long gone, as he is for so many post-Enlightenment thinkers; rather, he is the one slain Lamb of God now alive from the dead, the Master and Friend of each believer for time and eternity, the divine Redeemer who with the Father and the Holy Spirit is to be adored for ever and ever. It is common nowadays to define an evangelical in terms of a methodological commitment to the divine truth and trustworthiness of the canonical Scriptures and there are good historical reasons for starting the definition there;[4] but the heart of the matter is devotional and doxological commitment to the Christ of those Scriptures, in the terms adumbrated above.

What follows, then? This: that from the perspective of individual identity, all who understand Christianity as faith in, love for, and worship of Jesus Christ as their sin-bearing Saviour are evangelicals; all who affirm his sufficiency to save sinners are proclaiming evangelical theology; and every projection of trustful, grateful Christ-centredness as the true and only path of life for sinners is evangelical spirituality, even when justification by faith, salvation by grace, and Christ's threefold office as prophet, priest, and king are not articulated in an adequately biblical way. Theological deficiency here certainly needs correction, but the pattern of piety itself is already evangelical in type before the conceptual corrections take place. If 'catholic' is taken in a theological rather than denominational sense as signifying commitment to the universal over the local, occasional, eccentric and sectarian, then evangelical spirituality appears as authentically catholic, inasmuch as it represents the devotion of what has always been the central Christian flow.

Conscious acknowledgment of Jesus Christ as one's Saviour, of his Father as one's own Father through the grace of adoption, and of the Holy Spirit as Sustainer of this twofold fellowship, is of the essence of evangelical spirituality, and this trinitarian framework sets it apart from anything else that is called spirituality anywhere in the church or in the world.

Second: is the study of evangelical spirituality important? If so, why?

Competence in the field of spirituality is always important as a basis for pastoral care and direction, whereby penitents are pointed along the path of growth in Christ. Pastors, as the Puritans in particular never tired of insisting, are called to be physicians of the soul, promoting and guarding the spiritual health of God's people, and their work requires them to understand what it means for individuals to love and enjoy God through Jesus Christ. As physicians need knowledge of physiology in order to detect and treat pathological states, so pastors need insight into spirituality in order to teach and advise for the furthering of spiritual health and the overcoming of sin and folly in their many forms. Excellence in spiritual direction has been rare on both sides of the Reformational divide, and this seems to reflect the fact that studies of the dynamics of spiritual life have too often been crudely, simplistically, and carelessly done – a state of things that had to change, and has perhaps started to change already. Clearly, however, more competence in spirituality is being currently called for than is currently available.

Furthermore, a competent understanding of the spiritual life is needed today in order to vindicate in face of secular scepticism and post-Christian humanism the historic Christian contention that a life of faith, hope, love and worship, of fighting sin, struggling to pray, and denying oneself across the board, is our only true fulfilment in this world. That thesis has doubtless never sounded more paradoxical anywhere than it does in the permissive, materialistic modern West; yet it never was more true, and skill in spirituality is required in order to state it well, as it deserves to be stated, in our present world.[5]

III

All I can attempt in this brief essay is to specify three basic theological perspectives and three basic biblical themes that in my view need fresh attention if a fully evangelical spirituality is to flourish in our time.

The three theological perspectives are as follows:

(1) Thoroughgoing theocentricity

It is often and truly said that the gospel message, through the power of the Spirit of Christ that it mediates, turns people's lives upside down. Less frequently it is noted that the anti-God syndrome in our system called original sin has turned our lives upside-down already, so that this inverting change of heart by the Spirit, commonly called conversion, actually sets us right way up, to live in the way truly natural to us for the first time ever.

What happens is that in a sovereign act of grace that the New Testament theologizes as birth from God (John 1:13; 13:5–8; James 1:18; 1 Peter 1:23; 1 John 3:9; 5:1, 4), co-resurrection with Christ (Rom. 6:4–11; Eph. 2:1–10; Col. 2:13; 3:1–11), new creation in Christ (2 Cor. 5:17; Gal. 6:5) and regeneration (Titus 3:5), and that pietism highlights as *die Wiedergeburt*, God unites the individual to the risen Lord in such a way that the dispositional drives of Christ's perfect human character – the inner urgings, that is, to honour, adore, love, obey, serve and please God, and to benefit others for both their sake and his sake – are now reproduced at the motivational centre of that individual's being. And they are reproduced, in face of the contrary egocentric cravings of fallen nature, in a dominant way, so that the Christian, though still troubled and tormented by the urgings of indwelling sin, is no longer ruled by those urgings in the way that was true before.

Being under grace, the Christian is freed from sin (Rom. 6:14 – 7:6; Gal. 5:13–25; cf. John 8:31–36); the motivational theocentricity of the heart set free will prompt the actions that form the habits of Christ-likeness that constitute the Spirit's fruit (Gal. 5:22–23), and thus the holiness of radical repentance (daily abandonment of self-centred will), childlike humility (daily listening to what God says in his Word, and daily submission to what he sends in his providence), and love to God and humans that honours and serves both, will increasingly appear. This thoroughgoing intellectual and moral theocentricity, whereby Christians come to live no longer for themselves but for him who died and rose to save them (cf. 2 Cor. 5:15), is first God's gift and then the Christian's task, and as such it is the foundation not only of sound ethics but also of true spirituality.

Not surprisingly, the crusading secular humanists of the past hundred years have seen this self-abandoning theocentricity of faith, hope, and love as unnatural and impoverishing. Christians, however, experience it, despite the inward and outward conflicts in which it involves them, as joy, so long at least as their commitment to it remains clear-headed and whole-hearted, and the natural, Spirit-sustained functioning of their regenerate hearts is not inhibited by psychological blockage, hurt, or disorientation.[6] The knowledge that they live under the guarding, guiding, protecting and empowering hand of a loving almighty Creator, with a hope of glory assuring them that however good anything has been so far there is better to come, and that it will eternally be so, yields joy without end. In face of today's hedonistic secularism the 'solid joys' (John Newton's phrase) of thoroughgoing Christian theocentricity need to be stressed.

(2) Thoroughgoing trinitarianism

In contemporary reflection on the Christian life, lack of a rigorous biblical trinitarianism is a great widespread weakness – though there are signs that God is blending post-Barthian theology with charismatic experientialism in a way that should bring improvement here.[7] The weakness seems due to four causes. The first is an unawareness of the relevance of the Trinity for evangelical life as a result of rating it a theologoumenon of orthodoxy, to be upheld against heretics, and not seeing it as the structural frame of godliness itself.

The second cause is the 'humanitarian' Christology of liberalism, which sees Jesus as an exemplary God-filled man rather than a gracious divine Saviour,[8] plus the practical demythologizing of the Holy Spirit that was almost standard in the medieval doctrine of grace (maintained by Roman Catholics into this century) and that still breaks surface wherever the Spirit is referred to, whether by liberals or by conservatives, as 'it' (a supernatural influence) rather than 'he' (a personal agent).[9] Liberal theology, which was always implicitly unitarian, has had a baleful influence here.

The third cause is failure to appreciate what trinitarianism actually means – that, so far from being a kind of conundrum devised at Nicaea and Constantinople in order to squelch Arianism, it is in fact the joyful proclamation that, as a Puritan somewhere put it, and as John's Gospel shows, 'God himself is a sweet society', and that the purpose first of creation and then of redemption was to extend that fellowship of love by bringing creatures into it.

The fourth cause, linked with the third, is unawareness that the essence of the Christian life is involvement in the relational life of the triune Godhead, knowing the Father of the Son as one's own heavenly Saviour and Lord, and knowing the Holy Spirit, really though indirectly, as imparting vision and empowering devotion from which none should ever have lapsed. These causes have long combined to keep the church from seeing that a truly theocentric spirituality will be truly trinitarian. It is a happy thing that now at last, it seems, this obstacle to devotional right-mindedness is being overcome.

To say that sound spirituality must be fully trinitarian is to say that in our fellowship with God we must learn to do full justice to the part that each of the divine Three plays in the team job, as we may venture to call it, of saving us from sin, restoring our ruined humanness, and bringing us finally to glory. Should we neglect the Son, whether through some doctrinaire revisionist Christology or simply by lapsing into natural religion with Islam, so that we lose our focus on the Son's mediation, blood atonement, risen life, royal glory, and heavenly intercession, we shall slip back into legalism, a version of the treadmill religion of works, probably linked in these days with a syncretist theology.

Should we neglect the Spirit, losing our focus on the fellowship with Christ that he creates, the renewing of nature that he effects, the assurance and joy that he evokes, and the enabling for service that he bestows, we shall slip back into formalism, a version of the religion of aspiration and perspiration that lacks both inspiration and transformation, a religion of mechanical observances, low expectations, deep ruts of routine, and grooves that quickly turn into graves.

Should we neglect the Father, losing our focus on the tasks he sets and the disciplines he imposes (cf. Heb. 12:5-14), we shall become soft, lazy, self-absorbed, unsteady and erratic, with a dull and sleepy conscience - spoiled children, in the most literal sense, in God's family. As in human families, so in the divine: children who, for whatever reason, do not experience, along with love, moral strength and precision in their fathers carry character weaknesses with them throughout their lives. God's spoiled children will reveal themselves as exploitative egoists who make heavy weather of any troubles and setbacks that come their way, thus failing spectacularly to live out the self-denying theocentricity to which they pay lip-service.

True trinitarianism in the head and the heart can take us beyond these pitfalls; but anything less virtually guarantees a spiritual development that is one way or another stunted and deformed.

(3) Thoroughgoing two-worldliness·

New Testament Christianity is essentially two-worldly: not other-worldly in the sense of lacking interest in this world, but seeing life here as travel to, and preparation for, and indeed as a foretaste of, a life hereafter in which all without exception will reap what they sowed here in terms of their attitudes and decisions God-ward. Those who are Christ's will receive infinite enrichment in terms of joy in their God and Saviour; others face infinite loss, first of God's active kindness and then of all the good and pleasant things that this kindness brings now.

Death, or the return of Jesus Christ, whichever comes first, will effect a transition from the world of life-choices to the world where our Maker gives us what, fundamentally, we have chosen concerning him – either to be eternally with him, or eternally without him. And since our experience of the destiny we chose will be unending, and will in fact grow directly out of our life now, the whole of this present life should be lived in light of the future – which means, for Christians, living in the power of the magnificent hope of glory with Christ that the Father has given them.

Here is a further aspect of the naturalness to which regenerating grace restores us; for whereas the proverb says, while there's life there's hope, the deeper truth is that only where there is hope is there life. Man is a hoping animal, who lapses into gloom and apathy when he has nothing to look forward to. So Christ, who diagnoses living in the present with never a thought about death and the life to come as supreme folly (cf. Luke 12:5–21), directs us to lay up treasure, not on earth, but in heaven (Matt. 6:19–21; Luke 12:32–34) – in other words, to live, not in this-worldly, but in two-worldly terms, facing up to the issues of eternity as we have stated them. All Christians seem to have understood this, and laboured to act on it, until relatively recently.

But nowadays Christians have largely lost the two-worldly perspective of the Scriptures and have embraced for all practical purposes the Marxist, materialist, secular humanist assumption that this life is all that matters, because it is all there is. Creative Christian thought about spiritual live is now funnelled almost entirely into exploring spiritual and relational enrichment in this world, and Christians generally seem to have internalized the Marxist mockery of 'pie in the sky when you die', so that they feel deep down, just as Marxists do, that any serious reflection on the life to come is uncouth and unhealthy.

So we preach to each other, and write books for each other, about the path to present blessings in its various forms, and heaven and hell hardly get a mention. We treat any call to think seriously about the world to come, not as sober Christian realism, based on Scripture, but as sign either of escapism, if the focus is on heaven, or of vindictiveness, if it is on hell; and in both cases we see it as something regrettable. The wisdom, received from the Christian past, that only when one is ready to die is one ready to live, is forgotten; with the world, we treat continuance of life, as such, as the supreme value. Death finds us unprepared, and in daily life it is observable how little strength we have for the practice of detachment or renunciation in any form at all. Authentic spirituality, however, requires of us that we relearn the discipline of sitting loose to everything here in order to lay hold of glory hereafter, and our living cannot be in shape, Christianly speaking, until we have recovered the two-world perspective, with its attendant recognition of the eternal significance of all present action, that the New Testament exhibits to us.

IV

To these three basic theological perspectives for spirituality I now add three basic biblical themes, from which, as I see it, all that is essential for understanding what godliness is may be drawn. I merely point to, and generalize about, the wealth of material that awaits exposition under each head; this is, after all, no more than a brief programmatic essay. There will be some formal overlap with things already said, but they will be approached from a different angle.

(1) The new relationship: the Christian under God's covenant

All biblical religion has a royal covenantal form: that is, it is a matter of pledged mutual commitment, in which two parties give themselves to each other in total love and loyalty on the basis of promise, stipulations and requirements imposed by the superior party on the inferior, in this case by the divine king and benefactor on those he has saved. Every Christian believer, Jew and Gentile alike, lives under God's new covenant by virtue of being united to Jesus Christ, the specific seed of Abraham to whom specific promises were given when God covenanted with Abraham in the patriarchal age (see Gen. 12 – 13; 15; 17, interpreted by Gal. 3). The contrast between 'new' and 'old' covenants has to do with the greater range of God's promises, and the greater adequacy of his mediatorial arrangements in and through Christ, as compared with the provisional, typical arrangements that had gone before (see Heb. 1 – 3, and Jesus' words at the Last Supper: Matt. 26:28; Luke 22:20; 1 Cor. 11:25); it does not bear on Paul's insistence that the establishing of those who are in Christ as Abraham's seed and heirs of all that God's blessing of Abraham embraced was God's plan throughout (Gal. 3:14, 26–29).

Under the old covenant, the spiritually alive person trusted God and lived by faith in his promises, just as the New Testament believers were later to do, and godly character, as seen and modelled for us in the Psalms, had in it at least the following dispositional qualities: responsive attention to God's words of self-revelation, with loyal conformity to his commands and trustful hope in his gracious purposes (Ps. 119); adoring admiration of God's work in creation and providence (Pss. 46; 104; 107); submissive patience under God's afflictions (Ps. 102; cf. Job; Lam.); hearty gratitude for God's gifts (Ps. 118); active identification with God's cause (Pss. 101; 139:19–24); constant desire for God's fellowship (Pss. 16; 42) and joy in it as it is experienced (Ps. 23); committed solidarity with God's people (Ps. 7); prayerfulness at all times (Ps. 63); and neighbourliness with all one's fellows (see Lev. 19:13–18).

Under the new covenant none of this changes, and these qualities remain integral to godliness still. The profiles of New Testament saints, however, embody four further behavioural characteristics, each shaped by the enrichment of God's present grace to his people that the new covenant has brought. These characteristics are as follows: a personal relationship of faith and love towards Jesus Christ, the risen Saviour and Lord; a responsible use of the freedom from subjection to legal codes that God's gift of justification and adoption into his family has conferred; an active involvement in the church's every-member ministry, through receiving, discerning, and using the gifts (*charismata*) bestowed by the Holy Spirit; and a resolute detachment from pursuing this world's allurements of pleasure, profit, and position, a detachment maintained through the power of one's new-found love for God and one's hope of future glory with Christ (1 John 2:15–17; 3:2–3).

All this yields a basic definition of Christian spirituality as recognition of and response to the reality and power of God through Jesus Christ in the covenant of divine grace. This covenantal basis for communion with God was central to the Puritan understanding of the Christian life, and was spelt out clearly in the Westminster Confession, but less has been heard of it recently, and renewed exploration of it is currently needed. God's covenant with each Christian is a covenant of permanent friendship, like that between Jonathan and David (cf. 1 Sam. 1:3; 20:2), and of abiding fidelity, like that between husband and wife (cf. Ezek. 16:8; Mal. 2:14), and it defines the relationship in a definite way that has to be clearly grasped if the relationship itself is to grow and deepen. Here, then, is a major biblical agenda item for the renewing of evangelical spirituality today.

(2) The new creation: the Christian sharing Christ's life

The New Testament speaks emphatically of the 'newness' (*kainotēs*, from *kainos*, meaning 'of a new kind': see Rom. 6:4; 7:6; cf. 12:2) of the Christian's life in Christ, as compared and contrasted with all that went before. John, Peter and James, as we saw, present the start of this newness as a new birth, and Paul presents it as a new creation, as co-resurrection with Jesus, and as putting off the old person and putting on the new one (Eph. 4:4; Col. 3:10).

Putting off and putting on is the language of changing clothes, and when the NIV renders 'man' as 'self' it misses some of the meaning; what the

Christian has put off is solidarity with Adam, and what he puts on is Christ, or solidarity with Christ, as the source and principle of his new life (cf. Rom. 13:14; Gal. 3:28).

Each image entails the thought of a totally fresh beginning: one has ceased to be what one was, and has commenced to be what previously one was not. Paul then charts the course of this newness in terms of being restored as God's image (Col. 3:10), serving righteousness and God as bondslaves of both (Rom. 6:16–23), and bringing forth the fruit of the Spirit (Gal. 5:22–25); John speaks of walking in the light (1 John 1:7); and indeed the whole body of New Testament writers labour the thought that Christians are called to live in a radically different way from those around them, and from the way they themselves lived before. The proclamation of newness as both a divine gift and a Christian obligation is loud and clear.

We glanced earlier at the theological and psychological reality of this great change, which the dying-and-rising symbolism of baptism proclaims (cf. Rom. 6:3–4; Col. 2:12) and the Holy Spirit, by uniting us to the risen Christ, actually effects. Intellectually the change is an opening and enlightening of the blinded mind to discern what previously we could not discern (2 Cor. 4:3–6; Eph. 1:17–18; cf. Luke 24:25, 31, 45) – namely, the spiritual realities of Christ and his salvation. Motivationally, within the heart, the change is an implanting in us of the inclinations of Christ's perfect humanity through our ingrafting into him: this produces in us a mind-set and lifestyle that are not explicable in terms of what we were before. The Spirit-born person, as Jesus indicated, cannot but be a mystery to those who are not born again themselves; they can form no idea of what makes him tick (cf. John 3:8).

The New Testament enables us to form some idea of the characteristic exercise of heart that marks those whom God has thus brought into newness of life. Knowing the truth of the gospel, each will adore Christ as, in Newton's words,

> Jesus, my Shepherd, Husband, Friend,
> My Prophet, Priest, and King,
> My Lord, my Life, my Way, my End,

and will feel inwardly what Charles Wesley expressed when he wrote:

> Jesus, my all in all thou art;
> My rest in toil, my ease in pain,
> The medicine of my broken heart,
> In war my peace, in loss my gain,

My smile beneath the tyrant's frown,
In shame my glory and my crown:

In want my plentiful supply,
In weakness my almighty power,
In bonds my perfect liberty,
My light in Satan's darkest hour,
In grief my joy unspeakable,
My life in death, my heaven in hell.

Seeing themselves as travellers on the way home, they will live by hope – hope, quite specifically, of meeting their beloved Saviour face to face, and being with him for ever. Discerning sinful desires in themselves despite their longing to be sin-free, and finding that in their quest for total righteousness their reach exceeds their grasp, they will live in tension and distress at their frustrating infirmities (cf. Rom. 7:14–25). They will call on God as their heavenly Father, glorify and love him, honour and love other people, hate and fight evil in all its forms, grow downwards into a deeper and more childlike humility, and practise patience under pressure. All this is at the same time determined obedience to God's law, conscious imitation of Christ in attitude and purpose, and satisfying fulfilment of their own new instincts – in other words, naturalness in expressing their own new selves.

A further biblical agenda item for the renewal of spirituality in our time, in face of the misunderstandings of human nature that secular humanism sponsors and the whole western educational system assumes, is the study of the newness of the Christian person, and the naturalness of godliness when one is a new creature in Christ.

(3) The new community: the Christian in God's church

The gospel fosters individuality, in the sense of realization that as regards the present decisions that determine eternal destiny one stands alone before God; no-one can make those decisions for someone else, and no-one can enter the kingdom of God by hanging on to someone else's coat-tails. The individuality that consists of a sense of personal identity and responsibility Godward is a Christian virtue, making for wise and thoughtful behaviour, and is a necessity for mature life and growth in Christ. But it has nothing to do with individualism, which is actually a proud unwillingness to accept a place in a team of peers and to be bound by group consensus. The gospel condemns individualism as disruptive of the life of the divine family, the new community of believers together that God is building in each place where individual Christians have emerged. Harmonious consensus, undergirded by brotherly love, is to be the goal for every church, and individualism is to be overcome by mutual deference. So, at least, says the New Testament.

But the necessary protest of pietism in continental Europe and of Puritanism and evangelicalism in Britain against unthinking conformity to the routines of a state church on the supposition that this is all there is to Christianity have brought to birth not only much biblical individuality, but a great deal of unbiblical individualism as well. The latter is still with us, constantly spawning parachurch organizations accountable to no-one but their founders, and nowadays it is almost expected that persons of intense piety will want to sit loose to the structured life of the organized churches.

The modern lay movement, expressed in cursillo ministry, small groups, accountability and discipling relationships and all that goes with these, seeks to curb this individualism, but often falls victim to new forms of it, and the same has to be said of the charismatic renewal. The study of biblical principles and patterns for the involvement of the individual Christian in the worshipping and serving human units that, locally and ecumenically, make up the body of Christ is a further agenda item for a renewed spirituality.

The corporate aspect of Christian spirituality can be defined as practising mutual love and care in God's family on the basis that this is the life to which we are called and for which Christ equips us: each believer must be ready to lay down his or her life for Christ in others, and must be duly grateful when others lay down their lives and bear burdens for Christ in his or her own self. This is not, however, so well understood, nor so well practised, as it needs to be.

V

Though a gentle, patient, and tolerant person in himself, Klaus Bockmuehl saw contemporary Christians as called to battle – for truth in theology, for faithfulness in the churches, and for the wisdom and glory of God in a secular, apostate, and now mad world.

> Under the perspectives of good and evil, God and secularism, there is more drama in the twentieth century than would ever be necessary to give profile to our lives. Sometimes our days get dull, because we forget the perspective of the battle that is often waged so invisibly and silently. But it is above all in these struggles that we today find the concrete concerns for our prayer, intercession, proclamation, and teaching.[10]

The quest to recover true spirituality, which from another standpoint is the quest to recover authentic humanness, is part of this battle, both in the church and outside it, where secular humanism stands entrenched. I hope that Klaus would have approved my suggestions as to where we shall find resources for the fight.

Questions for study

1. What does Packer consider to be essential to a specifically evangelical spirituality?
2. Locate the following citation, and set it against its context: 'Conscious acknowledgment of Jesus Christ as one's Saviour, of his Father as one's own Father through the grace of adoption, and of the Holy Spirit as Sustainer of this twofold fellowship, is of the essence of evangelical spirituality.' What does Packer mean by this? And how does he develop this trinitarian frame of reference?
3. Why does Packer believe that evangelicals should become interested in spirituality?
4. According to Packer, what are the consequences of neglecting the person of the Holy Spirit in spirituality?
5. What does Packer mean by his call for evangelicals to recover 'the two-world perspective'. What are the two worlds in question? And what difference does this perspective make to spirituality?
6. Does Packer see evangelical spirituality as something which is individual, or corporate?

Notes

Preamble

1. See J. I. Packer, '"Keswick" and the Reformed Doctrine of Sanctification', *Evangelical Quarterly* 27 (1955), pp. 153–167. A later, and more eirenic, evaluation of the Keswick teaching may be found in his *Keep in Step with the Spirit*, Grand Rapids, MI: Fleming H. Revell; Leicester: Inter-Varsity Press, 1984, pp. 145–164.
2. Edward Farley, *Theologia: The Fragmentation and Unity of Theological Education* (Philadelphia: Fortress Press, 1983, pp. x, 7. The debate which resulted may be followed in works such as J. C. Hough and J. B. Cobb Jr (eds.), *Christian Identity and Theological Education* (Chico, CA: Scholar's Press, 1985); Charles M. Wood, *Vision and Discernment: An Orientation in Theological Study* (Atlanta: Scholar's Press, 1985); Farley, *The Fragility of Knowledge: Theological Education in the Church and University* (Philadelphia: Fortress Press, 1988).

Essay

1. Henry Rack, *Twentieth Century Spirituality*, London: Epworth Press, 1969, p. 2.

2. Scougal's work under this title was published in 1677, and was much appreciated by the Wesleys and Whitefield.

3. Klaus Bockmuehl, *Living by the Gospel*, Colorado Springs: Helmers and Howard, 1986; *Listening to the God Who Speaks*, Colorado Springs: Helmers and Howard, 1990.

4. See my *'Fundamentalism' and the Word of God*, London: Inter-Varsity Fellowship, 1958.

5. J. I. Packer and Thomas Howard, *Christianity the True Humanism*, Waco: Word Books, 1985, is a first attempt.

6. Some of these inhibiting factors are dealt with in James Houston, *The Transforming Friendship*, Oxford: Lion Publishing, 1989; *In Search of Happiness*, Oxford: Lion Publishing, 1990.

7. See three books by Thomas Smail: *Reflected Glory*, London: Hodder and Stoughton; Grand Rapids: Eerdmans, 1976; *The Forgotten Father*, London: Hodder and Stoughton; Grand Rapids: Eerdmans, 1979; *The Giving Gift*, London: Hodder and Stoughton, 1988.

8. I have discussed this in 'Jesus Christ the Lord', in *The Lord Christ*, ed. J. R. W. Stott, London: Collins, 1977, pp. 32–60, and in 'The Uniqueness of Jesus Christ', *Churchman* 1978/2, pp. 101–111.

9. One cannot but regret that Alistair Heron, *The Holy Spirit*, Philadelphia: Westminster Press, 1988, vii, pp. 173–176, argues for the impersonal usage.

10. *Living by the Gospel*, p. 119.

15. 'On from Orr: the cultural crisis, rational realism, and incarnational ontology' (1996)

The complex title of this mature piece of writing should alert its readers to the fact that they are in for some strong theological meat in this important essay. The background to the piece is the debate which broke out within the North American evangelical community in the 1990s over the question of the proper limits of dialogue or collaboration between evangelicals and non-evangelicals. The debate initially centred on the document 'Evangelicals and Catholics Together' (1994). From J. I. Packer's perspective, this statement built a platform on which evangelicals and Roman Catholics who shared a common faith in the Trinity, the incarnation, the atonement and new birth could unite and work together in reaching out to an increasingly secular society. In this context, Packer reaffirmed words once written by C. S. Lewis: 'When all is said (and truly said) about the divisions of Christendom, there remains, by God's mercy, an enormous common ground.'[1] For Packer, it was a matter of priority to work to occupy that common ground by seeking substantive convergence together, without forfeiting or fudging any specific truth.

For Packer, it seemed quite clear that 'Evangelicals and Catholics Together' was a parachurch document in which individual evangelicals and Catholics were invited to ally themselves for the work of Christian mission. Although the Protestant and Catholic church systems are opposed to each other on, for example, major aspects of the doctrine of salvation, Packer argued that those who trust and love the Lord Jesus Christ on both sides of the Reformation know that they are united in him, making some kind of collaboration entirely proper. Packer had always argued that the most fundamental level of ecumenical activity is to be involved in Christian mission, and saw the document as an important statement of the need to bear witness to Jesus Christ as Saviour to an apostate world.[2]

In Packer's view, the present needs of both church and community in the western world called out for some such collaboration across denominational divides. Two main considerations prompted this conclusion. First, that the 'slide into secularism and paganism that is so much a mark of current culture' demands that there should be some kind of 'alliance of all who love the Bible and its Christ'. A united Christian witness is necessary in the face of an increasingly secular cultural situation. Packer stresses that he is not advocating official collaboration between denominations, but individual alliances across denominational divides, along the lines of the parachurch coalitions already existing within evangelicalism itself.

Second, the historic division between 'relatively homogeneous Protestant churches and a relatively homogeneous Church of Rome' reflects a situation which no longer pertains. A new division has emerged within Christianity, which is of considerably greater importance – the division between theological conservatives (whom Packer prefers to term 'conservationists') who 'honour the Christ of the Bible and historic creeds and confessions' on the one hand, and 'theological liberals and radicals' on the other. This division can be seen within both the Protestant and the Catholic churches. Why should not conservatives form an alliance across the denominations, to fight liberalism and radicalism? 'Domestic differences about salvation and the church should not hinder us from joint action in seeking to re-Christianize the North American milieu.'

The document (and Packer's endorsement) gave rise to angry criticisms. One typical response was that Catholics and Protestants were antithetically opposed, with the result that neither could legitimately regard the other as being Christian with any integrity or honesty. Protestants should therefore treat Catholics as non-Christian or anti-Christian (and *vice versa*). It was a single-shot response, in that once this point had been made, no further discussion was possible. The result was that those who believed that such dialogue was dishonest refused to have anything to do with it, leaving those who disagreed with them to get on with the dialogue. The dialogue thus continued, without those who objected to it.

In the spring of 1995, Packer took this approach a stage further. He was invited to attend the Aiken Conference, organized by Orthodox Christians, which had been called to 'test whether an "ecumenical orthodoxy", solidly based upon the classic Christian faith, can become the foundation for a unified and transformative vision to the age we live in'. Packer's response to this question was strongly affirmative, and developed further his policy of collaboration within and across 'great-tradition Christianity', in the face of opposition from fundamentalists within Protestantism, Eastern Orthodoxy and Roman Catholicism. Packer offered his readers a vision of a 'transcendent new togetherness resulting both within and across denominational lines'. It is this essay which is reprinted for consideration here. It marks perhaps Packer's finest statement of his vision of 'great-tradition Christianity', and merits close – yet critical – consideration.

Related works by Packer

'Why I Signed It', *Christianity Today*, 12 December 1994, pp. 34–37.
'Crosscurrents among Evangelicals', in C. Colson and R. J. Neuhaus (eds.), *Evangelicals and Catholics Together: Toward a Common Mission*, Dallas: Word, 1995, pp. 147–174.

On from Orr: the cultural crisis, rational realism, and incarnational ontology

The announced aim of our discussions is to 'test whether an "ecumenical orthodoxy", solidly based upon the classic Christian faith, can become the foundation for a unified and transformative witness to the age we live in'.[1] The first thing I want to do is to state firmly that I believe it can, and to explain where I come from in saying that.

Starting-point

As an Anglican, a Protestant, an evangelical, and in C. S. Lewis' sense a 'mere Christian',[2] that is, as it is sometimes put, a 'small-c' catholic, I theologize out of what I see as the authentic biblical and credal mainstream of Christian identity, the confessional and liturgical 'great tradition' that the church on earth has characteristically maintained from the start. History tells me how reactions against abuses, syncretisms with secular culture, lack of theological competence, individual idiosyncrasies, and corporate deadness of heart, have on occasion led sections of the church to deviate from the great tradition. History also tells me, however, how the Holy Spirit, operating through the biblical Word of God, has again and again reformed and renewed lapsed sections and faulty facets of the church. My present hope is that the Holy Spirit is preparing to do this, indeed is beginning to do it, again in the English-speaking West and in those European countries that were once called Christendom, just as he is currently causing the gospel to advance by breath-taking leaps and bounds in Asia, Africa, and Latin America. *Pace* Nietzsche and some already outmoded moderns, I affirm that God is most certainly not dead, and the great tradition will most surely survive.

At the Reformation skewed western understandings of the church, the sacraments, justification, faith, prayer, and ministry were, as I believe, corrected; but the corrections took place within the frame of the great tradition, and did not break it. (Such, at least, is my theological judgment, as it was the judgment of the magisterial Reformers against the Anabaptists. The visible church, of course, fragmented, but that is another story.) The great tradition of Christian faith and life includes, as it has always included, the following:

- recognizing the canonical Scriptures as the repository and channel of Christ-centred divine revelation;
- acknowledging the triune God as sovereign in creation, providence, and grace;
- focusing faith, in the sense both of belief and of trust, on Jesus Christ as God incarnate; as our crucified and living Saviour, Lord, Master, Friend, life and hope; and as the one Mediator of, and thus the only way to, a filial relationship with God his Father;
- seeing Christians as a family of forgiven sinners, now supernaturally regenerated in Christ and empowered for godliness by the Holy Spirit;
- seeing the church as a single supernatural society, and the two dominical sacraments as necessities of obedience, gestures of worship, and means of communion with God in Christ;
- practising prayer, obedience, purity, love, and service, and sanctifying all relationships in the home, the church, and the wider world, as the Christian's proper individual lifestyle;
- reckoning with the personal reality of evil, and maintaining purposeful hostility to sin and the devil;
- expecting death and final judgment to lead into the endless joy of heaven, where the glorified saints will live with Christ and each other for ever.

The great tradition has from time to time embraced different ways of explicating these things, but the things themselves are the non-negotiables of Christianity according to Christ, and the reconceiving specifically of theological method, of salvation, and of the church in Reformation theology should be seen as an attempt – essentially, in my view, a successful attempt – to spell out all these themes in the most accurate way. The great tradition has witnessed many misconceptions (about the Trinity, and grace, and justification, for instance) which, if consistently held, would make true saving knowledge of Jesus Christ inaccessible, and responsible theology is motivated, in part at least, by the desire to prevent such a thing ever happening. Theological watchfulness for the sake of the gospel, such as Paul models in Romans, 1 Corinthians, Galatians, Colossians, and the Pastorals, and John and Jude in their letters also, is itself part of the great tradition, and there is nothing unspiritual about theological controversy and debate when gospel truth and evangelical life are at stake.

The Reformation split the western church, and nationalism, combined later with differences about church order and more recently with ventures in personal leadership, has given us a Protestant world now divided into a four-or-five-figure number of separate ecclesiastical organizations. About this state of affairs I would only say that convergence of faith and fellowship ought to be desired and sought wherever the world-wide visible church has come apart. However much historic splits may have been justified as the only way to preserve faith, wisdom and spiritual life intact at a particular time, continuing them in complacency and without unease is unwarrantable. To regard emergency arrangements as the normal order of things is defective thinking. So we are right to be seeking convergence now, for reasons both of theology (God's one family, scattered world-wide, ought to look and act like one family, as Jesus prayed it might), and also for reasons of strategy relating to our mission of witness and influence (divided we can only expect to fall, united we might hope to stand). In face of our own divisions, which are sad, and the resurgent paganism of our culture, which is sadder, let us, without forfeiting or fudging any specific truth as we see it, but in a fellowship that is shaped by our common anchorage within the great tradition, continue to seek substantive convergence together. As C. S. Lewis wrote to his one-time pupil, Dom Bede Griffiths: 'When all is said (truly said) about the divisions of Christendom, there remains, by God's mercy, an enormous common ground.'[3] We should labour to occupy that common ground properly, as a priority task.

The current cultural crisis

We are seeking to envision effective witness 'to the age we live in'. Though no sociologist, and thus no expert on cultural shifts, and therefore very dependent at this point on others' insights, my argument requires me to state here how I see the overall trend and trajectory of western intellectual life today. We are told that a major transition is in process: that modernism is giving way to postmodernism and secular hopefulness to cynicism, narcissism and despair. On this I have two remarks to make.

First: if a major cultural transition is indeed taking place in the West it will not be the first time the church has been involved in such a thing. Cultural transition is in fact a major part of the historic Christian story. The early church itself was a force for cultural change. When Christianity hit the Gentile world in the second half of the first century it faced Gnostic dualism, superstitious fatalism, and philosophical pessimism in myriad forms, and had to engineer its own cultural transition from paganism to Christendom— which it did, most brilliantly and successfully, with Augustine's *City of God* standing out as a monument to the process. Christendom, once established, then lasted for more than a millennium. But in the seventeenth century the West began to shake loose from its Christian moorings, and the secular rationalism of the Enlightenment, which we now call modernism, increasingly took control of the western mind and milieu. Enlightenment modernism elbowed the churches of the West out of cultural leadership in the eighteenth and nineteenth centuries, and this trauma produced different responses. Protestants divided; some maintained the great tradition against modernism by rearguard action, others recast the tradition in modernist terms, which really meant abandoning it, and many mediating attempts to square the circle by marrying the two points of view were made. Thus, confusion grew. Meantime, modernist hostility to the tradition reinforced the Roman Catholic siege mentality which the conflict with Protestantism had already induced. Rome put up the shutters, and until Vatican II resisted modernist pressure far better than Protestantism did. The irony now, however, is that great-tradition Protestantism if making a spectacular comeback in these latter years of the twentieth century, while Rome is having to struggle to survive the modernist inroads to which Vatican II wittingly or unwittingly opened the door. The present Pope has laboured mightily to counter this modernism by reasserting the Catholic version of the great tradition, and it is clear that his lead is being widely followed, though the long-term outcome remains uncertain. The Eastern Orthodox story has been different, but in the one-time Soviet world, despite two generations of enormous pressure from atheistic statist secularism, itself a product of the modernist mentality, the tradition has not been stamped out, and today Orthodoxy is being set forth with new energy.

Surely, I say again, we may be confident that whatever happens to current western culture the tradition will continue to survive. After all, if we are right, God is in it and with it. Christ has promised that the gates of hell will not prevail against his church, and they certainly have not done so in their modernist form. So we have no reason to panic as we look to the future.

Second: I grant that a genuine cultural transition from modernism to postmodernism is occurring in some places, if not everywhere, but I note that it is very differently analysed by different people, which is why I must lay before you my own understanding of it before I go further.[4] In a nutshell, what I think we have to face up to is this: In cultural modernism, and in the humanism that is its child, truth and value are thought to be determined by reason working empirically on the basis of observation and experiment. Reason, thus used, is called scientific, and the conclusions of scientific reason are made the lodestar for organizing education and all forms of community life. Optimistically assuming that everything can be improved by planning and technology and will in any case sooner or later evolve into something better, modernism has for two centuries sought to shape society through industrial development, social engineering, urban triumphalism, and materialistic enrichment. This process has been expected to bring health, harmony, and happiness to all the world; but the unmistakable witness of our barbaric twentieth century is that it has totally failed to do so, and moreover is totally lacking in resources for doing so in the future. So among intellectuals and particularly in the universities, which are of course the first units of society that intellectuals impact, there is understandably in progress a reaction of disillusionment against the modernist habit of mind.

What form does the reaction take? In place of the quasi-behaviourist ideal of rational objectivity creating a collectivist community of like-thinking, well-socialized human ants in smoothly functioning anthills, a new ideal of freedom and fulfilment for the individual has emerged. This ideal assumes the technological conveniences of the anthill as a given, but rejects the notion of universal public truth on questions involving values; muffles and scrambles all communication, oral or documentary, by a process of deconstruction; debunks other people's absolutes and values by playful or cynical negation; and reduces public disagreements to power plays and power struggles between competing subcultures and manipulators. In postmodernism, individualistic subjectivity is set in a critical relation to all forms of supposedly scientific and consensual objectivity, and the personal 'story' of each human being is allowed to stand in judgment over the corporate 'stories' of all human groups, both secular and churchly. Spirituality without truth, individuality without constraints, pluralistic pragmatism, whimsy claiming to be wisdom, desire masquerading as morality, and benevolent tolerance of any and every view that does not tell you that you yourself are wrong, thus constitute the essence of postmodern culture. Relativistic randomness replaces rationalistic purpose; to think, say, and do your own thing in conscious detachment from, and sometimes opposition to, conventional public humanism, now becomes the true heart of humanness. Such is the new view of reality that is sprouting all over the western world today.

That the shadows of French existentialism, Marxist atheism, and American hippiedom hang heavy over postmodernism, that reductionism rules its head while cynicism eats at its heart, and that its idea of political correctness makes it tyrannical towards dissentients much sooner than was ever the case with modernism itself are surely evident facts, and very disturbing facts too. Claiming to be a bracing disinfectant for the mind, postmodernism appears as a mode of intellectual anarchy, and in cultural terms as very much a dead-end street. Some Christians, seeking ways of effective witness, have welcomed postmodernism as enhancing the significance of personal testimony and dissolving cultural prejudice against the supernatural, but by and large the shift from modernism to postmodernism seems to be a move from the frying-pan into the fire so far as Christian existence and outreach are concerned, for it makes the necessary affirmation of absolutes twice as hard as it was before. Words from G. K. Chesterton's 'Ballad of the White Horse' may well round off our glance at the postmodernist mindset:

> I bring you naught for your comfort,
> Yea, naught for your desire,
> But that the sky grows darker yet
> And the sea rises higher.

Our present agenda is not, however, to develop jeremiads, but to seek the most effective way of united Christian witness in a world where modernism and postmodernism divide the control between them, and to this task I now turn. What has been said puts us in a position to sketch out a strategy, and at this point I want to introduce someone who should be better known than he is, namely James Orr, who I believe can help us in a major way.

About James Orr

Orr (1844–1913) was a Scottish theologian and apologist of real distinction who contended tirelessly for great-tradition Christianity in days before the first World War, when Ritschlian liberalism, Wellhausenite higher criticism, and philosophical idealism of a kind that would today be called panentheistic were riding high in the Protestant world, and the redemptive supernaturalism of mainstream Christian faith was being steadily dissolved away in the older evangelical churches. As a man of his time, Orr did not interact with Roman Catholics, who in those days had no place in Scottish theological life, nor with Orthodox, about whom he had no specific knowledge as far as one can tell; his battles were with the liberal and modernist academic leadership in German and British Protestantism, and here he fought most effectively. He was a polymath with a remarkable range of exact learning in philosophy, history, theology and biblical studies; he was thoroughly abreast of German theological literature, more so it would seem than any of his peers; and he established himself as something of a one-man band in traditionalist polemics. Because he was swimming against the stream in the British churches, on intellectual lines similar to those of his contemporaries at old Princeton Seminary but without the solid ecclesiastical support that the Princetonians could command; because most of his academic peers viewed him as an extremely able, but ultimately tiresome, dinosaur; and because his ability in high-level debate so far outstripped that of his conservative supporters that while approving him they were unable properly to appreciate him; he was not valued at his true worth in his own day. Since his death he has been largely neglected, as expositors of massive argument in a monochrome literary style all too often are.[5] But something of his quality can be seen from the following paragraphs, which I take out of Alan Sell's brilliant survey of eight turn-of-the-century Scottish Presbyterian teachers:

> Orr's was no unthinking, narrow traditionalism. If he ended, more or less, with the faith of his fathers, it was because, having departed thence for argument's sake, he had returned to base, after slaying numerous foes *en route*. He was in no sense one who needed the security of the blinkered. On the contrary, he was at his best when judiciously dissecting the view of those who were far removed from him in spirit ... of all our divines, Orr's interests were the most catholic ... in detailed knowledge of the Christian thought of the ages he outclassed them all.[6]

> [Orr's] conviction [was] that doctrinal theology cannot be expunged from Christianity. The fact is that 'there is a truth, or sum of truths, involved in the Biblical revelation, for [*sic*] which it is the duty of the Church to bear witness; that Christianity ... has an

ascertainable, statable content, which it is the business of the Church to find out, to declare, and to defend, and ever more perfectly to seek to unfold in the connection of its parts, and in relation to advancing knowledge; that this content of truth is not something that can be manipulated into any shape man's fancies please, but something in regard to which we should not despair of being able to arrive at a large measure of agreement ...'[7]

When he adds the comment, 'I venture to say that what the church suffers from today is not, as so many think, too much theology, but too little theology, of an earnest [i.e., serious] kind,'[8] it is difficult not to apply his words directly to our own time.

Orr defines doctrine as 'the direct, often naïve, expression by Christian faith of the knowledge it possesses, or the convictions it holds, regarding God and divine things.' Theology is the 'reflective exercise of mind upon the doctrines of faith.' 'Dogma' stands for 'those formulations of Christian doctrine which have obtained authoritative recognition in wide sections of the Church, and are embodied in historical creeds.'[9] Although the ultimate test of dogma is Scripture, Orr would have us remember that 'we are more dependent on the past than we think even in our interpretation of Scripture ...'[10] Other tests include the inner coherence of the dogmatic system, and its correlation with the vital experience, not of the isolated individual, but of the church as a whole; there is also the appeal to the practical results which have followed the upholding of dogma; and – what particularly concerns Orr – there is the 'practically unerring verdict of history ... the history of dogma is the judgment of dogma.'[11]

Orr's 'fundamental presupposition,' writes Sell, was that 'Christian truth forms an organism – has a unity and coherence which cannot be arbitrarily disturbed in any of its parts without the whole undergoing injury. Conversely, the proof that any doctrine fits in essentially to that organism – is an integral part of it – is one of the strongest evidences we have of its correctness.'[12] The point of Orr's appeal to the history of doctrine was that ongoing review and restatement in relation to intellectual life in both the church and the world will show up inadequacies and intrinsic incoherences as surely as ongoing use shows up the design faults of commercially manufactured objects. Continues Sell: 'While every part of the organism is sensitive to change in any other, the pivotal truth is that concerning God: "As a man thinks God to be, so will his theology be." "[13] Orr worked with the classic Christian notion of God, that of the great tradition, precisely grasped and lucidly set forth, and his contribution to apologetics and systematics was in consequence a vindicating and elaborating of old paths.

Orr, then, was in one sense a conservative; but it is important to see that he was not a confessional theologian in the manner of those Lutheran and Reformed writers, ancient and modern, who treat their own church's credal statement as their sole lookout point for surveying the church and the world. Orr, who actually helped to detach his original denomination, the United Presbyterian Church, from line-by-line adherence to the Westminster Confession,[14] should rather be thought of as a heritage theologian, whose pervasive sense that the times were out of joint philosophically and theologically led him to polemics that at every point constituted (to borrow the perceptive title of Glen Scorgie's book on Orr) *A Call for Continuity*. Orr's lifelong defence of continuity with the mainstream Christian past required him to argue, first, for holding to ontological and epistemological realism and rejecting both Kantian agnosticism and Hegelian idealism; second, for rating canonical Scripture as inspired revelation from God and rejecting lower estimates of it;[15] third, for viewing humanity as basically noble but actually sinful and lost without Christ, and for rejecting all forms of evolutionary optimism;[16] and, fourth, for affirming a generically Chalcedonian Christology and a generically Augustinian soteriology against all non-incarnational and non-mediatorial accounts of Jesus our Lord.[17] Orr wrote books criticizing Hume's reductionist epistemology, Ritschl's Kantian skewing of the gospel, Harnack's Ritschlian history of dogma, and J-E-D-P pentateuchal criticism of Wellhausen, Graf and Kuenen,[18] and in each of these clashes he showed himself to be a rational polemicist with a masterful line of counter-argument that made demonstrably better sense in biblical, logical and human terms than did the theories he was opposing. Orr's stature as an apologist for the historic faith is comparable to that of his much better-known contemporaries B. B. Warfield and Charles Gore; but his literary style was less weighty than Warfield's and lower-voltage than Gore's, and his peers took less notice of him than was the case with the other two. Scandalously, as I hinted earlier, by the end of his life he had won so many battles and become so formidable in debate that British theologians who could not answer him formed the habit of simply ignoring him, or treating him as an instance of academic bad taste. I urge now that it is time he was rediscovered, for Orr's stances in face of what he saw as the aberrant *Zeitgeist* of his day can I believe help us considerably as we face the incoherence of postmodern relativism and clever anti-intellectualism (I here call it by the name that fits) in our own day. Let me try to show how.

Unified and transformative witness

As I hope I have made clear, I do not maintain that Orr was the greatest turn-of-the-century Christian theologian, nor, certainly, that he was the most influential apologist of his time. It seems that in the flesh he was a lively debater, genial and commanding, with shafts of satirical humour and massive appeals to common sense adorning lucid and compelling argumentation; but on paper his admirable clarity hovers on the edge of dullness. He was not the equal of Warfield or Bavinck for expository weight, nor of Gore for pastoral passion, nor of Forsyth for evangelical eloquence, nor of Kuyper for intellectual vision, nor of Denney for rapier-like rhetoric. He was not so impressive in building up structures of truth as he was in showing up the irrationalities of error. Yet he had a wider range, a deeper philosophical involvement, and a more formidable array of learning, than anyone else at least on the British scene in his time, and I am venturing the claim that his work of a century ago models for us the kind of apologetic stance and strategy that can best serve us today. The rest of this presentation will be devoted to trying to make that claim good.

What would an Orr-type programme for persuasive Christian discourse look like? How would it give substance to our desire for a convergent conservative testimony to 'mere Christianity', unified and transformative, according to the announced terms of our quest together? As I try to answer these questions, I shall bear in mind the difference between the modernity of Orr's milieu and the postmodernity of ours, and I shall feel free to amplify and develop Orr's principles of procedure as I deploy and apply them. But here, now, are four basic guidelines for us that spring directly from Orr's own work.

(i) *Display the rational coherence of historic mainstream Christian beliefs, both as a crystallizing of the doctrinal content of the Bible and also as a full-scale, comprehensive, and satisfying philosophy of life: one that embraces all the facts of human experience, good and bad; that ennobles human existence; and that makes better sense than any known alternative.*

Orr's first and arguably greatest book, *The Christian View of God and the World as Centring in the Incarnation* (1893), hews to this line for nearly 500 pages, and does so with notable success. Of it Scorgie wrote: 'Charles Gore once claimed to be a philosopher in the sense that he felt compelled to try to make sense of existence and to discern his place within a framework of meaning. By such a definition, Orr also would have claimed to be a philosopher. And insofar as philosophy is understood to be a quest for a unified account reality, it is accurate to describe *The Christian View* as a work of philosophical apologetics.'[19] It was, in fact, the first attempt in Britain to articulate a full-scale Christian world-and-life view against modernist variants. Orr saw, with prophetic clarity, that

> the opposition which Christianity has to encounter is no longer confined to special doctrines or to points of supposed conflict with the natural sciences, – for example, the relations of Genesis and geology, – but extends to the whole manner of conceiving of the world, and of man's place in it ... It is the Christian view of things in general which is attacked, and it is by an exposition and vindication of the Christian view of things as a whole that the attack can most successfully be met.[20]

So he set himself to show

> that there is a definite Christian view of things, which has a character, coherence, and unity of its own, and stands in sharp contrast with counter theories and speculations, and that this world-view has the stamp of reason and reality upon itself, and can amply justify itself at the bar both of history and of experience.[21]

The strength of *The Christian View*, and of Orr's subsequent apologetic writings, which are best seen as so many detailed studies subordinate to *The Christian View*, lies in the precision and skill with which he follows out his self-imposed agenda, taking Jesus Christ – the Christ of the Scriptures, and of the church's historic faith – as his central point of reference. 'He who with his whole heart believes in Jesus as the Son of God', writes Orr, 'is thereby committed to much else besides ... to a view of God ... of man ... of sin ... of Redemption ... of the purpose of God in creation and history ... of human destiny, found only in Christianity.'[22] The detailed interactions involved in Orr's masterful treatment of these themes are inevitably dated and somewhat dull, but his identifying of the connections between one theme and another is as compelling today as ever it was.

Works of this kind, doing this job, are needed in every age if Christian testimony is to have credibility, and certainly such works are needed today. Despite the irrational and anti-rational posturings of many around us, the human mind as such, today as always, craves wisdom and understanding, so that no serious person can ever settle for living without a philosophy in the Gore and Orr sense, or with a philosophy that seems to them self-contradictory. One reason why historic Christianity has been put on the shelf in today's western world is that secular thinkers believe (often without looking) that it lacks internal coherence and cannot assimilate today's knowledge about the nature and history of the world, and is unable to account for the actual quality of human experience, with its tensions, tribalisms, hypocrisies, barbarisms, brutalities, traumas, disillusionments, madnesses and miseries. But when, with Pascal and Orr (to look no further), we insist that the basic dynamics of human existence are, first, sin – original sin, as Augustinians call it – corrupting all natural instincts and desires more or less, and then, second, God's grace in Jesus our Lord redeeming and restoring, the realities of our disordered human lives become intelligible; while theism, correctly – that is, biblically – formulated proves able to accommodate all the knowledge of historical events and physical processes in this world that modern study yields, or can yield. By explaining these things the rationality and viability of the Christian faith can be made clear. And because of the widespread anti-Christianity in the worlds of education and opinion-making, this is currently a major task.

Orr's arguments are a century old; have there been model apologists of his type more recently? Perhaps the most effective exponents of the rationality of the Christian faith in this century have been G. K. Chesterton and C. S. Lewis: both laymen, we may note. Francis Schaeffer addressed himself to his task, but his communicative style was comparable to that of the cartoonist, and his vivid popular presentations of biblical Christianity, with accompanying critiques of alternative views, though cogent for their own pastoral purpose, had academic limitations.[23] It is arguable, at least, that the present Pope comes close to qualifying as Orr's successor. But, however that may be, it is certain that without a flow of wide-ranging, well-focused, and magisterially combative declarations of the total Christian view of things as being supremely realistic and rational, apologetic renewal among us will not get very far. Gratefully to encourage, therefore, those who engage in authentically Christian philosophy, at both technical and broad-brush level, is a present-day priority for the people of God.

(ii) *Highlight the content and coherence of the Christian view of God in particular, as the focal and structural centre of the Christian understanding of everything else. Spell out trinitarian theocentricity as the foundational frame for Christian thought.*

'As a man thinks God to be, so will his theology be.' Alan Sell, as we saw, described this as the pivotal point for Orr; so indeed it was, and so it must be for every apologist and theologian worthy of the name. Theocentricity as a habit of mind and life is basic to Christianity. It is not enough to bring God in as predicative to something else which is the real focus of our concern. Cosmocentricity and anthropocentricity in any form are distorting perspectives, no matter how precisely Christian specifics are fitted into these frames. As God is the object of Christian worship, so he must be the controlling centre of Christian thought about everything; and he himself must be thought about in a rigorously biblical way. Orr discerned that an immanentist unitarian view of God underlay the liberal Protestant distortions against which he constantly battled, and firmly pointed out the greater intellectual adequacy, as well as the solider biblical basis, of trinitarian theism. Some of his sentences, written over a hundred years ago, are worth quoting here: the wisdom they express does not date with age.

> The doctrine of the Trinity is not a result of mere speculation ... still less, as some eminent writers would maintain,[24] the result of the importation of Greek metaphysics into Christian theology. It is, in the first instance, the result of a simple process of induction from the facts of the Christian Revelation ... Our faith in the Trinity does not rest even on the proof-texts which are adduced from the Scriptures in support of the Trinitarian distinction. These have their value as summaries of the truth we gain from the complex of facts of the New Testament Revelation, and serve to assure us that we are on the right lines in our interpretation of these facts, but the fundamental ground on which we rest is the facts themselves. The triune conception of God is justified when it is shown to be the conception which underlies the triuned Revelation God has given of himself, and the triune activity of the work of redemption.[25]

From this Orr moves on to make the now familiar point that unless one posits the eternity of the world it is impossible on unitarian principles to give substance to the thought of love as an eternal divine characteristic.

> What can love in God mean on the supposition of His absolute solitariness? What can be the object of God's love throughout eternity, if there is no triune distinction in God? ... Either, therefore, we must ... seek an object for God's love in the finite, created world, or recognise that God has an infinitely blessed life of love within himself, and this brings us to the doctrine of an immanent Trinity.[26]

A most significant development in contemporary theology is the emphasis increasingly being laid on the fact that God the Creator is essentially relational in his own being; in other words, that 'he' is 'they' within the unity of the Godhead, and that as these internal divine relationships are the vital clue to apprehending God so they are the vital clue to understanding in an existential way what it means for us humans to be made in God's image and then remade in it by saving grace after sin has marred and disfigured us. Prominent names in this recovery include such as Leonard Hodgson,[27] Robert Jenson,[28] Thomas and James Torrance,[29] Colin Gunton,[30] Millard Erickson,[31] Jürgen Moltmann,[32] and Wolfhart Pannenberg.[33] Three factors at least have prompted the recovery. The first is a growing recognition that unitarian thought-forms and New Testament data are out of sync with each other and can never be fitted together. The second is the insistence of modern psychology that personal relationships constitute the essence of personal lives, which forces us to ask whether the same is not true of the God whose image we bear. The third is the emergence of the isolation of the individual as an increasingly agonizing problem in our increasingly unstable and fragmented western society, which obliges the church to muster its resources for ministering to this condition. The bottom line is a renewed awareness that a consistent and thoroughgoing trinitarianism is basic both to authentic Christian discipling – that is, to evangelism, and nurture, and pastoral care, all leading into the life of prayer, purity, and praise, which is our true spiritual health.

So I am bold to believe that the subliminal unitarianism that has been at the heart of liberal theology ever since Schleiermacher is finally on its way out.[34] Certainly, process theology, which is a finite-God mutation of the unitarian view and the most recent form of it to generate anything like a school of thought, is losing ground.[35] And while there are currently on offer many personal theologies of a radical kind, no 'politically correct' alternative to classical theism can claim establishment status in the way that evolutionary panentheism could and did within the older Protestant churches in Orr's day. This gives heritage Christians a great opportunity to highlight the 'social Trinity' of the Cappadocians, of Augustine (who if I read him right stood on Cappadocian shoulders), of Calvin and John Owen, and of the present-day theologians just mentioned, as our resource for discipling, for personal spiritual growth, for rebuilding human and humane community in the family and the church, and for the rescue of Christian worship from the swamps of subjectivity in which it is today so frequently bogged down.

Orr, were he alive now, would I think tell us emphatically that this is an opportunity that all heritage Christians – conservative, if you wish to call us that – should take, not only for the restoring of spiritual health to individuals and communities, but also for the purging and re-forming of our respective theological traditions and thereby the furthering of their convergence: the convergence out of which alone, as I see it, contemporary witness to God that is sufficiently strong and significant can emerge. To continue at this point on the trajectory of Orr's thought thus seems to me a priority task at the present time.

(iii) *Stress that the incarnation, atonement, bodily resurrection and ascension, present heavenly reign and future public return of Jesus Christ are central to the Christian story, and by projecting this biblical Christocentricity establish the fact that the Christian gospel is first and foremost news of redemption for lost sinners.*

For Orr, belief in the reality and centrality of the Christ of the New Testament was crucial. His first book, as we saw, presented the Christian view of God and the world as 'centring in the Incarnation'. He there categorized the truth of the Trinity as 'the first of the corollaries of the doctrine of the Incarnation',[36] thus displaying his awareness that Christian trinitarianism is essentially affirmation about Jesus Christ. In a published speech delivered in 1904 he declared war on all forms of naturalistic Christology,[37] and followed this up with two substantial volumes, *The Virgin Birth of Christ* (1907) and *The Resurrection of Jesus* (1908); and his last major piece of writing, in fact his main contribution to the five-volume *International Standard Bible Encyclopaedia* which he organized and edited and which was published shortly after his death,[38] was the book-length article, 'Jesus Christ', which was in effect a full-scale life of Christ based on a harmony of the Gospels with a minimum of polemical interactions.

Always Orr argued Christianity's credentials on the basis that as the apostolic witness to Jesus' divine saviourhood grew out of the historical impact that the historical Jesus had made on his first followers, so the evidence for the truth of the gospel was and is space-time phenomena, to be assessed by the historical type of argument that looks for causes adequate to produce the events under study. The anti-miraculous presuppositions that operated as blinders on the minds of so many of Orr's theological contemporaries, keeping them from discerning the weight and the force of the historical evidence for Jesus, could, he believed, be shown to be unreasonable and inappropriate, while the Gospel accounts of Jesus had a certain self-authenticating quality that would surely be recognized once they were viewed as a coherent whole. What had to be explained was the fact that Christianity began and spread as the worship of a Creator-God truly manifested in a risen, living, miracle-working divine Saviour who forgives sins and bestows the divine Holy Spirit, thereby transforming believers into loving, rejoicing, praying, worshipping persons who lived in an unquenchable hope of sharing Christ's heavenly glory for ever. This characteristic new life, Orr argued, requires the supernatural Christ of the Gospels and Epistles to explain it; no other hypothesis is adequate. His argument seems unanswerable, and perhaps against our twentieth-century background of resurgent barbarism world-wide it is easier for us to see that than it was for the children of the evolution-besotted, perfectionist culture with whom Orr had to deal. The liberal fancy, that Christianity is in essence mankind's natural religion, coming naturally to all who live in relatively civilized communities, is clearly a nonsense. As in yesterday's Roman empire, so today in both East and West, the Christian life involves a wholesale reversal of what comes naturally out of the egocentric human heart, and cannot be accounted for in terms merely of education and social conditioning. Living in pre-narrative theology days, Orr did not use the phrase 'the Christian story' as theological shorthand in the way that we do; but his thought is fully in line with our use of it. Redemption through the Christ of the Gospels and Epistles for sinful human beings, flawed and foolish, guilty, vile and helpless, with our shameworthy and blameworthy track records and our pathetic inadequacies for the business of living, is for Orr the authentic Christian story, and any affirmation of it and apologetic for it must be historical and redemptive throughout. That is as true today as it was when Orr wrote a century ago, and as it was in the first century when this affirmation and apologetic first broke through the lips of Paul and his apostolic peers on a culturally dying world.

Orr's witness to Jesus Christ did not stop here, however, and neither must ours. In *The Christian View*, having shown most effectively that the New Testament is unanimous in viewing Jesus as a person to be worshipped, and thereby acknowledged as divine, and having drawn out of this a basic trinitarianism, Orr then spends half a chapter exploring the cosmic role of the Son of God, linking the creating and upholding of things with redemption 'as parts of one grand whole'.[39] Introducing this section by posing the old question, whether there would have been an incarnation of the Son had there been no sin, he frankly acknowledges that Scripture always relates the incarnation to our need of salvation, and to the Father's purpose that the Son should ultimately head up a redeemed and remade universe. But then he affirms:

> God's plan is in reality one, and it is but an abstract way of thinking that leads us to suppose otherwise ... we speak as if God had first one plan of creation – complete and rounded off in itself – in which sin was to have no place; then, when it was foreseen that sin would enter, another plan was introduced, which vitally altered and enlarged the former. But ... the plan of the universe is one, and ... however harsh the expression may sound, the foresight and permission of sin were from the first included in it ... God has chosen to create a universe into

which it was foreseen that sin would enter; and the Incarnation is part of the plan of such a creation. This being so, it may well be conceived that the Incarnation was the pivot on which everything else in this plan of creation was made to turn ... Christ's relation to the universe cannot be thought of as something adventitious and contingent; it is vital and organic. This means that His Incarnation had a relation to the whole plan of the world, and not simply to sin.[40]

Facing as he did non-supernatural hypotheses about the life and identity of Jesus on the one hand, and non-trinitarian conceptions of the divine on the other hand, Orr was skilfully hitting his way out of trouble by insisting that the historical and cosmic dimensions of New Testament faith in Jesus Christ are inseparable parts of a single whole, so that neither can be fairly and adequately assessed save in the light of the other, and the final assessment must be of both together. And in doing this Orr was doing more than pursuing a tactic for evading trouble; he was showing what is involved in this or any age in facing the full reality of the New Testament witness to Jesus. Here, then, is a guideline for our testimony today. In explaining and commending Christ to positivistic modernists and relativistic postmodernists alike there is need to bring together both the evangelists' account of the Son of God's life in this world – his words, works, ways, and wars – and the apostolic conviction of his co-creatorship with the Father; of his activity as the upholding source of our existence and life every moment; of his identity as 'the truth' in the sense of being the final source and goal of the cosmos, the ultimate answer to all ultimate questions; and of his destiny as the person through and in whom the whole universe is to find its perfection when he reappears in glory. The Christocentricity of the world in this sense is an integral part of the Christian understanding of Jesus, and must ever be set forth as an integral element in the Christian witness to Jesus. Both the coherence of our own faith and its correspondence with the faith of Christianity's founders depend on the clarity and firmness with which we grasp that this is so, and practise the principle accordingly.

So here is a further pointer to the way our current witness must go.

(iv) *Celebrate the life-changing impact of the gospel of Jesus Christ as an integral part of our testimony.*

Let Orr himself introduce this section with his account of the gospel's original triumph in the Roman Empire.

Christianity won the day because ... it met the deepest necessity of the age into which it had come. It met the deep craving of the age for spiritual peace and rest, its need of certainty, its longing for redemption, and for direct communion with God. To these wants it brought a satisfaction which no other religion of the time could pretend to offer. It did not meet them by teaching merely – as if Christ were a new Socrates – but it met them by the positive exhibition of the redeeming love of God in Christ, by the setting forth of the personal Jesus in His life, death and resurrection, by the proclamation of the forgiveness of sins through Him, by the bestowal of the power of the Holy Spirit. It was not a doctrinal religion merely, but a religion of dynamic – of power. It did not only tell men what to do, but gave them power to do it.[41]

Today, a quest for spirituality – that is, as the word is used, for some transforming contact with the transcendent, whatever that may be – has once again become a feature of western culture: which means that the door for declaring the nature and quality of Christian spiritual life is now once more wide open. Deep craving for inner peace and rest, for certainty and hope, for rescue from oneself and for fellowship with God, is widespread, and within the churches, Protestant, Catholic and Orthodox, serious study of life in the Spirit has again begun to take hold. Maximize this, Orr would urge; the life-changing power of the gospel, or rather of the Christ and the Holy Spirit of whom the gospel speaks, is something to make much of; the transcultural unity of the Christian experience of prayer over two millennia, and the proven capacity of Christian conviction to sustain itself through cultural change and persecuting pressure, constitute weighty *prima facie* arguments for the claim that Christianity is true.

Here, surely, is a project that can both express and further convergence of our traditions in Christian testimony. Nothing is nearer the heart of the great tradition, and therefore more purely and gloriously ecumenical, than loving the Lord who in love died for us and now lives in us, and with that hating sin, and practising repentance, and testifying that we live by being forgiven, and proving God's power to enable us to resist sin's down-drag. Protestant liberalism, with its enfeebled notions of God and sin and redemption, lost this supernaturalizing of daily life, substituting for it a culture of moralism and *bonhomie*, and the various liberation theologies of our time are in process even now of undergoing a similar loss. For the exponents of classical Christian orthodoxy to recover and display these inner aspects of classical Christian orthopraxy is a clear and urgent call from God at this present time. The world needs to know of the supernatural action whereby God transfigures personal life in Christ and imparts resilience for righteousness and liberty for love in a way that makes believers a mystery to those who do not share their faith. When Jesus told Nicodemus that with those born of the Spirit it was like the wind – 'you hear its sound, but you cannot tell where it comes from or where it is going' (John 3:8) – he was referring to bewilderment on the part of unbelievers as to what makes Christians tick; true life in Christ will always have a supernatural quality that generates such bewilderment. Part of our calling is to unite to tell the world of this supernaturalizing of the natural, and of the Christ who brings it to pass; and with that to demonstrate through the devotion of our own lives the supernaturalizing of which we speak. 'Make your light shine,' says Jesus, 'so that others will see the good that you do and will praise your Father in heaven' (Matt. 5:16, CEV).

Conclusion

Can conservative Protestants, Eastern Orthodox, and Roman Catholics of mainstream type join together in bearing witness to all that I have spoken of? I urge that we can, despite our known and continuing differences about the specifics of the salvation process and the place of the church in that process. From the great tradition, or rather from the Scriptures as they have always been read within that tradition, we receive shared understanding of ruin, redemption, regeneration, and the reality of fellowship with our risen Saviour, that suffices for the purpose, and if we can agree as a rule of procedure to base our testimony directly on what we can find in Scripture as we exegete and expound it together we shall be home and dry. To be sure, fundamentalists within our three traditions are unlikely to join us in this, for it is the way of fundamentalists to follow the path of contentious orthodoxism, as if the mercy of God in Christ automatically rests on persons who are notionally correct and is just as automatically withheld from those who fall short of notional correctness on any point of substance. But this concept of, in effect, just-ification, not by works, but by words – words, that is, of notional soundness and precision – is near to being a cultic heresy in its own right, and need not detain us further now, however much we may regret the fact that some in all our traditions are bogged down in it.

I would have liked at this point to be able to draw from Orr a fifth guiding principle for our present-day witness, which would have read as follows:

(v) *Highlight the international supracultural phenomenon of the church, the new human race that is committed here and now to worship, to brotherhood, to loving and serving, and to spreading the gospel, while anticipating the future joy of endless loving fellowship with the Father and the Son through the Spirit, and in and through God with one another.*

This principle, I believe, is needed to complete the programme that Orr has so far suggested to us: for despite the church's many shortcomings, past and present, this new society that God is constantly building embodies in itself impressive evidence of divine power at work on the grand scale. The evangelizing and nurturing church has had a uniquely unifying, humanizing, and civilizing impact on world history. It seems to me that the transcultural solidarity of the church's corporate demonstration in experience of worship, prayer, suffering, resolute hope, faithfulness even to martyrdom, and divine enabling for righteousness and ministry, gives *prima facie* credibility to the claim that the institutional church is home to a supernatural life in Christ, and is thus powerful evidence for the truth of the gospel. But I cannot draw this principle from Orr, because to my knowledge he never voiced it. Like most other Protestants, Orr is robustly aware that God is building the believing community for his glory, and that we all need the church for our nurture; yet, like many other Protestants, he does not appear as a man whose imagination has been caught by the church, so that he sees the church as integral to his evidential scheme. Perhaps in Orr's Scotland, heavily imbued as it was with Presbyterian formalism, it was harder to sense the unique quality of true church fellowship than it is for us today; but certainly, the full strength of Orr's cerebral argument for the truth of the faith is only likely to be felt where it is backed up by the watching world's perception in the first Christian century – 'see how these Christians love one another!' As myself, like Orr, a Protestant – that is, a catholic Christian protesting against what appear as un-catholic specifics – I urge that we need this fifth principle as a guideline if we are to achieve in our day the coherent cogency of classical Christian understanding that Orr was contending for throughout. Unified and transformative witness to a world in which the deep-level loneliness of the individual has become an epidemic disease requires celebration of the new community in which through new creation 'there is neither Jew nor Greek, slave nor free, male nor female, for you are all one in Christ Jesus' (Gal. 3:28) – with transcendent new togetherness resulting, both within and across denominational lines. May such witness be forthcoming from now on; we need it, desperately.

What success can we expect from such a united witness here in the West, where the departure from us of the glory of God seems such an obvious fact? Perhaps not much, at any rate in the short term. But the call at present is surely to resolve to do our best, in collaboration as close as we can make it, and to commit the outcome to God – and then to emulate Orr, who never doubted that he was on the victory side, but who knew that anyone maintaining the faith in its classic biblical form was in for the long haul. In an article titled 'Prevailing Tendencies in Modern Theology', published in 1906, Orr declared that in face of the current flowing of the western intellectual stream against the faith of the fathers 'what was needed in the way of a proper response was "above all, a cool head, strong faith, a little patience, action like that of the mariners with Paul, who when they feared lest they should have fallen among rocks, and when for many days neither sea nor star appeared, sensibly dropped four anchors, and waited for the day." '[42] Wise advice, surely! Let us, then, like Orr, resolve to work and wait, together, and see what God will do.

Questions for study

1. Set out, in your own words, what Packer understands by 'great-tradition Christianity'.
2. Packer argues that his arguments are to be set against the backdrop of a 'cultural crisis'. Set out, in your own words, the main themes of that crisis. Why does this crisis lend legitimacy to Packer's proposals?
3. The central figure in this discussion is James Orr (1844–1913). Why does Packer regard Orr as so important to his theme?
4. The proposal which Packer is considering is that 'conservative Protestants, Eastern Orthodox, and Roman Catholics of mainstream type join together in bearing witness' to the doctrinal and ethical truths of the gospel. How realistic do you consider this? What are the main objections to this proposal? What are its strengths?
5. Give a critical account of the way in which Packer uses church history to illuminate our present situation, and evaluate options. Why does Packer appeal to history so often, when most evangelical writers tend to bypass it as an outdated irrelevance?

Notes

Preamble

1. C. S. Lewis, *Christian Reflections*, London: Bles, 1967, p. vii.
2. The statement can be studied in C. Colson and R. J. Neuhaus (eds.), *Evangelicals and Catholics Together: Toward a Common Mission*, Dallas: Word, 1995, pp. xv–xxxiii.

Essay

1. From the brochure advertising the conference, 'Not of This World'.
2. The phrase means a generic Christian who does not see denominational distinctions as a matter of prime importance. Lewis took the phrase from the ecumenically minded Puritan Richard Baxter, who was happy to describe himself as a 'meer Catholick'.

3. C. S. Lewis, *Christian Reflections*, ed. Walter Hooper, London: Geoffrey Bles, 1967, p. vii.

4. I have been helped here by essays in David Dockery (ed.), *The Challenge of Postmodernism: An Evangelical Engagement*, Wheaton: Victor Books, 1995, and by G. E. Veith Jr, *Postmodern Times*, Wheaton: Crossway Books, 1994.

5. The most significant studies of Orr have been Alan P. F. Sell, *Defending and Declaring the Faith: Some Scottish Examples, 1860–1920*, Exeter: Paternoster Press; Colorado Springs: Helmers and Howard, 1987, pp. 137–171, and Glen G. Scorgie, *A Call for Continuity: The Theological Contribution of James Orr*, Macon: Mercer University Press, 1988. See also Scorgie on Orr in Walter A. Elwell (ed.), *Handbook of Evangelical Theologians*, Grand Rapids: Baker Book House, 1993, pp. 12–25.

6. Sell, p. 141.

7. Sell, p. 145, quoting James Orr, *The Progress of Dogma*, London: James Clarke, 1901, pp. 8–9.

8. Orr, p. 9 n.

9. Orr, pp. 12–13.

10. Orr, p. 15.

11. Orr, p. 17. The whole extract is from Sell, pp. 144–145. The final sentence from Orr is an adaptation of Schelling's dictum, 'the history of the world is the judgment of the world'.

12. Orr, *God's Image in Man and its Defacement in the Light of Modern Denials*, London: Hodder and Stoughton, 1907, pp. 260–261, quoted from Sell, p. 150. This sentiment belonged to Orr's larger vision, in which both the common-sense and idealist philosophies that nurtured him academically would support him, of the coherence of all knowledge. 'The mind for him was just the instrument for the unification of all truth within our reach.' James Denney, 'The Late Professor Orr', *British Weekly*, 11 September 1913, p. 567.

13. Sell, pp. 150–151, quoting Orr, ibid., p. 7.

14. See Scorgie, pp. 39–46.

15. *Revelation and Inspiration*, London: Duckworth, 1910.

16. *God's Image in Man* (see n. 12 sup.) and *Sin as a Problem of Today*, London: Hodder and Stoughton, 1910.

17. *The Faith of a Modern Christian*, London: Hodder and Stoughton, 1910.

18. *David Hume and his Influence on Philosophy and Theology*, Edinburgh: T. and T. Clark, 1903; *The Ritschlian Theology and the Evangelical Faith*, London: Hodder and Stoughton, 1897; *Ritschlianism: Expository and Critical Essays*, London: Hodder and Stoughton, 1903; *The Problem of the Old Testament*, London: James Nisbet, 1906.

19. Scorgie, pp. 48–49, referring to *The Christian View of God and the World as Centring in the Incarnation*, Edinburgh: Andrew Elliot, 1893.

20. *The Christian View*, p. 4.

21. Ibid., p. 16.

22. Ibid., p. 4.

23. See Ronald Ruegsegger (ed.), *Reflections on Francis Schaeffer*, Grand Rapids: Zondervan, 1986.

24. Orr had Edwin Hatch and Adolph Harnack in his mind. We today might add Rudolf Bultmann.

25. Orr, *The Christian View*, pp. 263–264.

26. Ibid., p. 274.

27. Leonard Hodgson, *The Doctrine of the Trinity*, Welwyn, UK: James Nisbet, 1943.

28. Robert Jenson, *The Triune Identity: God according to the Gospel*, Philadelphia: Fortress Press, 1982.

29. Thomas F. Torrance, *The Trinitarian Faith: The Evangelical Theology of the Ancient Catholic Church*, Edinburgh: T. and T. Clark, 1993; *Trinitarian Perspectives: Toward Doctrinal Agreement*, Edinburgh: T. and T. Clark, 1994. See also James B. Torrance, 'Contemplating the Trinitarian Mystery of Christ', in J. I. Packer and Loren Wilkinson (eds.), *Alive to God*, Downers Grove, IL: InterVarsity Press, 1992, pp. 140–151, and Alistair I. C. Heron (ed.) *The*

Forgotten Trinity, British Council of Churches Study Commission of Trinitarian Doctrine Today, London: BCC/CCBI, 1991.

30. Colin Gunton, *The Promise of Trinitarian Theology*, Edinburgh: T. and T. Clark, 1991; *The One, The Three, and the Many*, Cambridge: Cambridge University Press, 1993.
31. Millard Erickson, *God in Three Persons*, Grand Rapids, Baker Book House, 1995.
32. Jürgen Moltmann, *The Trinity and the Kingdom of God*, San Francisco: Harper and Row, 1981.
33. Wolfhart Pannenberg, *Systematic Theology*, Grand Rapids: Eerdmans, vol. 1, 1991, vol. 2, 1994.
34. Cf. Alister McGrath, *The Renewal of Anglicanism*, Harrisburg, PA: Morehouse Publications, 1993, pp. 33–47, 71–75, 95–113, 121–124.
35. See R. G. Gruenler, *The Inexhaustible God: Biblical Theology and the Challenge of Process Theism*, Grand Rapids: Baker Book House, 1987; Ronald Nash (ed.), *Process Theology*, Grand Rapids: Baker Book House, 1989.
36. *The Christian View*, p. 262.
37. See Scorgie, pp. 124–127.
38. *International Standard Bible Encyclopaedia*, ed. James Orr, 5 vols., Chicago: Howard-Severance Co., 1915.
39. *The Christian View*, p. 276.
40. Ibid., pp. 279–281.
41. James Orr, 'The Factors in the Expansion of the Christian Church', in J. B. Paton et al., *Christ and Civilization*, London: National Council of Evangelical Free Churches, 1910, pp. 218–219; quoted from Sell, p. 144.
42. Scorgie, p. 166, quoting Orr in *Review and Expositor* 3 (1906), p. 571.

16. 'Living truth for a dying world: the message of C. S. Lewis' (1998)

Our final text for study takes the form of a lecture given by J. I. Packer at the Oxford conference to mark the centenary of the birth of C. S. Lewis (1898–1963). The lecture is a brilliant analysis of the significance of Lewis for Christianity in the third millennium, and merits close study, both for its appreciative interaction with Lewis and for its shrewd judgments concerning the contemporary cultural scene.

Yet the lecture can be read at another level. Packer had, by this late stage in his career, established himself as a powerful representative of 'great-tradition Christianity', and clearly sees in Lewis another representative of this genre. Packer's lecture can therefore be seen as a highly significant analysis of the potential for a theologically orthodox Christianity – what Lewis terms 'mere Christianity' – in the future. Packer's analysis of Lewis can be seen as an indirect assessment of the form of Christianity which Lewis and Packer represent, in different manners, and which they propose as a resource for the future. Packer's musings on Lewis can easily be transposed into a critical reflection on the challenges facing the Christian faith and churches in the next few decades, and a sober evaluation of the resources which will be required to deal with them.

The readers of *Christianity Today*, when invited to nominate the Christian writers who had exercised the greatest impact on their lives, placed Lewis at the top of their lists, and Packer as runner up. This lecture will be a gem for such readers, bringing together the two minds they valued most. As will be clear, it is a thoroughly productive interaction, involving both looking *at* Lewis (Who was he? What was his achievement?) and looking *along* Lewis (What does he say to us as we engage with the issues of our day?).

Related works by Packer

'Is Christianity credible?', in D. Stacey (ed.), *Is Christianity Credible?* London: Epworth, 1981, pp. 64–72. (Essay 10 in this collection.)

Living truth for a dying world: the message of C. S. Lewis

I owe C. S. Lewis a lot, and I am grateful. To be sure, my introduction to him was something of a false start: in 1939 I read *Out of the Silent Planet* because as a boy I liked space-travel stories, but I thought Oyarsa's theology was part of the fantasy, and its significance totally passed me by. At that time I was no more than a churchgoer who had no clue as to what Christianity really was. By 1943, however, *The Screwtape Letters*, read at my state school (yes!) as a sample of comic literature (imagine!), along with the three little books that later became *Mere Christianity*, had led me to something approaching orthodoxy, and soon after I was born again in 1944 *The Pilgrim's Regress* cleared my head regarding the intellectual milieu of which I was a part. Also it was Lewis who subsequently put me on to Charles Williams, to my mind the truest though certainly the most uneven genius in the Inklings circle, and that was a huge gift. As a Reformed evangelical, English by genes, Canadian by choice, and with, I think, something of a mid-Atlantic mindset, I am glad to acknowledge my debt to Lewis, a fellow-Oxonian, a fellow-Greats man, and a fellow-Anglican, whose clarity of mental and moral insight, both as a human being and as a Christian, continues to astound me the more I read and re-read him. That is where I come from as I approach my theme.

The aim of this paper is to seek Lewis's help for our own task of what we may call 'encultured discipling' – the complex activity of outreach that includes apologetics, pre-evangelism, evangelism proper, pastoral bonding, and the foundational elements of Christian nurture. To that end, if I may use a Lewisian distinction, we shall look both at him and along him. So away we go.

Lewis was an extraordinary man; not simply for asking to be called 'Jack' when his baptismal names were Clive Staples, but for the mix of powers that made him up. One side of him was his brilliant analytical intellect, honed first by the rationalist W. T. Kirkpatrick, tutor of his teens, and then by idealist philosophers at Oxford in the days before linguistic analysis took over. He had the Irishman's love of conversation and debate, which meant his ideas were constantly strengthened by being put into the ring beside and against other views. English language and literature in the medieval and Renaissance periods was his academic specialty, but as a generalist he was fully conversant with all English literature, western philosophy, and first-world cultural development up to his own day. He was widely read, and had a retentive and almost photographic memory for whatever he found in books. As a professional critic he was enterprisingly independent, and challenged the conventional right, left and centre. Thus, he rejected as 'chronological snobbery' all forms of the idea that what comes later will be truer, wiser, and of better quality than what came before. Also, he rejected the notion that there was a great cultural divide between the Middle Ages and the Renaissance, while insisting that there was such a divide between the world of Jane Austen and Sir Walter Scott, with its fixed values and cosmic certainties, and the de-absolutized, de-Christianized, de-personalized world of his own day. He rescued literary criticism from the clutches of relativistic sociology by finding the significance of written works in what they do for their readers, and he challenged any number of academic assessments that had not been made from this standpoint. As well as all this, he had a Chestertonian flair for pithy, pointed utterances of a commonsensical sort, and wrote many occasional articles for what we would call 'thought journals'. As a lecturer, tutor, critic and journalist he was never less than formidable, and he made his mark in a way that few scholars can match.

But there was more to Lewis than this. Deep inside him was a pictorial, dramatic, poetic, story-forming imagination of a Celtic type, childlike in its directness and simplicity and colourfully vivid in its verbalizing. From this imagination flowed a stream of what Lewis was happy to call fairy tales for both children and adults. Each mode of the resultant blend – fantasies narrated with the critic's clinical precision, arguments clothed in poetic images – makes fascinating reading, even when interest in the subject-matter itself is small; while Lewis's ability to grasp the implications of an idea and then to imagine the behaviour of people living by it yields material that again and again strikes one as stunningly prophetic. Such, then, was the man whose message we are to explore now.

When Lewis recovered the Christian faith he had lost almost two decades before, he at once set himself to share it. 'Ever since I became a Christian,' he wrote in 1952, 'I thought that the best, perhaps the only service I could do for my unbelieving neighbours was to explain and defend the belief that has been common to nearly all Christians at all times.'[1] Thus he became, willy-nilly, a theologian; not indeed in the post-Enlightenment professional sense of an academic in a guild of peers where biblical and ecclesiastical problems, proposals, and enquiry for its own sake form the agenda (Lewis disclaimed everything of this sort); but a theologian in the more basic sense of a person who proclaims the opinions about God by which he or she seeks to live – in other words, a responsible Christian communicator. Lewis claimed no identity save that of a 'mere Christian', lay and untutored; but he was identifiably a High Church Anglican, orthodox and mainstream, whose Christian mind was shaped mainly by the heritage of Plato, Athanasius, Augustine, Thomas Aquinas, Thomas à Kempis, Richard Hooker, Thomas Traherne and William Law, plus the Scotsman George MacDonald. Apart from MacDonald, this roster of giants had been shaping Anglican minds long before Lewis's day, and all that was distinctive to Lewis was his adhering to this heritage at a time when it was fashionable to leave it behind.

Nor did he merely state and defend it in logical and didactic form. Myths, to Lewis, were a class of stories that impact receptive souls as reflecting and pointing to transcendent realities which are felt without as yet being focused. Myths trigger what Lewis called 'joy', that is, delightful desire for that which they, so to speak, smell of; and Lewis's theology has a place for pre-Christian myths in various cultures as 'good dreams' of God, holiness and heaven, God-given dreams that bring awareness of the sort of life that we need and want and do not have and so prepare minds and hearts for the gospel. From Lewis's Roman Catholic friends, Tolkien and Dyson, he had received the thought that did most to lead him to full Christian faith, namely that a myth found in pre-Christian cultures worldwide, the myth of a dying and rising deity through whose ordeal new life comes to others, had become redemptive fact in Christ. Believing this, and knowing first-hand how the gospel of Christ functions under God as myth still, imparting inklings of the reality, beauty, and goodness of God that go beyond left-brain conceptual knowledge and the power of words to express, he found his knowledge of Christ generating within him new 'good dreams' – stories, that is, which, by reflecting Christian fact in a fantasy world, might stir the wish that something of this sort were true in our world, and so beget readiness to learn that it actually is so. Thus were born the space trilogy, *Out of the Silent Planet, Perelandra*, and *That Hideous Strength: A Modern Fairy-Tale for Grown-ups*, and the seven Narnias; and *Till We Have Faces: A Myth Retold*. All these are myths in the defined sense, and all of them are fairy tales in the sense Lewis had in mind when he wrote his article, 'Sometimes Fairy Stories May Say Best What's To be Said.'[2] *The Pilgrim's Regress*, too, though formally an allegory,[3] is in intention, and for me at least, in achievement, myth; for allegory becomes myth when it conveys the mythic message to the heart.

Since Lewis spoke so forthrightly for mainstream Christianity, and since historic evangelicals (Christians, that is, who find their identity within the Reformational-Puritan-Pentecostal mix) belong to the mainstream, it is hardly surprising that for many of them Lewis has something like icon status, despite his smoking and drinking, his belief in purgatory and his quiet but decided sacramentalism, his use of confessional to keep himself honest, his non-inerrantist view of Scripture, and his unwillingness to speak of penal substitution and justification by faith alone when affirming forgiveness and salvation in Christ.

What evangelicals most love in Lewis is his depiction of Aslan, the Christly lion of Narnia; his strong defence of biblical supernaturalism, personal new birth, Christ's return to judgment, the reality of Satan, heaven and hell, and the certainty that we all are inescapably *en route* for one or the other, according to what each does with such light from God as reaches us. Evangelicals love too Lewis's squelching of secular modernity and the 'Christianity-and-water' religion of professed liberals; his stress on repentance and actual submission to Christ as the heart of Christianity; his openness about his conversion from atheism, and his concern to help others make the same journey; his mental vigour in seeking to make every thought captive to Christ by thinking everything out in terms of God's revealed truth; and the wit, humour and playfulness with which he pursues this solemn task. Tuning in to all of this, evangelicals claim Lewis as essentially 'one of us' – and who should want to stop them doing that? The only proviso must be that since Lewis aimed (successfully, I think) to be, in the words of a recent book title, *A Christian For All Christians*,[4] the claim cannot be exclusive.

This is enough of preliminaries; we move on now to what I take to be Lewis's central message, to his own contemporaries and to ourselves.

Inside the cover of his first Christian book, *The Pilgrim's Regress*, is a fanciful Mappa Mundi (map of the world). The world in question is the personal world of wandering and return that the story explores. Explaining this in his Preface to the third edition, Lewis speaks of the map as diagramming 'the Holy War as I see it'. At both the top and the bottom of the map is a Military Railway, evidently there to carry supplies, reinforcements, and new resources for 'the double attack from Hell on the two sides of our nature' (the intellectual and the instinctual).[5] Bunyan certainly, Chesterton probably, perhaps Milton, plus Lewis's own war service, contributed to this imagery; but spiritual warfare – God against Satan, good against evil, light against darkness, and each human individual under threat from known and unknown forces of malice and destruction – is a biblical theme, and one that Lewis pursues from various angles not only in *Regress* but also in *Screwtape*, and in the space-travel and Narnia stories, and in *The Great Divorce*, to look no further. From one standpoint, to be sure, Lewis's central theme is the redemptive grace of God in Jesus Christ that brings us to heaven, but the idea of the Holy War is what gives shape and perspective to Lewis's output as a whole; so I make this idea the peg on which I hang my account of the main things Lewis had to say.

Beginning at the beginning, we first ask: why is there a Holy War at all? If God's rational creatures were made for loving fellowship with their Creator, how is the state of war to be explained?

Lewis's reply is that three factors are currently operating, as follows:

1. Universal Satanic antagonism to God the Creator

Following the classic Christian understanding, as imaginatively spelt out in Milton's *Paradise Lost*, Lewis affirmed the reality of angels (unembodied rational creatures) and the factuality of a pre-cosmic revolt by some of them, under 'the Bent One' of *Out of the Silent Planet*, 'Our Father below' of *Screwtape*, the Dark Power who was made good but went wrong and became bad and now leads an army of demons (fallen angels like himself) against God and all that God is up to. Satan labours as a spoiler to ruin souls and thus frustrate God's goal of having humans know and love him, and to that end he twists out of shape all that through God's gift is good, beautiful, and true. This world is enemy-occupied territory, where Screwtapian ingenuity is constantly being employed to block and dissolve historic Christianity as a formative force in people's lives, to turn everyone's cultural environment into a corrupting influence, to fill human minds with anti-Christian ideas and attitudes, and to lead people away from reason in the old moral sense (that is, thoughtful, responsible, prudent living). Satan battles God by systematically corrupting and destroying humans; our own story of universal personal temptation and the downward slide to hell is thus one facet of a larger conflict. Satan's hostility to God is the first factor in the Holy War.

2. Universal human antagonism to God the Creator

Factor number two is original sin, the anti-God allergy of our fallen race.

Lewis affirmed that mankind is a 'spoiled species' due to a historical, space-time act of self-willed disobedience which became the mould in which human nature was thereafter set. Lewis expounds this, very strikingly along Augustinian lines by positing that God in judgment adjusted his way of upholding the human individual so that the personal integration that existed before was now lost.

Here is Lewis saying that in his own way.

Thus the organs, no longer governed by man's will, fell under the control of ordinary biochemical laws and suffered whatever the inter-workings of those laws might bring about in the way of pain, senility and death. And desires began to come up into the mind of man, not as his reason chose, but just as the biochemical and environmental facts happened to cause them. And the mind itself fell under the psychological laws of association and the like which God made to rule the psychology of the higher anthropoids. And the will, caught in the tidal wave of mere nature, had no resource but to force back some of the new thoughts and desires by main strength, and these uneasy rebels became the subconscious as we now know it. The process was not, I conceive, comparable to mere deterioration as it may now occur in a human individual; it was a loss of status as a species. What man lost by the Fall was his original specific nature. 'Dust thou art, and unto dust shalt thou return.' ... Thus human spirit from being the master of human nature became a mere lodger in its own house, or even a prisoner; rational consciousness became what it now is – a fitful spotlight resting on a small part of the cerebral motions. But this limitation of the spirit's powers was a lesser evil than the corruption of the spirit itself. It had turned from God and became its own idol, so that ... its inclination was selfward. Hence pride and ambition, the desire to be lovely in its own eyes and to depress and humiliate all rivals, envy, and restless search for more, and still more, security, were now the attitude that came easiest to it. It was not only a weak king over its own nature, but a bad one; it sent down into the psycho-physical organism desire far worse than the organism sent up to it. This condition was transmitted by heredity to all later generations, for it was not simply what biologists call an acquired variation; it was the emergence of a new kind of man – a new species, never made by God, had sinned itself into existence. The change which man had undergone was not parallel to the development of a new organ or a new habit; it was a radical alteration of his constitution, a disturbance of the relation between his component parts, and an internal perversion of one of them.[6]

The result is that 'we inherit a whole system of desires which do not necessarily contradict God's will but which ... steadfastly ignore it'[7] – and we always find in ourselves some measure of reluctance and resistance to any form or degree of obedient self-surrender to God, a stubbornness that is only ever overcome through help from God himself. For obeying God is contrary to human nature as human nature has now become.

How did Lewis see our inbred anti-God inclination expressed in the world he knew between the 1920s and his own death in 1963 – an era punctuated by the Second World War and embracing two distinct post-war communities? What report did he bring from the ideological battlefield, where, despite his efforts and those of others, post-Christianity as a perspective was steadily advancing? Here are three blossomings of post-Christianity of which Lewis took particular notice.

First, Lewis observed a growing separation of sensibilities.

The Mappa Mundi, mentioned earlier, shows enemies of the soul coming from both the North and South. These, said Lewis, represent 'equal and opposite evils, each continually strengthened and made plausible by its critique of the other'.[8] Both are mindsets among intellectuals seeking reality in light of the Freudian suspicion that conventionality is a cover-up for conflicts we need to face. The Northern mindset is intellectualist, elitist, purist, doctrinaire, and lacking in humility and humanity. 'The Northerners are the men of rigid systems whether sceptical or dogmatic, Aristocrats, Stoics, Pharisees, Rigorists, signed and sealed members of highly organized "Parties".' Southerners, by contrast, equate feeling with insight and celebrate sensuality as revelatory. They are 'boneless souls whose doors stand open day and night to almost every visitant, but always with the readiest welcome for those ... who offer some sort of intoxication ... Every feeling is justified by the mere fact that it is felt: for a Northerner, every feeling on the same ground is suspect.'[9] 'D. H. Lawrence and the Surrealists have perhaps reached a point further "South" than humanity ever reached before.'[10] Were Lewis with us today, he might well conclude that some current exponents of sex as self-expression yielding self-discovery have outdone even Lawrence. But his point is not that one of these pathologies is worse than the other; it is, rather, that both unfeeling intellectualism and unthinking sensualism actually dehumanize. So: 'With both the "North" and the "South" a man has, I take it, only one concern – to avoid them and hold the Main Road ... We were made to be neither cerebral men nor visceral men, but Men'[11] – persons in whom the sensibilities of thought and feeling combine to produce reverence, wisdom, and joy. As, however, the last pages of *The Pilgrim's Regress* declare, this only happens where egocentricity gives way to God-centredness and the self-willed backtrack into a life of repentance, faith in Jesus Christ, and receiving and giving love. That remains eternally true.

Second, Lewis observed an ongoing slippage into subjectivism. Subjectivism means rejecting any idea of universal standards of truth and right in favour of everyone doing what seems good in their own eyes each moment. Lewis saw this as a great evil and fought it with the gloves off; we see him doing so in his Durham lectures, *The Abolition of Man*, in his major article, 'The Poison of Subjectivism',[12] and in his adult fairy tale, *That Hideous Strength*. Subjectivism was to him a replay of the revolt in Eden, where humans sought wisdom by defying their Maker; and as then, so now, the outcome is loss of all life's prime values – freedom and truth and beauty and goodness and joy.

Specifically, the loss is threefold. To start with, the Tao (Chinese for Way) is lost. The Tao, for Lewis, is the basic moral code (beneficence, family loyalty and respect, justice, truthfulness, mercy, magnanimity) that all significant religions and stable cultures maintain, and that Christians know from the first two chapters of Romans to be matters of God's general revelation to our race. Lose this, says Lewis, and we are lost indeed, at least in life-quality terms. 'Unless we return to the crude and nursery-like belief in objective values, we perish.'[13] Next, with the loss of the Tao the chest is lost. The chest is Lewis's image, lifted from a medieval writer, for 'emotions organized by trained habit into stable sentiments', so that we 'feel pleasure, liking, disgust and hatred at those things which are pleasant, likeable, disgusting, and hateful'.[14] Loss of the Tao makes such moral training impossible, for all questions of moral values then become matters of personal taste, and sober folk do not try to dragoon each other on matters of taste. So moral education will go to the wall, and the result will be – indeed, in some quarters already is – 'Men without Chests', marked by 'defect of fertile and generous emotion':[15] in other words, adults who never experienced moral formation and so now lack moral character. And, lastly, where subjectivism prevails a legacy is lost – namely, the heritage of Tao-based, time-tested moral, social, and familial landmarks bequeathed to us by our Graeco-Roman-Christian western culture. Subjectivism appears as a call to cast off the shackles of the past by relativizing yesterday's absolutes, which sounds like a siren-song inviting us to freedom; but the effect is to turn each individual into a cultural castaway, rootless and directionless, a voyager lost in the cosmos. By undermining the moral authority of our communal heritage and telling us that, whatever we do, we must not be bound by it, subjectivism impoverishes us more grievously.

Were Lewis with us today, he would weep, I think, at the progress subjectivism has made during the last half-century. The indifference to truth that calls itself tolerance, and is enforced under the name of political correctness; the prevalence in educational circles of the deconstructionist dogma that human discourse never conveys public truth, but is only a power play; and the emergence of Men without Chests of leadership to the political, socio-economic and ecclesiastical life of the West; all point to a degree of cultural decadence beyond anything Lewis knew.

Third, Lewis observed an ominous slide into scientism.

Scientism was Lewis's term for being devoted to science and technique as one's God and to using science for world-change as one's religion. Lewis imagined utopian scientists being given their head to reconstruct the human race, and was appalled. In *The Abolition of Man* and *That Hideous Strength*, both composed in the Hitler era under war conditions against a background of British babble about science the saviour, Lewis projected his vision of the Tao-less tyranny to which such action would lead. Neither book is really a success: in *Abolition* (the text of three guest lectures at Durham University) he tries to say more than he has room for, and *That Hideous Strength* attempts to be at the same time a realistic novel about marriage, a satirical pageant of evil on the march, and a fantastic myth in which King Arthur's magician Merlin and five planetary celestials combine for cataclysmic judgment – which artistically is just too much to fit together. Charles Williams, with whom Lewis discussed the book in its early stages, might have brought it off; Lewis simply couldn't. But Lewis's picture of the callous, banal, demeaning idiocy of the clever men planning to reconstruct the British people is brilliant, as is his crystallizing of the mindset of scientism's devotees in *Abolition*:

> There is something which unites magic and applied science while separating both from the 'wisdom' of earlier ages. For the wise men of old the cardinal problem had been how to conform the soul to reality, and the solution had been knowledge, self-discipline and virtue. For magic and applied science alike the problem is how to subdue reality to the wishes of men: the solution is a technique; and both, in the practice of the technique, are ready to do things hitherto regarded as disgusting and impious such as digging up and mutilating the dead.[16]

(Lewis has the representative of scientism reanimate a bodiless human head in *That Hideous Strength*; his presentation encourages his readers to feel disgust at such nastiness.) The truth is that the agenda of scientism (masterminds using their technique to change the rest of the race according to their wish) always views people as objects for treatment rather than as personal subjects, and so inevitably it attacks human dignity and disrupts human relationships. Lewis saw it as expressing the power-madness of original sin, and delineated it accordingly.

There is less overt scientism today than once there was, for most people, scientists included, now see that the world's problems are greater than applied science as such can ever solve, so that facile utopianism is totally out of place. Yet remarks sometimes heard about what genetic engineering and human cloning might achieve show that the dream is not quite dead yet.

Lewis, then, diagnosed both the North-South extremes of personal and inherited wisdom, and also the subjectivist rejection of moral absolutes and inherited wisdom, and with that the chilling pretensions of applied science and technology, as three post-Christian British expressions of original sin, the self-deifying, God-resisting disposition in humankind that is Satan's resource and chief ally in the Holy War. Original sin, of course, takes countless forms in both individuals and communities, so this threefold pin-pointing is exemplary and not exhaustive. As demonstrations of the arrogant inanity, not to say insanity, of original sin, however, he might well have accorded these modes of it classic status.

The third factor in the war is God counter-attacking: thwarting Satan, overcoming sin in the human heart, and moving into the wholesale reconstruction of his spoiled world; in other words –

3. Universal divine antagonism to Satan and sin

What Lewis has to say about the way in which the three persons of the holy Trinity have acted, are acting, and will act to overcome the demonic and racial rebellion that darkens our planet spiritually need not detain us long, for the assertions are familiar, however novel and striking their expression. The following extracts from *Mere Christianity* crystallize Lewis's testimony to God the Restorer.

> Enemy-occupied territory – that is what the world is. Christianity is the story of how the rightful King has landed, you might say landed in disguise, and is calling us all to take part in a great campaign of sabotage. When you go to church you are really listening-in to the secret wireless from our friends: that is why the enemy is so anxious to prevent us from going.[17]

Why is God landing in this enemy-occupied world in disguise and starting a sort of secret society to undermine the devil? Why is he not landing in force ...? Well, Christians think he is going to land in force; we do not know when. But we can guess why he is delaying. He wants to give us the chance of joining his side freely.[18]

What is the difference which [Christ] has made to the whole human mass? It is just this; that the business of becoming a son of God, of being turned from a created thing into a begotten thing, of passing over from the temporary biological life into timeless 'spiritual' life, has been done for us.

Humanity is already 'saved' in principle. We individuals have to appropriate that salvation ... One of our own race has this new life: if we get close to him we shall catch it from him.

Of course, you can express this in all sorts of different ways. You can say that Christ died for our sins. You may say the Father has forgiven us because Christ has done for us what we ought to have done. You may say that Christ has defeated death. They are all true.[19]

Christ says, 'Give me All. I don't want so much of your money and so much of your work: I want You. I have not come to torment your natural self, but to kill it. No half measures are any good. I don't want to cut off a branch here and a branch there, I want to have the whole tree down. I don't want to drill the tooth, or crown it, or stop it, but to have it out. Hand over the whole natural self, all desires which you think innocent as well as the ones you think wicked – I will give you a new self instead ...'[20]

When a man turns to Christ and seems to be getting on pretty well (in the sense that some of his bad habits are now corrected), he often feels that it would now be natural if things went fairly smoothly. When troubles come along – illnesses, money troubles, new kinds of temptations – he is disappointed. These things, he feels, might have been necessary to rouse him and make him repent in his bad old days; but why now? Because God is forcing him on, or up, to a higher level: putting him into situations where he will have to be very much braver, or more patient, or more loving, than he ever dreamed of being before. It seems to us all unnecessary: but that is because we have not yet had the slightest notion of the tremendous thing he means to make of us ...

If we let him – for we can prevent him, if we choose – he will make the feeblest of us into a god or goddess, a dazzling, radiant, immortal creature, pulsating all through with such energy and wisdom and joy and love as we cannot imagine, a bright stainless mirror which reflects back to God perfectly (though, of course, on a smaller scale) his own boundless power and delight and goodness. The process will be long and in parts painful; but that is what we are in for.[21]

The more we get what we now call 'ourselves' out of the way and let him take us over, the more truly ourselves we become ... He invented – as an author invents characters in a novel – all the different men that you and I were intended to be. In that sense our real selves are all waiting for us in him ... I am not, in my natural state, nearly so much of a person as I like to believe: most of what I call 'me' can be very easily explained. It is when I turn to Christ, when I give myself up to his personality, that I first begin to have a real personality of my own.[22]

Thus Lewis witnesses to the incarnation, the redemption, the church, the gospel invitation, the transforming relationship to Jesus Christ, the call to holiness, and the hope of glory – the set of truths, or perhaps we should say, the set of emphases within the one truth, which, viewed within a trinitarian frame,[23] make up the essential and unchanging Christian message. Thus he surveys the divine initiatives that rescue sinners from Satan's control and prepare them to share God's coming victory. This holy-war perspective is thoroughly biblical, thoroughly coherent, and consistently illuminating to any who want to know how a Christian mind should work and what constitutes a Christian outlook on life. Some wish Lewis had said more about the societal order; I wish he had said more about justification by faith; but all must surely agree that in holy-war terms he gives us a brilliant overview of what in Christianity does not change with the passing years, and a brilliant battle manual on faithfulness to God in a hostile world. From his holy-war perspective we see why he thought the post-Christian Britain of his day was dying, and how he hoped that reasserting the truth of Christ would remedy that state of affairs.

We have looked at Lewis long enough; it is now time briefly to look along Lewis, to see what his exertions and example might have to say to us as we tackle our own God-given, anti-Satanic task of evangelism and nurture in an English-speaking world which, both sides of the Atlantic and in the southern hemisphere also, has gone further down the post-Christian road since Lewis's day. Accepting that Christians are God's resistance movement, Jesus Christ's underground army, called to be spiritual subversives in face of enemy occupation, we ask: how are we to do our job? What might Lewis say in answer to our question, were he here to advise us?

Stay at your post, Lewis would certainly counsel; stand steady and don't be discouraged, for truth, fact, and Christ the living Lord himself are on your side. Rather, devoted yourself to countering current claptrap by doing two things.

First, affirm the truth

Evangelism is our task ('woe to you if you do not evangelize,' said Lewis to theological students in 1959).[24] But evangelizing today requires, first, a focusing on truth rather than on experience – after all, New Age, music, and drugs provide experiences – and, second, a recognition of the rationality of Christian supernaturalism as a whole, otherwise the space-time incarnation, the once-for-all atoning death, the bodily resurrection, the present heavenly reign and the future triumphant return of our Lord Jesus Christ will seem simply incredible. We must therefore be ready to vindicate the Christian message as real truth, in the sense of its being a map, diagram, and index of temporal and external reality; as revealed truth, in the sense of its being truth that God himself has told us and shown us; as rational truth, in that it is coherent in itself and makes sense of everything else that we know; and as redemptive truth, in that it mediates a life-transforming relationship with the Redeemer himself, in person.

Second, cultivate the Chest

In an age of moral relativism, inculcating a Tao-oriented mindset in young and old alike is vitally important, partly because acknowledging moral absolutes opens the door to a realistic recognition of one's sin and one's need of forgiveness and help, partly because appropriate reactions to good and evil are basic to all truly Christian obedience and all truly Christian influence. Yes, but how can this mindset be induced? Partly, at least, said Lewis, through stories that engage the imagination and model those appropriate responses: poems like Spenser's *Faerie Queeene*, novels like those of George MacDonald, and mythical fantasies like the chronicles of Narnia. For many moderns Spenser and MacDonald will be lead balloons, but Narnia's appeal seems universal. Says Doris Myers: 'the didacticism of the Chronicles consists in the education of moral and aesthetic feelings ... to prevent children growing up without Chests'; and she reviews the series to show how in each one 'a particular virtue or configuration of virtues is presented, and the reader is brought to love it through participating in the artistry of the tale':[25] courage, honour, and limitless kindness in *The Lion, the Witch, and the Wardrobe*; personal nobility (Reepicheep the Mouse) and public responsibility (Caspian the captain) in *The Voyage of the Dawn Treader*; bravery in face of loss and death in *The Last Battle*; and so on.

The deep point here is that, both for the glory of God and for pre-evangelistic conditioning and for back-up in the nurture of converts and indeed for human well-being across the board, the cultural milieu needs to be impregnated with Christian – that is, authentic human – values in every possible way, family life, public education, and popular reading being three prime areas where this must be done. So letting loose Christian perceptions and valuations within the culture has real evangelistic and discipling relevance. Lewis, being a writer, set himself to inject fictional embodiments of Christ and Christian truth, including the Tao, into the world of popular reading; both for children (Narnia) and for adults (the space trilogy); others with other skills must seek to impact communal culture in other ways. Declaring and defending the gospel of Christ, and developing people's Chests every way we can, sound like two distinct activities, but Lewis saw them as aspects of one, namely full-scale, full-orbed, 'enculturated' disciple-making; and surely he was right.

Who follows, now, where Lewis led?

Questions for study

1. Compare Packer's writing style in this lecture with that of his 1954 article on 'Revelation and Inspiration', reprinted as the first essay in this collection. How would you describe them? What factors help account for the development in Packer's writing style over the near half century which separates them?

2. What does Packer consider to be Lewis's central message? Try to state this in your own words, rather than just repeat Packer's.

3. What is 'scientism'? Why is it such a threat? And what does Lewis offer in response, according to Packer?

4. What does Packer mean when he urges his readers to 'cultivate the Chest'?

Notes

1. *Mere Christianity*, London: Collins Fontana, 1955, p. 6.
2. *Of Other Worlds*, New York: Harcourt Brace Jovanovitch Harvest, 1975, pp. 35–38; first published in the Children's Books section of *The New York Times Book Review*, 18 November 1956. The wording of the title is unlikely to be Lewis's.
3. Subtitle: 'An Allegorical Apology for Christianity, Reason and Romanticism'.
4. Andrew Walker and James Patrick (eds.), London: Hodder and Stoughton, 1990.
5. *The Pilgrim's Regress*, London: Geoffrey Bles, 1944; from 'Preface to Third Edition', p. 14.
6. *The Problem of Pain*, London: Geoffrey Bles, 1940, pp. 70–71.
7. Ibid., pp. 86–87.
8. *The Pilgrim's Regress*, p. 11.
9. Ibid., pp. 11–12.
10. Ibid., p. 12.
11. Ibid., p. 13.
12. *Christian Reflections*, London: Geoffrey Bles, 1967, pp. 72–81; first published in *Religion in Life*, Summer 1943.
13. Ibid., p. 81.
14. *The Abolition of Man*, London: Geoffrey Bles, 1967, p. 16. The medieval writer is Alanus ab Insulis.
15. Ibid., p. 21.
16. Ibid., pp. 52–53.
17. *Mere Christianity*, p. 47.
18. Ibid., p. 63.
19. Ibid., pp. 152–153.
20. Ibid., pp. 163–164.
21. Ibid., pp. 170–171.
22. Ibid., p. 187.
23. The last four quotations come from Book Four of *Mere Christianity*, 'Beyond Personality: or First Steps in the Doctrine of the Trinity'.
24. *Christian Reflections*, p. 152.
25. Doris T. Myers, *C. S. Lewis in Context*, Kent, OH: Kent State University Press, 1994, p. 126. See the whole section, pp. 126–181.

Sources of citations

A full bibliography of the writings of J. I. Packer to 1996 may be found in Alister E. McGrath, *J. I. Packer: A Biography*, Grand Rapids, MI: Baker Book House, 1997. United Kingdom edition published as *To Know and Serve God: A Biography of James I. Packer*, London: Hodder and Stoughton, 1997, pp. 293–308.

The following pieces are used by permission of Dr Packer, and any holders of publishing rights for this material.

1954

'Revelation and Inspiration', in F. Davidson, A. M. Stibbs and E. F. Kevan (eds.), *New Bible Commentary*, London: Inter-Varsity Fellowship, 1954, pp. 24–30.

1959

'Christianity and Non-Christian Religions', *Christianity Today*, 21 December 1959, pp. 3–5.

1962

'The Nature of the Church', in C. F. H. Henry (ed.), *Basic Christian Doctrines*, New York: Rinehard and Winston, 1962, pp. 214–217.

1963

Keep Yourselves from Idols, London: Church Book Room Press, 1963.

'What is Revival?', in D. Winter (ed.), *The Best of Crusade*, London: Victory Press, 1963, pp. 89–93.

1969

'The Problem of Universalism Today', *Theolog Review: Australian Journal of the Theological Students Fellowship* 5/3 (November 1969), pp. 16–24.

1974

'What did the Cross achieve? The Logic of Penal Substitution', *Tyndale Bulletin* 25 (1974), pp. 3–45.

1975

'On Knowing God', *Tenth: An Evangelical Quarterly* (July 1975), pp. 11–25.

1977

'Jesus Christ the Lord', in J. R. W. Stott (ed.), *Obeying Christ in a Changing World*, London: Collins, 1977, pp. 32–60.

1981

'Is Christianity credible?', in D. Stacey (ed.), *Is Christianity Credible?* London: Epworth, 1981, pp. 64–72.

1987

'A Modern View of Jesus', *Faith Today* (January 1987), pp. 28–30, 32–33.

1990

'An Introduction to Systematic Spirituality', *Crux* 26/1 (March 1990), pp. 2–8.

The Problem of Eternal Punishment, The Leon Morris Lecture, 1990,

Camberwell: Evangelical Alliance (Victoria), Inc., 1990.

1991

'Evangelical Foundations for Spirituality', in M. Bockmuehl and K. Burkhardt (eds.), *Gott Lieben und seine Gebote halten*, Basel: Brunner Verlag, 1991, pp. 149–162.

1996

'On from Orr: The Cultural Crisis, Rational Realism, and Incarnational Ontology', *Crux* 32/3 (September 1996), pp. 12–26.

1998

'Living Truth for a Dying World: The Message of C. S. Lewis', *Crux* 34/4 (December 1998), pp. 3–12.

CPSIA information can be obtained at www.ICGtesting.com
Printed in the USA
LVOW07*1119060715

445116LV00006B/27/P